Contestable Concepts of Literary Theory

By the same author:
The Secular Lyric in Middle English
The Frontier Mind

Contestable Concepts of Literary Theory

Arthur K. Moore

Louisiana State University Press

BATON ROUGE

ISBN 0–8071–0057–9
Library of Congress Catalog Card Number 73–77654
Copyright © 1973 by Louisiana State University Press
Manufactured in the United States of America
Printed by Heritage Printers, Inc., Charlotte, North Carolina
Designed by Dwight Agner

To My Mother

Contents

Introduction / 3

I   Lyric Voices and Ethical Proofs / 12

II   Lyric Personae and Prying Critics / 32

III   Rhetoric's Wrung Neck / 56

IV   The Case for Poetic Obscurity / 73

V   The Literary Status of the English Popular Ballad / 99

VI   Medieval English Literature and the Question of Unity / 126

VII   Formalist Criticism and Literary Form / 155

VIII   The Instruments of Oracular Expression / 175

IX   The Theoretical Liabilities of Literary Criticism / 209

Index / 235

Acknowledgments

All but the last essay originally appeared in journals and, aside from the addition of a few supporting references and the correction of a number of typographical errors, are preserved substantially unchanged. To the several editors who accepted the articles in the first place and subsequently granted permission to reprint I am indeed grateful and hereby make acknowledgment: "The Literary Status of the English Popular Ballad," *Comparative Literature*, Vol. 10 (1958); "Rhetoric's Wrung Neck," *Western Humanities Review*, Vol. 17 (1963); "Lyric Voices and Ethical Proofs," *Journal of Aesthetics and Art Criticism*, Vol. 23 (1964–65); and in the same journal, "Formalist Criticism and Literary Form," Vol. 29 (1970–71); "The Case for Poetic Obscurity," *Neophilologus*, Vol. 48 (1964); "Lyric Personae and Prying Critics," *Southern Humanities Review*, Vol. 1 (1967); "Medieval English Literature and the Question of Unity," *Modern Philology*, Vol. 65 (1967–68), copyright 1968 by the University of Chicago; "The Instruments of Oracular Expression," *Diogenes*, No. 82 (Summer, 1973).

I am indebted to the University of Kentucky Research Foundation for grants in the summers of 1965 and 1966; otherwise, this book has been accomplished in the course of normal academic activity. To my long-time colleague Robert D. Jacobs I am especially grateful for perceptive criticism and substantial support from the outset and also to Monroe C. Beardsley, who, encouraging me to persevere at midpoint, appraised my sometimes disconcerting arguments with the tolerance becoming a complete philosopher.

Arthur K. Moore

Atlanta, 1973

Contestable Concepts of Literary Theory

Introduction

Invention having disappointed my search for a portentous Gothic symbol to focus these essays, I settled for a title which, though plain, aptly suggests both the considerable range and the relatively abstract character of the whole. My concern has been to subject leading concepts of contemporary literary criticism to logical scrutiny and in some instances to devise theoretical correctives. If the exposition at times appears excessively economical and sparing of illustrative matter, my main excuse is that extensive elaboration often dulls the point of an argument and leads to the confusion of crucial issues with irrelevances. Abbreviation is in any case a respectable rhetorical mode, particularly effective in exposing central propositions to appraisal for truth or falsity. The concepts which I have elected to examine are theoretically interesting and, for a wide variety of critical approaches, practically important. Contestable, though not readily dismissible, my verdicts challenge several sectors of applied criticism to produce improved warrants. Appearances notwithstanding, my guiding purpose has not been to unsettle the critical enterprise; indeed, contending critics have left nothing to be accomplished in that regard. Rather, I have preferred to reflect on the confusion which critics have produced, usually from drawing ideologies into consideration or proceeding with faulty inferences. The conclusions, while often pronounced forcefully in the interest of persuasion, are necessarily provisional, leaving the door fully open both to rebuttal and, hopefully, to refined extension.

My biases have been freely developed, which is as much as to say that the arguments owe little to prior inclinations to preserve literature in any of the esteemed perspectives or to afford satisfaction to dogmatic critical circles. I have proceeded on the assumption that literature is indestructible and inexhaustible and that criticism, while an inevitable accompaniment of literary experience, is in principle ephemeral and forever liable to distort what it pretends to master. This is not to suggest that criticism must need fail to justify its existence but only that the critic labors under the continuing obligation of demonstrating that his mediatorial services in truth serve understanding rather than eccentric preference. Although broadly implicated with the world's concerns, literature yet stands in no certain relation to its supposed references; it testifies incontestably not to religious, ethical, or social goods but only to human capacity for formalizing human predicaments in the medium of language. To be sure, literature serves many conventional and probably many strange interests; but neither personal nor institutional uses can be reasonably allowed to define literary art or to justify its disciplinary study. While selected specimens can be invoked in support of every cherished value and of every system of belief, literature collectively denies what it affirms and affirms what it denies, much to the confusion of critics who would force art into a servile condition. The moral (and immoral) values which literature presumably embodies are not aesthetic values, and critics who have supposed the contrary have regularly foundered in equivocation and contradiction. While modern apologists for humane studies proclaim the benefits to be derived from literary consumption, Platonic objectors survive; and in truth the effects of literature on the individual and on the collectivity are not well understood even after two and a half millennia of claims and counterclaims. What justifies criticism as a discipline is the incontestable fact that literature is a complex and universally interesting verbal phenomenon, possessing in its multitudinous exemplars common properties sufficient for systematic study. If general knowledge of literature can only be probable and less than adequate to the varieties of individual experience, criticism is no more liable to ultimate uncertainty than the physical sciences. It is a reasonable conjecture that the present theoretical understanding of literary art leaves much to be accomplished short of that point at which no further questions and thus no further answers are possible.

Composed in locations far distant from the centers of advanced critical thought, these essays have been spared the stultifying effects of overly weighty group opinion and denied, by the same token, the benefits of continuing informal appraisal. While perhaps given under the circumstances to overstatement, I have been able to hold steadily in consideration the possibility that criticism in any and all of its contentious divisions might be in fundamental error. Somewhat awkward, if not graceless, a skeptical attitude usually wins small favor; nonetheless, it has an obvious sanction when theoretical thinking is in a state of disarray. Skepticism is particularly disagreeable because it tends to produce theories in negative (and hence interdictive) form and to leave out of serious account their larger disciplinary consequences. Although the possibility seems never to be denied that falsifiable assumptions may lurk in the fabric of any branch of systematic knowledge, revisionary views, since necessarily posing a threat to standard views, are seldom received with equanimity. Disciplines—by no means the humanities exclusively—which have accumulated large quantities of applied research without secure theoretical foundations are especially vulnerable to negative theory and especially prone to irrelevant, if not irrational, response. Plausible correctives, whatever their origin in personal dissatisfaction, are possible only in consequence of demonstrable defects in customary ways of observing and ordering data. The history of modern thought teaches nothing if not that old theories are doomed to be superseded by new, but this lesson seems often to be lost on scholars who have acquired a large stake in threatened approaches. Perhaps most methodologies represent significant advances in theoretical thinking, and perhaps most incorporate untested assumptions which, when perceived, call for correction. Theories succeed best by offering new perspectives which accommodate the formerly intractable elements of observation; but, as twentieth-century criticism attests, the solutions which problems evoke beget other problems and therewith the need for improved theoretical formulations. Benign skepticism, the handmaiden of free inquiry, upholds uncertainty against the very human urge to bring speculation to a halt at some congenial point and, when reason fails, to sustain methodology by dogmatic assertion or appeal to antique authority.

Objectivity is a condition difficult to achieve and more difficult to sustain over an extended period, and I cannot pretend to having remained equally patient and fair with the several prominent critical attitudes. My concern, however, has usually been not with critical schools and their representatives but with general concepts which are not identified exclusively with unified theoretical positions. I have remained sensible of the important contributions of— and documented my large debt to—the contending factions without being drawn into a specious pluralism. These essays were not moved by the familiar passion to synthesize and reconcile but by a simple interest in identifying real problems and non-problems and exploring the implications of such solutions as had been attempted. Each component of the book resulted from a separate inquiry, without necessary relation to or dependence on any other; if the whole suggests steady development, it is not a consequence of conscious effort to smooth inconsistencies or to defend stage by stage the ground previously claimed. I consider that I have engaged in the traditional exercise of attempting to prove and disprove theses. Acceptance or rejection of one part entails nothing with respect to the other parts, and I shall be completely satisfied with partial concurrence. Indeed, I should be melancholy if the whole were felt to constitute a whole in the sense of being a unified deterrent to critical investigation; for theoretical labors are largely futile unless opening as well as closing lines of inquiry. I should like to think that mine, in clearing the ground somewhat, actually promote the search for improved concepts of literary art.

Undertaking to prepare a sketch indicative of the general trend of my arguments and of the total accomplishment, I first came to realize how indefatigably I had asserted the relative indeterminacy of literature and contested the a priori assumptions by which critics have thought to overcome semantic and formal perplexities. Negatively, my essays expose defects in several critical methods; positively, mine has been an enterprise of liberation, logically extricating the literary work from extraneous circumstances of production and allowing its import to vary unpredictably with individual experience. While constructed as contestations, these essays yet set forth varyingly general theories, which define a critical position and provide some suggestions for the development of less vulnerable— and, unavoidably, more austere—methods of analysis. Perhaps fortunately for the continuation of interest in literary scholarship, my theoretical understanding, as that of others, can serve only at the pleasure of unregarded anomalies and unforeseeable innovations in literary construction.

The first four essays of this book examine the relation of the author to his work and the question of his public responsibility; the conclusions have the effect of invalidating several kinds of inferences which have figured importantly in modern criticism. "Lyric Voices and Ethical Proofs" sketches the circumstances which brought the lyric speaker into prominence and encouraged biographical critics to speculate about the poet's sincerity. Nothing knowable and nothing demonstrably significant for artistic accomplishment, sincerity under logical scrutiny turns out to be not a legitimate value criterion but simply a conjectured disposition which can be used to create the presumption of merit. A general theory of the relation of poet to poem appears in "Lyric Personae and Prying Critics" and therewith a pair of criteria governing the admission of background data to critical consideration. According to the argument of this essay, the original intention of the poet, even if available, is misleading and in all cases irrelevant to critical appraisal. The identification of the speaker with the poet has served much less to advance understanding of lyric art than to implicate it with supposed auctorial views. "Rhetoric's Wrung Neck" briefly explores the long-standing and largely unjustified prejudice against rhetoric and concludes that the term in much modern criticism is not in function descriptive but abusive. Nonetheless, the objection to rhetoric, conceived as ordered expression with persuasive ends, raises a question about the rationality of poetic discourse; and this matter receives some attention in a later chapter. "The Case for Poetic Obscurity" responds to certain modern critics who would impose upon poets the burden of being universally intelligible. Judged by the criterion of clarity, the greatest of recent poets receive low marks; but they have excellent classic company and therewith a long precedent for speaking to the more discerning.

The problem of form, which occupies large space in the last four chapters, first arises in "The Literary Status of the English Popular Ballad." The efforts of latter-day communal theorists to preserve the Child collection as a special genre, defined (and limited) by origin and form, cannot overcome the simple logic of the case or the evidence of unremarkable literariness. Those ballads most frequently anthologized neither define a distinct genre nor require excuses for the assumed inelegance of their authors. "Medieval English Literature and the Question of Unity" analyzes a supposedly indispensable property of good literature in connection with the efforts of period specialists to discover unity in (and thus vindicate the art of) a considerable number of loosely constructed narratives. Insufficiently reflective though remarkably ingenious, these studies find that unity, which is a necessary condition of any perceivable object, consists in many strange and unlikely relations. It is scarcely necessary to observe that unity is demonstrated usually at considerable expense to credibility. Statements about form are as contestable as statements about unity, as "Formalist Criticism and Literary Form" makes plain. Unfortunately for claims to objectivity in explication and interpretation, form is not a fixed and determinable property of any literary work but varies unpredictably with perception. Analysis answers to prior formal decisions, but these, arising in intuition, can never escape arbitrariness. "The Instruments of Oracular Expression" begins as a historical consideration of the pretensions of romantic seers, proceeds to an examination of their theorizing with particular respect to logic and rhetoric, and then, after sketching a theory of figuration as an instrument of perception, provides a demystified description of what might be called seer-writing. By this account, nothing is lost to romantic art except a set of useless superstitions, and much is gained for the poets' knowledge of the forms of immediate experience. The last chapter —"The Theoretical Liabilities of Literary Criticism"—describes the institution of literature as a serious obstacle to theoretical thinking and as an ill-conceived monument of opposition to science. By the definition thereafter proposed, literature in principle resists the best efforts of critics to establish meaning with exactitude or even to sort out the significant parts of a literary work without falling into arbitrariness.

The rather full documentation of this book, besides registering my very extensive indebtedness, calls particular attention to the varied and resourceful critical thought of the period since World War II; hopefully, it will direct students of literature to highly stimulating books and articles which, though occasionally included in bibliographies, are probably not often admitted to consideration in standard courses. If my arguments sometimes prove difficult to follow, the explanation may be not so much my abbreviated style as unfamiliarity with the resources upon which I have drawn. Once supposed to stand in imminent danger from criticism, literary study has accommodated new concepts only very slowly and without radical transformation of customary procedures. Unfortunately for the better understanding of literature, innovation has been dictated more often by social concerns than by theoretical considerations of an aesthetic kind. Though widely admitted to graduate study, criticism has not been adequately integrated with it; and the history of criticism running not much beyond Matthew Arnold has often been thought to suffice. Modern literary theory as such seems to have no recognizable place. The convenient division of literary study along national lines doubtless works against the recognition of theory, which, like mathematics, overflows the boundaries of language and geography. Ironically, in a period when theory confronts traditional practices with a multitude of caveats, students of English have increasingly persuaded themselves that language study is no necessary part of preparation for research. In truth, the spread of theoretical studies threatens to embarrass all but a handful of very gifted linguists. Translations, even when available, cannot be supposed to preserve the nuances of complex speculative thought. In any case, modern theoretical work stands to be neglected in the absence of official recognition of its importance. Criticism has been further complicated by the increasing intrusion of supposedly alien disciplines. Philosophers, psychologists, linguists, and anthropologists have drawn attention to problems which, though perhaps sometimes trivial, often have considerable theoretical interest and the potentiality for modifying critical methodologies. While the vast accumulation of speculative scholarship may be thought to impose an intolerable obligation on the student of literature, it yet suggests a multitude of alternatives to old and largely exhausted types of research. Moreover, the unstable realm of theory, far from being closed by determined system-makers, has never been more open to imagination and resourcefulness. It is scarcely necessary to observe that the popular enterprise of practical criticism can be inattentive to theory only at the risk of invalidation.

By comparison with scientists and even historians, literary scholars (including critics) have been rather indifferent to the issue of validity. Methods have languished less on account of theoretical objections than on account of the exhaustion of usable subject matter; and perhaps few have altogether disappeared. The arguments which have flared up among literary theorists and philosophers over the nature of literature and the propriety of various kinds of criticism seem to have been unnoticed—or at least unheeded—by the majority; even the practicing critics have been inclined to leave to the aestheticians the logical perplexities which afflict critical work. The forces of radical change identified by Thomas S. Kuhn in the *Structure of Scientific Revolutions* (2d ed., 1970) have been largely resisted in literary study, though from no lack of theories which cast doubt on the significance of traditional problems as well as on the methods used to solve them. It is, of course, arguable that no new methodology has so far succeeded in accommodating the whole range of observable literary properties as to merit general acceptance and that, therefore, various methods (and accompanying theories) can be defended under existing circumstances. For literary historians, however, the competing critical theories offer only a choice of evils, as none confers great honor on the mountainous accumulation of background studies. The effect of modern critical thinking has been generally to exclude from consideration historical data lacking immediate and demonstrable relevance and to trivialize utterly such studies as stand at several removes from the literary object. It is scarcely possible that a strictly literary theory can be devised which will remove the suspicion of irrelevance from literary history and validate the myriads of genetic explanations of artistic accomplishment; but literary scholars, in contrast to scientists, seem unprepared to accept the extinction of old methods together with their exemplary applications. While the theoretical understanding of literature has considerably improved of late, the direction of literary studies is unlikely in any case to shift radically until patently more fruitful (and satisfying) methods of analysis are provided. Disciplinary change awaits widely acceptable alternatives, for the lack of which imperfect procedures are preserved out of hard necessity.

Chapter *I*

Lyric Voices
and
Ethical Proofs

The lyric is the most privileged and in some important respects the least plausible of literary kinds. Whereas the epic ostensibly builds on secular or celestial history, and the drama offers to imitate in some sense real life, the lyric as such is required neither by definition nor by plain precept to announce any sort of rational justification. In other words, the lyric (singing) voice, while loosely responsible to decorum and to such general limitations as apply to all poetry, has the largely unrestricted privilege of verbalizing any experience, however improbable or trivial, without directly appealing to any value or set of values approved by custom. To be sure, lyric poets, whether ancient or modern,[1] have not often exercised to the fullest their long-standing and perhaps universally sanctioned liberties of expression, but rather have incorporated, even if sometimes very subtly, more or less defensible grounds of value. It is possible to hold that on this account the bulk of lyric verse—and in particular that composed before the nineteenth century—is the less pure, though to do so invites, if it does not compel, the awkward conclusion that the lyric ought not only to be exempted but also prohibited from expressing —at least overtly—any sort of value claim apart from experience considered as an aesthetically realizable phenomenon. If the privilege of the lyric has never been interpreted quite so tyrannously, there has yet been since the romantic revolt an inclination to purge it of the typical reliances of conceptual discourse and of direct statements of uncontested or commonplace values.

The extremely narrow view of the lyric mode taken by Emil

1. It scarcely matters that the lyric has been defined as a genre only in relatively modern times, for the West has always known lyrical poetry, though under a wide variety of labels.

Staiger may suit European aesthetic presuppositions better than British or American; and yet in denying, as it seems, the appropriateness of any form of justification dependent upon objective values, he has merely accepted a limitation which is probably implicit in expression theory: "Wer sich an niemand wendet und nur einzelne Gleichgestimmte angeht, braucht keine Überredungskunst. Die Idee des Lyrischen schliesst alle rhetorische Wirkung aus. Wer nur von Gleichgestimmten vernommen werden soll, braucht nicht zu begründen. Begründen in lyrischer Dichtung ist unfein, so unfein, wie wenn ein Liebender der Geliebten die Liebe mit Gründen erklärt."[2] *Gleichgestimmte*, which in this context is perhaps best rendered by *kindred spirits*, seems at first glance to be a substantial qualification; but Staiger actually asserts without the protection afforded by the term (1) that the lyrical properly excludes the rhetorical, and (2) that *Gründe* are crude, essentially unlyrical elements. The first proposition probably entails the second, for rhetoric, as persuasive speech, needfully incorporates grounds, which are of course claims to value and as such claims on interest. But if the lyric is an instrument of intelligible purpose and not merely a collection of unsorted verbal fragments, it issues claims to value of some kind and becomes by that fact persuasive and hence rhetorical.

Staiger's "Idee des Lyrischen" appears to suffer from the logical disabilities which vitiate all concepts of *poésie pure*, but his statement is valuable in defining quite clearly the thrust of a good deal of modern criticism and for suggesting at least one explanation of twentieth-century obliquity and indecisiveness. If it is accepted that premeditated expression, including that directed to oneself, necessarily incorporates justifications or rationalizations, that it is in some sense *begründet*, then it can hardly be expected that a modern lyric should achieve even a modicum of intelligibility without adumbrating a ground of value. What can be reasonably expected is that modern poets should feel compelled to employ

2. Emil Staiger, *Grundbegriffe der Poetik* (5th ed.; Zürich, 1961), p. 49.

inobvious strategies of validation. Traditional validating methods, while yet visible, are much complicated by the fluctuating and often ambiguous relationship of poet to speaker and of poet to poem. If the modern poet cannot be so far identified with the voice of his poetry as to permit certain biographical inferences, the distinction between the two is often hopelessly blurred. This confusion is a subject for separate discussion, but it is needful to observe here that the very character of modern verse tends to prevent critics from making a clear-cut distinction between poet and speaker.

1   It is perhaps possible to assert without seriously offending against the several theories of literary value that lyrics are vouched for simply—that is, regardless of ethical import or aesthetic quality—through intelligible relationships to activities, conditions, occasions, lives, ideologies, and states of consciousness into which interest enters. There is historical presumption that verbal constructs exhibiting one or more of these relationships have, or may have, value;[3] but the degree of value varies not only according to the quality of the formal arrangement but also according to the character of the claim made on interest. It is hardly deniable that the value of a poem as aesthetic object stands in some degree of contingency to the external values which it embodies;[4] its achievement, however, is ultimately determined less by the quality of these values than by the manner in which the relationship is demonstrated. It should be perfectly evident from a multitude of examples between Wordsworth and Auden that not even the noblest sentiment and the noblest language can rescue a poem which rests on an unconvincing proof or on a proof which, for whatever reason,

3. See R. B. Perry, *General Theory of Value: Its Meaning and Basic Principles Construed in Terms of Interest* (New York and London, 1926), p. 116.

4. This difficult subject has recently been reargued by Herbert Wutz, *Zur Theorie der literarischen Wertung: Kritik vorliegender Theorien und Versuch einer Grundlegung* (Tübingen, 1957), pp. 53–56.

invites ironical contemplation. Although it may be possible to illustrate very nearly every mode of validation from the verse of a given period, the acceptability of different sorts appears to vary with prevailing presuppositions about the function and ontological status of poetry and about the importance and authority of the poetic voice. It is reasonable to suppose that the values addressed by poems will be those least debatable and the relationship of poems to values most explicit in times, such as the Middle Ages, when the status of literature is uncertain. The truth of the converse is less evident, though it is observable that modern poets sometimes leave doubts about what values are being invoked and about what means are being employed to establish the relationship between poem and values.

Medieval lyrics—to begin with relatively simple exemplars— usually appeal directly to approved social and religious sympathies and, by comparison with modern lyrics, require for validation very little interest in formal innovations or in the special case of the speaker. Inasmuch as the values invoked admit of little question within the circle of the intended audience and of little variation in attitude, the possibility of marked self-consciousness is precluded. Form tends to be conventional and sets fairly narrow limits on the varieties of relationships which may be established between poems and values. This is in no way to deny the excellence of medieval lyrical poetry but only to call attention to an aspect of it which is in the context of the present discussion a formal limitation. When not assuming the mask of the courtly lover, the poet is likely to be Everyman registering typical religious experiences or safe and secure commonplaces. Religious lyrics are vouched for not by the individual experiencing *I* but by subjects (e.g., the Crucifixion, the Blessed Virgin, Doomsday) or by states of consciousness—penitential or devotional—shared by the Christian community. What chiefly vouches for the chansons of the troubadours and trouvères is not the unexceptional postures of the lovers or their analyses of li duz mal de amer but the pretended usefulness of the pieces to the conduct of courtly love. As ceremonial gestures designed to induce cooperation, they make conventional professions and appeals and often take epistolary form. Insofar as lyrics can be, medieval exemplars are self-effacing; the voice may in fact be the poet's, but it is most evidently that of a well-defined social or religious predicament. The Middle Ages took pleasure enough in lyrics, but the rationale was surely lacking for admiration of the aesthetic object as such or of its maker made manifest as such. If proof by use and proof by the sanctity of the external reference were often only thin pretexts for poetic expression, they nonetheless tended to distinguish serious poetry and to relieve medieval misgivings about profane and idle songs.

Renaissance lyrics, by contrast, depend for validation upon formal proofs rather more than upon public attitudes and gain a measure of autonomy thereby. The medieval poet's assertions and exclamations, by reason of being addressed to approved values, require slight internal support in the way of argument. The Renaissance poet assumes little more than the integrity of reason and stakes his case on the persuasive force of rational progression. Whether pleading, praising, scolding, or moralizing, he levies systematically upon the arts of language with the object of constructing a self-contained whole, which from the excellence of its diction and formal arrangement will prove a delight in the mind. An anonymous Tudor piece, which takes the form of a sorites, illustrates the extreme possibilities of internal validation and at the same time suggests the rationalistic bias of the period:

The longer life, the more offence;
The more offence, the greater pain;
The greater pain, the less defence;
The less defence, the lesser gain.
The loss of gain long ill doth try,
Wherefore come death, and let me die.[5]

5. J. W. Hebel and H. H. Hudson, eds., *Poetry of the English Renaissance, 1509–1660* (New York, 1946), p. 45, stanza 1.

Abstractness is not, of course, an unavoidable accompaniment of formal proof, as the verse of John Donne frequently demonstrates. In the facetious lyric "The Flea," for example, he uses what is technically a polysyllogism but fuses it with an elaborate analogy. It scarcely matters to the Renaissance sensibility that one of these poems is moral and the other immoral or that neither is quite serious, for both are pre-eminently intellectual exercises and as such largely exempt from ethical criticism. The characteristic manner of the verse of the period presupposes an audience like neither the medieval nor the modern, but with sufficient intellectual detachment to allow arguments to discover their logical, if sometimes perverse, conclusions. The apparent toleration of even irresponsible virtuosity implies no failure to discriminate between poems of greater or lesser magnitude or moral significance but only a large concern for formal excellence. Whether serious or unserious, Renaissance verse presupposes an efficient methodology for finding and ordering suitable matter, and it is validated to the satisfaction of the period by the skillful application of methodology rather than by the quality of its external references or the assumed disposition of its composers.

Lyrics in general could be conveniently and perhaps advantageously classified on the basis of modes of validation did they but issue, as a rule, simple and direct claims to value. Whatever the case with pre-romantic lyrics, which in this regard are not always unequivocal, validation since Wordsworth and particularly in the twentieth century has been achieved, or at least aimed at, more often than not by a mixture of modes and through the self-conscious posture of the poet either as or alongside the speaker. This circumstance considered, it is not so strange that the focus of modern lyrics should often seem to shift illogically. Frost, for instance, is given to stating a proposition which appears to call for and is probably often amenable to formal proof; but his argument —usually adumbrated through a series of economical observations— tends to be so wavering and indecisive that the conclusion remains problematic. This is not to maintain that a lyric must need have a firm logical line or even a suggestion of resolution; but a lyric containing a proposition cast in polemical form arouses a legitimate expectation of some sort of demonstration. Frost's inconclusiveness, considered as strategy, has the effect of focusing attention on the *persona*—ordinarily in the more famous poems the homely philosopher who knows somewhat more than he discloses—and it is his supposed wisdom that chiefly bears the weight of validation. Some of the verse of Dylan Thomas provides an instructive contrast to Frost's, for, general impressions to the contrary, it is usually more broadly and decisively validated. The lyrical *I*, which in Thomas' verse allegedly merges with the empirical *I*, ordinarily puts forward an unembarrassed claim for self as value; at the same time, the *I* speaks to external values which are significant and largely incontestable and frames the argument with a marked degree of rigor. The result in such poems as "And Death Shall Have No Dominion" and "A Refusal to Mourn the Death, by Fire, of a Child in London" is a progressive shift of focus away from the *persona* and a corresponding broadening of the base of validation. It is fair to observe, however, that Thomas' strategy, though on logical grounds sounder than Frost's, entails degrees of commitment and resolution rather in excess of modern preference.

Modern poets, including Frost, sometimes augment their value claims (and incidentally embarrass definitions of lyric poetry) by using, in addition to conventional artifices of amplification, various formal features of narrative and drama, both of which tend to be, by historical presumption, self-validating. "The Love Song of J. Alfred Prufrock" is in truth a love song and accordingly the literary record of what may be called, for the lack of a more felicitous phrase, a lyrical experience; but the form—essentially interior monologue—has the effect of adding to whatever value can be claimed for private expression such interest and plausibility as inhere in dramatic representation. The speaker is clearly not the poet but an individualized victim of the social order, confessing with convincing candor his weaknesses, frustrations, and longings. The conversational and somewhat clinical cast of his reflections appears to deny the proximity of the poet and the employment of artful contrivances, and yet the argument is scarcely less firm than that of Donne's "Loves Deitie," which employs formal proof to set forth a similar protest. What is particularly to be observed is that Eliot has given "Prufrock" very broad validation without noticeably implicating himself as a value factor. Yeats and Ransom sometimes use the ballad form and superficial aspects of narrative for what is not essentially narrative but lyrical poetry. Although their mixture of literary kinds is less perilous than Eliot's to definitions of the lyric, they leave a more marked impression of personal involvement. Ransom's "Bells for John Whiteside's Daughter" claims value as a fairly credible and pathetic story poem, but it is the tone which counts; and the tone makes a particularly strong value claim on behalf of the poet's sensibility and insight. Tone becomes of crucial importance whenever gaps occur in the logical line—as often the case in this century—which cannot be bridged without inferences regarding the speaker's (and ultimately the poet's) attitude. While it may not afford a certain key to interpretation, tone perhaps gives reliable evidence of the poet's good intentions and thus sets at rest suspicions about obscure effects. But insofar as he may be required, whether by critical methodologies or simply the uneasiness of critics, to vouch for poetic experience, the poet in some sense claims self as value. Modern lyrics issue, often to the point of confusion, multiple and even competing claims to value; but such is the disposition of critics that the poet as empirical person is seldom unimplicated in final assessments.

If the lyric is conceived to be not illusion, not imitation, but essentially expression, then interest (and therefore value) necessarily attaches to the speaker, whether thought of as the poet or not; and under these circumstances there can be no legitimate objection to his unembarrassed assertion of self as value. Indeed, criticism has to take account of poems in which very nearly all significance inheres in the individualized poetic voice. It is unnecessary at the moment to examine the aesthetic and cultural implications of literary theory which rationalizes the speaker's strongly self-conscious involvement; but the point should be made that most modern poets invite to themselves in consequence of their ambiguous relationships to their speakers and poems a form of ethical inquiry which in the Middle Ages and Renaissance would have been largely irrelevant. Criticism of poets as opposed to criticism of poems can hardly be defended, and yet it has a kind of appropriateness whenever the poet claims self as value.

To be sure, a poem cannot be unaffected by the moral character of its poet; but to insist greatly on this self-evident truth is to make the poet's supposed intention and attitude a ground of value competitive with form (considered as rational argument or demonstration) and with content (considered as a set of external references). The idea of the poet set forth in Wordsworth's "Preface" leaves the distinct impression that excellence of character is a prior condition of poetic achievement and not inferior to craft in the scale of values which can be held to vouch for poetry. It is significant of this view that Wordsworth rejects decorative artifice less because it abuses art than because it allegedly reveals in the poet an intent to deceive: "It is not, then, to be supposed that any one who holds that sublime notion of poetry which I have attempted to convey, will break in upon the sanctity and truth of his pictures by transitory and accidental ornaments, and endeavor to excite admiration of himself by arts, the necessity of which must manifestly depend upon the assumed meanness of his subject." Wordsworth is not, of course, depreciating self as a value but only stipulating that it should be made manifest through the poetic vision rather than through artifice, which he associates with dishonest purposes. Whatever the validity of his notion of composition, he here raises an issue which was originally argued in relation to rhetorical practice. Quintilian took much the same position but with oratory in mind and the employment of the arts of language to affect public sympathies:

> Now a bad man cannot help speaking things other than he feels. On the other hand, the good will never be at a loss for honourable words or fail to find matter full of virtue for utterance, since among his virtues practical wisdom will be one. And even though his imagination lacks artifice to lend it charm, its own nature will be ornament enough, for if honour dictate the words, we shall find eloquence there as well. (*Inst.*, XII.i.30) [6]

It can be said for Quintilian, without excusing the Longinian cast of his argument, that he was not opposed to rhetorical methodology but only to what the ancients recognized as display oratory and to the sacrifice of ethical considerations to the exigencies of persuasion. It is arguable that the character of the orator cannot be a matter of indifference because orations come into existence and exist only as instruments of social or political purpose. Whether the critic can view the poet analogously without degrading the poem to the same mode of existence as the oration is a question of some importance.

Support of a kind for Wordsworth's heavy stress on the character of the poet as a validating factor appears in Aristotle's *Rhetoric* (I.ii). Of the several proofs available to oratory—proof by the character of the speaker, by persuasive tactics, and by logical demonstration—the first or ethical proof, as R. C. Jebb renders the Greek, carries perhaps the most weight with audiences:

> Ethical proof is wrought when the speech is so spoken as to make the speaker credible; for we trust good men more and sooner, as a rule, about everything; while, about things which do not admit of precision, but only of guess-work, we trust them absolutely. Now this trust, too, ought to be produced by means of the speech,—not by a previous conviction that the speaker is this or that sort of man. It is not true, as some of the technical writers assume in their systems, that the moral worth

6. Trans. H. E. Butler, Loeb Classical Library (Cambridge, Mass., 1958).

of the speaker contributes nothing to his persuasiveness; nay, it might be said that almost the most authoritative of proofs is that supplied by character. (I.ii.4)[7]

Intelligence, virtue, and good will, as evidenced by the speech, satisfy Aristotle's requirements and constitute ethical proof (*Rhet.*, II.i.5). This argument obviously verges on circularity, for the only admissible evidence of character must come somehow from the values evoked by the speech. But whatever the case with the orator, self-consciousness and the assertion of the speaking self as value call attention to the poet and create an impression of his acceptable character. Ethical proof in Wordsworth's verse, for example, takes the form of pointed references to the empirical *I*, the affectation of singular and singularly enlightened attitudes, and the pronouncement of pious commonplaces with striking fervor or solemnity. It is not without significance, however, that the terms[8] —and especially *sincerity*—available to the critic for registering his acceptance of ethical proof presuppose logically unwarranted conjectures about the intention of the poet.

2   It is surely accurate to state that the sincerity of the poet became of major importance to literary criticism (as opposed to purely moral criticism of literature)[9] only with the progress of the Romantic Movement and with the increasing reliance on ethical proof in the lyric. There may be some doubt that sincerity became in actual practice, as M. H. Abrams insists, the "primary criterion, if not the *sine qua non*, of excellence in poetry,"[10] and yet the case could hardly have been otherwise. The claim of the speaking self to value, if admitted to court, seemingly calls for ethical inquiry

7. Trans. R. C. Jebb, *The Rhetoric of Aristotle* (Cambridge, 1909).
8. See W. K. Wimsatt, Jr., and M. C. Beardsley, *The Verbal Icon: Studies in the Meaning of Poetry* (Lexington, Ky., 1954), p. 9.
9. For example, the poets of the Pléiade condemned the insincerity of the Petrarchan mode but imitated the style, as R. J. Clements shows in "Anti-Petrarchism of the Pléiade," *Modern Philology*, XXXIX (1941–42), p. 16.
10. M. H. Abrams, *The Mirror and the Lamp: Romantic Theory and the Critical Tradition* (New York, 1953), p. 318.

and a judgment, however hazardous, about the good intentions of the author. The alternative is to disregard what appears to be in a good many poems the only significant value claim. That sincerity survived as a major criterion into the twentieth century must have been owing not to its demonstrable validity but to the circumstance that the new poets favored the same mode of validation—ethical proof—as the much-depreciated romantics. Modern critics generally avoid Tolstoy's extravagant claim for sincerity in *What Is Art?* (Ch. 15), but there can be little doubt of their continuing concern with this problematic quality. Indeed, Henri Peyre maintains with particular reference to French literature, that the notion of sincerity is the "most potent *idée-force* in the literature and psychology of our age."[11] F. S. Flint, following Rémy de Gourmont, stated long ago what has continued to be in English and American criticism a popular view in this matter: "The test of poetry is sincerity, the test of sincerity is style, and the test of style is personality."[12] Flint's circle of interlocking propositions is obviously a logical box and a flagrant instance of intentionalism,[13] but it may not be altogether avoidable by the critic who judges the bulk of modern lyrical verse more or less on its own terms and accordingly reckons with the problem of sincerity.

Authority as diverse as Croce, C. S. Lewis, and M. C. Beardsley[14] exists for utterly rejecting sincerity as a literary criterion; but its persistence suggests that it serves a definable need. Henri Peyre,

11. Henri Peyre, *Literature and Sincerity* (Yale Romanic Studies, 2d Ser. 9; New Haven and London, 1963), p. 14.
12. Quoted by René Taupin, *L'influence du symbolisme français sur la poésie américaine (de 1910 à 1920)*, Bibliothèque de la *Revue de Littérature Comparée*, LXII (Paris, 1929), p. 128. Cf. Ezra Pound's declaration, "I believe in technique as the test of a man's sincerity"—*Literary Essays*, ed. T. S. Eliot (London, 1954), p. 9.
13. For the classic critique, see Wimsatt and Beardsley, *op. cit.*, pp. 3–18.
14. See Benedetto Croce, *Aesthetic as Science of Expression and General Linguistic*, trans. Douglas Ainslie (2d ed.; London, 1929), pp. 53 ff.; E. M. W. Tillyard and C. S. Lewis, *The Personal Heresy: A Controversy* (London, 1939), pp. 1–30, 120; and M. C. Beardsley, *Aesthetics: Problems in the Philosophy of Criticism* (New York, 1958), p. 29.

though sensible of the risks the employment of the term entails, nevertheless asserts its continuing usefulness—indeed indispensability: "The truth is that, in spite of half a dozen moves of revolt against the romantics staged since 1830, most lyrical poetry still is judged relatively to the romantic, and that the concept of sincerity is for us inseparable from literature." [15] Peyre doubtless has a point, and it is only fair to consider under what circumstances the sincerity of the poet, whether plainly visible in his work or perhaps discoverable by inference, ought to be taken into account. If a poem directly addresses local and controversial matters and embodies an appeal for a change of attitude which may lead to significant action, then the sincerity of the poet seems to demand attention, though perhaps no more so than his virtue and intelligence. It is arguable that such verse as this is essentially propaganda and therefore doubtfully literary; for, like the oration, it seems to be preeminently an instrument of political or social purpose. Yet this argument begs the question whether art and propaganda are necessarily incompatible. Whatever may be the case generally, to decide in the affirmative is to depreciate not only blatant demagoguery but also such prayerful exhibits as Milton's "On the Late Massacre in Piemont" and Auden's "Petition." The principle is surely establishable that what the poet intends is significant in some way for what he writes, though the relationship can be crucial for criticism only if ethical proof is admitted. Whether the poet's sincerity has broad cultural importance may be considered doubtful unless it can be demonstrated that poetry is likely to make something happen.

It may be feasible to reject the poet's or *persona's* claim of self as value and to dispose therewith of the question of sincerity, but this solution slights the circumstance that modern society allows great value to the individual as individual and accordingly to his utterances. If complete justice is to be done the poet who in fact

15. Peyre, *op. cit.*, p. 140. But see Patricia M. Ball, "Sincerity: The Rise and Fall of a Critical Term," *Modern Language Review*, LIX (1964), pp. 1–11, for the confused use of *sincerity* in the nineteenth century.

speaks for himself, what he says cannot be judged absolutely but only relatively—according to the correspondence of his expression to the thought and feeling which produced it. In this connection, sincerity has a technical signification, defining the relationship of the poetic self to the formalized products of the imagination and rationalizing the claim of self as value irrespective of moral absolutes. Wordsworth, to be sure, associated sincerity with morality; his poet, like Quintilian's orator, is sincere because he is in the conventional sense good. But Rousseau more nearly reflects the romantic toleration of dubious character and its unembarrassed self-analysis.[16] He seeks to validate the *Confessions* not by a demonstration of good character—at least not in Aristotle's sense—but by a disposition to complete candor: "Voilà ce que j'ai fait, ce que j'ai pensé, ce que je fus. J'ai dit le bien et le mal avec la même franchise. . . ."[17] This declaration is not inconsistent with the high valuation which the later eighteenth century came to place on the individual and especially on the inspired eccentric. Moreover, if literature is held properly to be more or less literal reproduction, rather than imitation, of experience, Rousseau's implicit claim has compelling logic. Logic notwithstanding, critics since Rousseau have doubtless been of Peyre's opinion that "sincerity in a writer never sufficed to give merit to a work of art."[18] The question remains, however, whether critics are even yet inclined to Wordsworth's opinion: "And indeed where the internal evidence proves that the writer was moved, in other words where this charm of sincerity lurks in the language of a tombstone and secretly pervades it, there are no errors in style or manner for which it will not be, in some degree, a recompence. . . ." (*Upon Epitaphs* II).

16. Ernst Beer, *Thomas Stearns Eliot und der Antiliberalismus des XX. Jahrhunderts*, Wiener Beiträge zur englischen Philologie, LXI (Vienna, 1953), pp. 37 ff.

17. Cf. Thomas Mann, *Joseph and His Brothers*, trans. H. T. Lowe-Porter (New York, 1948), pp. 694–95—"What would become of men if each would live only in the sincerity of his own desires, claiming for them the dignity of truth and unwilling to be strict with himself to his own improvement?"

18. Op. cit., p. 339.

What conspicuously survived in the twentieth century of romantic criticism was, in the opinion of Laurence Lerner,[19] expression theory and with it an abiding concern with sincerity. Whether the connection of this theory with sincerity is altogether necessary deserves some consideration. Whatever else objectification of the inner reality may entail, it assuredly limits manipulation and revision of language and focuses attention on the relationship of the poem to its cause. To the extent that the integrity of this connection must be judged, the poet's supposed intention becomes a value factor competitive with form and content and in some measure compensation for recognizable faults of execution. In actual practice the critic seldom need stake everything on determining the quality of the intention. For the reason that poets seldom rely exclusively on ethical proof, the critic can ordinarily reach acceptable decisions by employing more or less classical criteria. A great difficulty arises, however, when the objectification of the inner reality is so faithful and therefore original as to resist comparison with models of established worth. While perhaps only Surrealism has produced really extreme instances of this sort, so-called modernist poetry often escapes familiar classifications and understandably raises doubts whether its expression can be appropriate to any conceivable experience. To label such poetry insincere and thus to call in question the integrity of the connection between experience and expression is to allow excessive weight to doubt bred of ignorance. On the other hand, to take for granted the sincerity of the innovator is to run the risk of imposition and consequent embarrassment. Yet it may be that intelligence and sensitivity are sufficient safeguards. At any rate, it is Peyre's view that as a criterion sincerity "is neither worse nor better than the mind of the person who makes use of it."[20]

19. Laurence Lerner, *The Truest Poetry: An Essay on the Question What is Literature?* (London, 1960), pp. 63, 110.

20. *Op. cit.*, p. 332.

3   The importance of sincerity granted provisionally, it is yet not clear precisely what this quality consists in or how it is to be recognized. Even if advocating the essential correspondence of poetic experience and poetic expression, critics cannot intend that sincerity dictate a literal transcription of the jumbled content of experience, for the product could owe nothing necessarily either to art or to intelligence. Indeed, absolute sincerity could be so interpreted as to leave the poet without responsibility for his work and the critic with dubious warrant to make value judgments.[21] It may be that critics mean only that the poet should not falsify experience by admitting in the process of composition those "transitory and accidental ornaments" which Wordsworth decried, although this stipulation, besides limiting somewhat the poet's right to revise, authorizes the critic to judge poetry exclusively on the basis of its relationship to its cause. This interpretation appears to have the support of I. A. Richards' definition: "It [sincerity] may perhaps be most easily defined from the critic's point of view negatively, as the absence of any apparent attempt on the part of the artist to work effects upon the reader which do not work for himself."[22] The common name for these effects in modern criticism is *rhetoric*, which signifies a style that errs and errs on account of the author's insincerity. Sir Herbert Read's comments on Eliot's development is a case in point: "It has been a long search for sincerity of utterance—sincerity of *poetic* utterance: a long disciplined effort to avoid the artificiality of rhetoric."[23] It may be doubted whether the issue of sincerity can be legitimately raised against so dramatic a poet as Eliot, who stakes very little on ethical proof.

21. W. K. Wimsatt, Jr., and Cleanth Brooks, *Literary Criticism: A Short History* (New York, 1957), pp. 499–519, sift these issues in connection with Crocean aesthetics.

22. I. A. Richards, *Principles of Literary Criticism* (5th ed.; New York, 1934), p. 271.

23. Herbert Read, *The True Voice of Feeling: Studies in English Romantic Poetry* (New York, 1953), p. 142. Arthur Symons, one of the early influences on the imagists, set rhetoric and sincerity in plain opposition in *The Symbolist Movement in Literature* (rev. ed.; London, 1908), p. 84.

For that reason, the possibility is worth considering that *rhetoric*, in Read's usage, stands for an ethical rather than a technical judgment. The basis of his objection, in that event, is not the relationship of the experience to the expression but simply the experience —that is, the hopeless world of the early Eliot. It is not without interest that Odette de Mourgues notes Richards' definition with apparent approval and at the same time acknowledges that "we are accustomed to test the sincerity of a poem by the value of the personal experience it expresses."[24] What led to this statement was the awkward circumstance that *précieux* poetry, whether sincere or insincere, comes out much the same stylistically. Even if modern styles afford more reliable evidence for determining sincerity, the question yet arises whether the term is not used mainly to evaluate experience rather than the relation of experience to expression. It might be possible to evaluate experience according to emotional discharge, but it is more reasonable to suppose that value in De Mourgues' usage refers to the attitudes and notions implicit in the posture of the experiencing self. This is not to say that the question of sincerity has never been aimed specifically and exclusively at pompous and overly ingenious diction but only that in addition it often involves evaluation of a poet's views.

Yet it is a trifle strange that sincerity should be a major critical concern in view of the widespread contention that in the twentieth century the empirical *I* is distinct from the lyrical *I* and that the poetic experience becomes significant only as it becomes *überpersönlich*.[25] The explanation may be related to the circumstance that modern lyrics are notably rich in concrete particulars and notably poor in generalizing links, which provide reasonably safe guides to interpretation. But even when lyrics yield discernible arguments and address significant values, their final import may be clouded by those characterizing figures of the twentieth century

24. Odette de Mourgues, *Metaphysical, Baroque & Précieux Poetry* (Oxford, 1953), p. 114.
25. See Hans Jaeger, "Subjektivität und Objektivität der Lyrik," *PMLA*, XLVII (1933), pp. 252–56.

—ambiguity and irony. If the element of uncertainty discourages overt consideration of argument and external values, a critic can yet manage an oblique judgment of these validating strategies by raising the question of sincerity. It should be noted, however, that the reluctance of critics to deal with poetry at more general levels may be owing in some measure to the influence of the French symbolists and imagists, who introduced an enduring bias against ideas in art. While just evaluation of some lyrics may appear to require only analysis of imagery and more or less informed conjectures about the causative states of consciousness, preoccupation with the causative mechanism leads to criticism of poets rather than of poems and invites Elijah Jordan's acrimonious summary: "The tragic failure of modern criticism lies in the assumption that a poem as a work of art can be explained by enumerating and describing and celebrating the hypothetical states of mind of the poet, on the superstition that these states as 'experiences' constitute the substance of the poem."[26] In guarding against the temptation to treat poetry either as philosophy or as mere verbal apparatus, the critic can hardly afford to ignore the fact that poetry may be both philosophical and methodically rational. This is not, however, to minimize the problem presented by lyrics in this century. Very often the poet, perhaps out of regard for the extreme aversion of the times to didacticism and value judgments, seems strongly inclined to blur both argument and external references and to create the impression that his poetry claims value chiefly as rather private expression.

Admittedly, the twentieth century could not tolerate a poetry validated like the medieval chiefly by external values or a poetry validated like that of the Renaissance by rigorous argument. The former presupposes assured values and tends to didacticism and banality; the latter, besides doing somewhat less than justice to the element of feeling, threatens to become an exercise in technique. Ethical proof above all other modes of validation suits

26. Elijah Jordan, *Essays in Criticism* (Chicago, 1952), p. 376.

modern times because it presupposes the value of undiscriminated human nature, the one value that has survived thus far the widespread skepticism about all values. And possibly the lyric nowadays puts a truer face on reality inasmuch as it supposedly issues more directly than before from the poetic consciousness. Ethical proof nonetheless involves the critic in much the same difficulties as *argumentum ad hominem*. Sincerity can hardly be regarded as a reliable criterion if it requires some sort of ethical analysis of style as a basis for highly problematic inferences about intention. The fact, moreover, that a poet's reputation for sincerity can alter with the times, as Peyre admits,[27] strengthens the suspicion that the word, like *rhetoric*, is less a criticism of art than of sensibility and ideology. While it is not to be imagined that responsible critics allow the presumption of sincerity to excuse the lack of craft, the issue has remained unresolved since Wordsworth; and enough careless art has been extolled on account of its sincerity to give substance to the extravagant claim of Roger Caillois that in some modern poetry "la sincérité tient lieu de tout effort et de tout mérite."[28] The most serious defect of ethical proof as now accepted is that it is allowed to consist of a show of good intentions alone without implication of virtue or intelligence, which Aristotle included. Quintilian was doubtless wrong in supposing a necessary connection between good character and the disposition to speak candidly; but critics, far from facing up to the central issue, tend to allow the presumption of sincerity to excuse a very great deal and the presumption of insincerity to damn all else, whether of character or of art. Moreover, criticism leaves unargued the basic assumption that in the context of literature sincerity equals goodness.[29] Of course, it may be thought that Western society in subscribing to the essential goodness of human nature has answered the question

27. *Op. cit.*, p. 11.
28. Roger Caillois, *Les impostures de la poésie* (Paris, 1945), p. 25.
29. Richards, *loc. cit.*, equates sincerity with truth, though it should be obvious that sincere ignorance can speak the truth only by accident or by a very loose interpretation of truth.

in the affirmative, even though this equation rationalizes the literary expression of the most revolting experiences.

There can be no doubt of the usefulness of ethical proof both to poets and to critics. It is a means by which the poet can seek the mitigation of adverse judgments of his craft and a means to compel the critic to judge his work in the small universe of its conception. Ethical proof in lyrics of obscure import is a convenience for critics lacking intellectual confidence, for they are thereby enabled to issue brave judgments which cannot be effectively refuted. Yet the risks are also great, for lyrical poetry which appears to deny its relevance for the larger world of experience and which employs, instead of *personae* of established significance, the unmasked and unique state of consciousness stands a good chance of becoming, like a great deal of romantic verse, merely clinical material. If the test of sincerity enables the critic to reduce the risk of his being imposed upon, it also limits his objectivity and accordingly the significance of his work. Though it is hardly fair in any discussion to summon up the inverted platitudes of Oscar Wilde, Gwendolen's quip in the *Importance of Being Earnest*—"In matters of grave importance, style, not sincerity, is the vital thing"— contains an important point and ought to be taken more seriously than it was uttered. For if it is accepted that style and content are inseparably unified and that accordingly improvements in the one produce improvements in the other, it follows that a poet may be able by artful tinkering to transform what was originally individual and therefore limited into universally valid expression. The question of the poet's sincerity is irrelevant when a poem can be evaluated at a general and abstract level.

Chapter II

Lyric Personae
and
Prying Critics

Systematic criticism of lyric poetry entails a decision as to the degree of autonomy properly allowable to the speaker, considered in relation to the author, and the decision taken biases in some measure description, interpretation, and consequently evaluation. The condition of the speaker as determined by the critic tends to define the kinds of data relevant to criticism and accordingly to establish the context of critical inquiry. When the speaker, whether represented as "I" or as an impersonal voice, is closely associated with the poet as empirical person, background data, chiefly from the poet's biography, break through the boundaries of the poem and to some degree modify its formal qualities. When the speaker is allowed by the critic to speak for himself as a generalized person, the poem preserves its aesthetic shape but may appear to lack immediate reference to real experience and to the sensible world. While no one seems to maintain in principle the absolute identity or the absolute non-identity of poet and speaker, critics incline toward one pole or the other, usually without explicit acknowledgment or strict consistency. Warrant exists for both critical dispositions in the practice of poets and, indeed, in the very logic of the cases; notwithstanding, the grounds for neither are secure.

The autonomous speaker is something of a philosophical puzzle and perhaps not wholly credible; on the other hand, identification of the speaker with the poet encounters logical obstacles no less formidable and raises, besides, questions about the location of and responsibility for poetry and even about the decorum of criticism. The former approach, though probably less open to radical objections, may yet be uncongenial to many critics because it narrows the context of criticism and grants large prerogatives and exemptions to speakers whose utterances embody social, political, or religious concepts of a contestable character. But even if every consistent view of the speaker entails some warping of perspective, it does not follow that all views are equally defensible or have equally acceptable consequences for poetry. What every discussion of the matter must finally take into account is the possibility that a verbal construct acquires the special quality termed "literary" only as the speaker becomes disengaged from the circumstances of his creation and thus escapes the finite order. This proposition, it is scarcely necessary to observe, restricts the interchange of background and constituent data and thus embarrasses historical, sociological, and other genetic approaches to literary art.

1   Prior to the romantic movement the speaker presented no practical problem because he was commonly a genuine persona declaiming or arguing the commonplaces of his times within the limits of conventional form. The romantics, by affecting spontaneity and sincerity as opposed to artificiality, brought in question the autonomy of the speaker and furnished critics with pretext enough for locating the poet in the poem and the poem in the biography. There is, of course, no strong necessity for taking the romantics on what appear to be their own terms; their verse, as frequently demonstrated, is amenable to contextualist or formalist criticism and as often as not none the worse for it. Even so, nineteenth-century lyrical verse taken in the lump leaves the impression of subjectivity, and biographical data can sometimes be applied persuasively to its explication. Although the modernists have attempted, with the cooperation of a good many critics, to restore the speaker's autonomy,[1] enough ostensibly personal poetry has appeared in this century to leave the speaker's location and the critic's privilege in doubt. Nor has it been altogether a matter of the lyrics of the last two centuries, as the stereotyped personae of

1. G. T. Wright, *The Poet in the Poem: The Personae of Eliot, Yeats, and Pound* (Berkeley and Los Angeles, 1960), p. 50.

Shakespeare and Donne have sometimes been violated as freely as Wordsworth's and Shelley's. Three decades ago Hans Jaeger argued for the essential objectivity of the lyric genre and protested the identification of the speaker with the poet.[2] His view has been affirmed from time to time,[3] though usually in connection with the related problem of intention. M. C. Beardsley fairly represents the considerable number of recent critics who in practice draw a perceptible line between poet and speaker: "In general, the correct principle seems to be that the speaker of a literary work cannot be identified with the author—and therefore the character and condition of the speaker can be known by internal evidence alone—unless the author has provided a pragmatic context, or a claim of one, that connects the speaker with himself."[4] This principle, at least in the form stated, must always be vulnerable to the testimony of poets. The late Gottfried Benn, for instance, stated without qualification, "And so, basically, there can be no other subject for lyric poetry than the lyric poet himself."[5] Whether or not Benn meant to place the empirical "I" squarely in the center of the poem, he assuredly provided support for critics who rely on biographical evidence. Yet the poet who identifies his speakers with himself is vastly oversimplifying a complex ontological problem, and the critic who takes him at his word accepts as true a relationship which is possible but hardly probable.

A verbal system of literary description presupposes an author

2. Hans Jaeger, "Subjektivität und Objektivität der Lyrik," *PMLA*, XLVIII (1933), pp. 252–54.
3. See Manfred Kridl, "Observations sur les Genres de la Poésie lyrique," *Helicon*, II (1939), p. 149; Marcel Raymond, *De Baudelaire au surréalisme* (new ed.; Paris, 1940), p. 344; Käte Hamburger, *Die Logik der Dichtung* (Stuttgart, 1957), pp. 184–86; and Victor Erlich, "The Concept of the Poet as a Problem of Poetics," ed. D. Davie *et al.*, *Poetics* [International Conference of Work-in-Progress Devoted to Problems of Poetics, I, Warsaw, 1960] (Warsaw, 1961), pp. 707–17.
4. M. C. Beardsley, *Aesthetics: Problems in the Philosophy of Criticism* (New York, 1958), p. 240.
5. Gottfried Benn, "Problems of Lyric Poetry," trans. Edgar Lohner, *Western Review*, XXIII (1958), p. 15.

able and willing to accomplish it; all other relationships are problematic. As irreversible process, writing is convertible neither in part nor in whole into the content of mind or the structure of intention. The unity of consciousness, considered as the matrix of composition, can be only a matter of conjecture and never of fact; but even if ascertainable and ascertainably stable, it could not account precisely for a verbal event because language offers options which may satisfy general purposes equally well and yet produce rather different textural effects. So much accepted, the speaker can be certainly defined only in the context of his verbal production; and his relationship to the author is determinable neither by the literary critic nor by the psychologist. These natural limitations on knowledge of the relationship of the consequence to the cause of writing occasion no difficulty when the efficacy of completed compositions can be tested empirically. In the case of literature—and especially lyric poetry—which, in contrast to practical writing, is not in any usual sense of the word testable, the posture of the author is a tempting, though doubtful, source of clues as to import and ultimately to value. But all that the biography ordinarily testifies to is the author's probable capability for accomplishing what in fact has been accomplished. The quality of the verbal action, including the "meaning," is of course attributable to the author as artist; but to seek its explication in the special predicament of the author as person is to assume as true an unprovable relationship, which, if insisted upon, can only relocate his work in a nonaesthetic dimension.[6]

Granted that poets realize themselves in their verse, the relationship is unlikely to be level, but, rather, oblique or skewed. The formalist critic risks nothing by agreeing with Benn that "A poem is always the search for the 'I,' " since his further remark—"all the sphinxes and images of Sais are mixed in the answer"[7]—underscores

---

6. Stephen Ullman, "Style and Personality," *Review of English Literature*, VI (Apr., 1965), pp. 21–31, surveys and largely depreciates recent attempts in stylistics to connect style and author.

7. *Op. cit.*, p. 10.

the futility of attempting to match the poetic content with the turbulent processes of the creative mind.[8] Nor is it a great deal safer to interpret the life in light of the work, for, as Jaeger argues, what the poem reflects is partial and even misleading: "Und wie die Summe vieler Momentaufnahmen kein einheitliches Porträt ergibt, so vermittelt auch die Lyrik nur mehrere, vielfach gänzlich unähnliche, zufällige und daher durchaus nicht immer besonders charakteristiche Bilder des Dichters. . . ."[9] It is doubtless possible to associate biography and poetry convincingly, but critical biographies seldom succeed wholly as biography or as criticism. When viewed largely in its literary relationships, the life suffers misrepresentation. When the life is mingled with the art, the art suffers because the tension which holds together its formal properties is to some degree released. Yeats, rather through his own fault, has become so intimately involved with his speakers that his poems stand in danger of being read as documents attesting to a particularly colorful career; and this is the case even with those which are exemplary embodiments of timeless themes. Hopkins, cast or miscast by critics as the suffering (or contented) Jesuit priest, now intrudes so far on his speakers as to claim as empirical person the solicitude of his readers.

If poetry is fabrication and not more or less faithful verbalization of experience, the speaker is not a person but a persona. In the lyric, it is not so much a mask held before the face of an actor as a disembodied voice speaking of the possibilities—not the actualities—of thought and feeling. If the lyric persona may be said to derive ultimately from the poet, it is most immediately a product of language and is wholly defined by the content of its utterance. The "voice of the poem" is no less an abstraction than the agent desig-

---

8. F. W. Bateson, *English Poetry: A Critical Introduction* (London, 1950), p. 69, observes, "The psychological processes inside the poet as a result of which the black marks are on the paper include so much that is not recorded there that they cannot be equated with the poem, though they are, of course, related to it."

9. *Op. cit.*, p. 252.

nated in such phrases as "voice of doom" and vox *populi,* but among sophisticated readers it is more liable to hypostatization. When hypostatized, the lyric voice points in the most obvious direction—that is, toward the poet himself—and inevitably borrows something from his personal experiences and attitudes. Whatever the intention of the poet may be, his poem is likely to consist *in embryo* of unsorted shards of language. The full-fledged persona cannot be said to exist *ab initio* but must arise as a by no means predictable consequence of the poet's contriving. This is not to register a doubt that language can be manipulated precisely to serve practical ends or even that a poet may sometimes create a persona substantially in his own image; but the fact remains that the persona receives its identity from the completed verbal system, which, in the case of imaginative literature, is built up from linguistic options. If it is too much to say that language takes charge of the poet,[10] his solution of verbal problems assuredly leads to unforeseeable results. Between the interval of reflection with which a poem begins and the perfected work stands the artistic process— that is, the conscious use of the arts of language in a framework of intuitions and tentative plans—and such are the vagaries of creation that a finished poem must come as something of a surprise to the poet himself. Since writers generally do not admit failure of purpose, it is reasonable to suppose that they adjust their original intentions to accord with actual results and accept their personae as finally made manifest by art.

Logical obstacles notwithstanding, interpretation often appears to benefit—that is, to gain in plausibility—from inferences drawn from data not directly relatable to the literary work itself. If it stands to reason that critical decisions are best made on the basis

10. Notice should be taken, however, of the possibility suggested by Ivan Fónagy, "Informationsgehalt von Wort und Laut in der Dichtung," *Poetics,* ed. D. Davie et al. (Warsaw, 1961), p. 591: "Der Dichter ist nur so lange frei, bis er nicht nach der Feder greift. Der erste Versfuss bestimmt die metrische Gestalt des Gedichtes, mit jedem Wort wird die Wahl der folgenden Wörter mehr eingeengt, bis der Dichter zuletzt in diesem Netz der Bindungen verwoben das Gedicht seinem eigenen Schicksal überlassen muss."

of all reliable information, criticism must yet vary radically according to the weight allowed that class of data which gives not direct knowledge of a literary work but only knowledge of the generating milieu and particularly the circumstances of the author. Data of this sort acquire the status of evidence only in the context of posited composer-composition relationships, and these, except as indicated, must always fail of logical necessity. Literary history assuredly has its sanctions and indeed makes possible many sorts of inferences useful to criticism; at the same time, it has little to say of rules of evidence for the guidance of critics. If the critic may usually accept the historian's explanation of (say) a topical allusion, the same privilege cannot be reasonably extended to the bulk of circumstantial evidence of literary relationships which may be supposed to aid interpretation. Although never recoverable, the totality of biographical detail, including the author's reading, must account in some way for his literary production; but to say how is to presume to order into a causal complex what presents itself as a largely undiscriminated mass of fact. And yet a designing intellect has to be reckoned with, unless literary products are to be regarded as mere accidents of nature, detached from the circumstances which brought them into being. So much conceded, the use of background matter ought yet to be governed by the criteria of probable (not possible) relationship and literary relevance. Probable relationship, though not always acknowledged in practice, seems incontestable. No less incontestable, literary relevance presupposes a delimitation of context. If a literary work is essentially a self-contained aesthetic object rather than a fragment of biography or history, facts about the author and his milieu, even though inferentially connectable to his works, may or may not be relevant; and the critic must assume case by case the burden of proof. These are the conditions under which the attitudes and experiences of the author may be properly allowed to infringe the speaker's autonomy and thereby to contribute to the "explanation" of his utterance. Yet, even under such circumstances as these, logical difficulties

arise, for external evidence is clearly admissible only as it is confirmed by poetic content.[11] All that it seems safe to grant is that
background data can legitimately enrich—not dictate—the critic's
understanding of a poem and thus of its speaker.

If "criticism can hardly do without a kind of literary psychology
connecting the poet with the poem," as Northrop Frye maintains,[12]
the connection can consist only of such inferences as effects permit
concerning their causes; and inferences thus drawn can logically
contribute nothing to the understanding of effects. It is doubtless
a convenience for discussing poetry—and especially lyric poetry—
to establish a connection between poet and poem and to identify
the speaker with the poet, but these relationships must always be
uncertain and therefore a flimsy basis for interpretation. In the
absence of significant (as opposed to trivial) general laws under
which supposed causes and artistic results can be subsumed, literary
psychology can consist of little more than preferred explanations
among less appealing alternatives. (This is not, of course, to deny
the very great importance of psychology for the understanding of
such human predicaments as literature actually embodies.) For
example, the attempts to account in terms of personal experience
for the failure of much of Wordsworth's later poetry, while varying
in plausibility, share alike the status of mere opinion. Whatever
may be revealed by the psychological probing which Frye sanctions
relates to the poet and only conjecturally to his verse: "Part of this
[literary psychology] may be a psychological study of the poet,
though this is useful chiefly in analysing the failures in his expression, the things in him which are still attached to his work."
Whether failure ever has so narrow a cause may be doubted; but,
more importantly, this line of inquiry, which is a questionable
attempt to surpass the knowledge provided by the work of art,

11. For example, *The Listeners* can hardly be said to confirm the account of
its origin—a class reunion—which Walter de la Mare supplied. See J. M. Purcell,
"de la Mare's *The Listeners*," *Explicator*, IV (1945–46), item 31.
12. Northrop Frye, *Fables of Identity: Studies in Poetic Mythology* (New
York, 1963), p. 11.

entails hypotheses impossible of validation and ends with "solutions" not properly literary. Such attempts inevitably carry the critic into other universes of discourse; though what he discovers may be independently interesting, it cannot be translated into aesthetic (and hence into value) terms. Frye proposes for critics a scientific methodology,[13] but seeking in literature the psychological cause of its aberrations is scarcely less futile than searching for the first cause of gravitation in a fallen apple. If criticism is to be in any sense a science, critics have no alternative to setting boundaries to their province and limiting themselves to statements actually susceptible of verification. This is the price of scientific status, and of course it may be too high.

Granted that rummaging in the biography and milieu of the poet may be a largely disinterested endeavor to provide a context in which his art can be the better understood and appreciated, the fact remains that prior knowledge of the art, insofar as it may induce expectations about the poet's character, biases background research. Work of this kind can hardly advance without at least vague presuppositions as to the relationships which generally obtain between compositions of a given tenor and their composers, but these have a doubtful validity simply because literary quality cannot be deduced from traits of character. The point of departure is perhaps usually the assumption that the speaker is the poet or some penetrable disguise thereof; and whether admitted or not, the search tends to be for that essential or "true" self capable of accomplishing the poetry attributed to the public person. But the "true" self is only an intuition, and attempts to locate it may lead to infinite regress. While it is possible by means of a tenuous string of inferences drawn from the public acts and statements of the poet to map his private domain, such knowledge as may be gained cannot logically explain his artistic productions. Whatever may emerge from the unconscious becomes inextricably mingled with and unpredictably modified by such conventions, borrowings, and

13. *Ibid.*, pp. 7 f.

artifices as the poet consciously employs. Moreover, if the critic insists on locating the "true" self in the labyrinth of the unconscious, where no rules apply and no art exists, he thereby relieves the public person of much of the responsibility for his artistic accomplishment. So considered, the poet tends to become a mechanism registering in conventional language the tensions and anxieties peculiar to his time and place and accordingly deserves neither praise nor blame. By this deterministic view the "true" self is little more than a voice speaking out of historical circumstances, and its location is, to use Taine's terms, in the *race, milieu,* and *moment.* While the case for author psychology may not be quite so desperate, it is perfectly evident that there is no methodology by which the formal result of the creative process can be described in terms of its ultimate cause. The critic surely errs when he fabricates a poetic self out of conjectured psychic contents and allows it to usurp the role of the speaker.

Criticism can pretend to exclusive competency to deal with literature only because the formal consequences of creativity cannot be deduced from background data. Were the case otherwise, defensible descriptions of literary events could be given by reference to causes and in nonaesthetic terms. But without covering laws, such disciplines as anthropology, psychology, history, and sociology are incompetent to describe the formal construct as a product of personal and cultural influences and can only cite its content as evidence of those influences. As such, however, literature is less reliable than documents and letters. In contrast to the poet, the author of a letter may be assumed to speak directly through the "I" of his communication to a definite time and occasion. Poetry is not so easily located, and its contemporary relationships are usually problematic. Although behavioral scientists are privileged to evaluate art as cultural material, it is the prerogative of the critic to determine precisely how far the cultural legacy as known impinges upon the work of art and affects its value as such. Edward Stankiewicz has recently asked, "For what can prevent literary analysis from endless proliferation, from considering the totality of human culture as a gloss to any single line of a poem?"[14] The answer is acceptance of logical limits to critical inquiry. A line of poetry is, properly considered, a gloss to human culture, but a cultural datum can be admitted as a gloss to a line of poetry only if it satisfies the criteria of probable relationship and literary relevance.[15] The "Ode on a Grecian Urn," for instance, presupposes knowledge of aesthetic objects but not of Grecian urns, and nothing in the history of ancient art can gloss the poem in any way necessary to its understanding. Nor can Keats's demonstrated interest in the Elgin Marbles modify the lyric voice, which is entirely constituted of thought and feeling about art and beauty and the truth status thereof. The critic as critic can only accept the cultural and philosophic context as described and judge the literary value of the poem from the quality of its experience and expression.

A methodology of whatever kind imposes limits on inquiry and thus on understanding. The poem may be considered as an aesthetic object, autonomous and autotelic, or as a document evidencing and exerting influences; but there is no system capable of containing it under both aspects. The claims of history and the behavioral sciences to understand literary works as cognitive contents cannot be denied; what can be denied is the interchangeability of aesthetic and nonaesthetic terms and the convertibility of nonaesthetic value into aesthetic value.[16] While the content of a poem, considered as a set of implicit or explicit statements, can often be related with fair plausibility to general cultural circumstances and appraised accordingly, the formal construct, considered as a fusion of thought and feeling ordered rhetorically, can be plausibly de-

14. Edward Stankiewicz, "Poetic and Non-Poetic Language in Their Interrelation," ed. D. Davie et al., *Poetics* (Warsaw, 1961), p. 23.

15. See C. S. Lewis, "The Anthropological Approach," ed. Norman Davis and C. L. Wrenn, *English and Medieval Studies Presented to J. R. R. Tolkien on the Occasion of His Seventieth Birthday* (London, 1962), pp. 219–30.

16. For example, equating moral "good" and aesthetic "good" fails of logical necessity.

scribed and evaluated only in terms of formal relationships. This is in no way to deny the value of literature for an understanding of institutions and human predicaments or its potential influence for good or ill but only to define the conditions of artistic success and failure. If these limitations on the critical function preclude synoptic views and therewith claims to total understanding, they assuredly protect the integrity of the aesthetic object against those for whom literature subserves other concerns. And if the critic is logically compelled to assume the separate role of moralist in order to discriminate the sanitary from the unsanitary, his purely professional reports must be all the freer of statements of mere opinion and preference.

2 Rehearsing the more or less familiar arguments against adulterating criticism with inappropriate dimensions and with unwarranted deductions from background data is unlikely to result in widespread adoption of logically defensible (and therefore constrictive) approaches. The simple fact that contemporary poets derive from and exist in largely knowable cultural locations makes feasible, if it does not justify, the very broadest inquiry into the relations between their verse and the circumstances surrounding its production. For the last century and a half, moreover, the prevailing genre has been the lyric; and the forms which it has taken, rather in contrast to pre-romantic specimens, frequently leave a marked impression of subjectivity and sometimes of special pleading. Often ideologically implicated, or seemingly so, and at the same time afflicted with a degree of indeterminacy, modern lyrics force attention on their authors as likely sources of clues to import and intent. Understandably, critics can claim that they have no alternative to interpreting the lyric speaker in some significant relationship to the poet, even at the risk of confusing these two logically discrete entities. It should be perfectly evident from the reception of Wimsatt and Beardsley's exemplary refutation of

intentionalism[17] that many very talented critics are simply unwilling to sacrifice to methodological nicety such advantages (and doubtless satisfactions) as accrue to biographical inquiry. The liberty to inquire into and to conjecture the poet's intention is of crucial importance to any variety of criticism which admits genetic and teleological factors to major consideration. Though ordinarily a matter of opinion rather than of fact, the poet's intention affords the critic a pretext for and a means of constructing an *ad hoc* system, which, with respect to description and explanation, may incorporate plausibly the bias of his own preferences. The question "what was intended?" does not of course entail the question "why was it intended?" or "should it have been intended?" but critical assessments complicated with biographical data are unlikely to be free of ethical considerations. Granted that clinical objectivity is neither possible nor desirable in literary criticism, it is yet proper to protest any system of criteria which incorporates concessions to the quality of intention as opposed to achievement. At worst, such a system can be a means of enhancing the reputation of a poetaster who happens to make agreeable ideological responses; at best, it introduces to critical appraisal biases which may appear perfectly absurd in the cool perspective of literary history.

The question whether the critic must need on occasion take the poet as purposeful person fully into account probably admits of no definite answer, but it is well to recall that the understanding of lyrics from earlier centuries has not been noticeably impeded by a dearth of biographical data. The explanation may be, at least for the Middle Ages, that poets, presumably lacking a strong sense of individuality, make through their speakers negligible demands for recognition as empirical persons. Whether signed or unsigned, medieval lyrics are in an important sense anonymous, and their authors are identifiable, if at all, by craft rather than by obtrusive sensibility. What is especially instructive for modern criticism is

17. First published as "The Intentional Fallacy," *Sewanee Review*, LIV (1946), pp. 468–88.

not so much the achievement of these early lyrics as the inferable postures of their authors, speakers, and audiences; for these, by contrast, define the tensions which affect the production and criticism of poetry in this century. The relative unity of medieval life assumed in those affairs which bear most significantly on art, the conventionality of medieval lyrics is most plausibly to be explained by reference to the stability of the matrix of their production. This is to say no more than that the number of voices (that is, sets of values) available to poets was sharply limited and defined by what would now be described as a "closed society." The verse presupposes a fund of shared convictions and attitudes which poets could exploit without embarrassment and without much fear of protest. While there are exceptions to this generalization (e.g., sporadic clerical strictures on secular songs), the community of interest and agreement was such that the line of communication from the poet through the speaker to the audience could run unambiguously. The voice of a medieval lyric is, very nearly out of necessity, a commonplace of thought and feeling; and the author, though doubtless having gained therapeutic benefits from composition, is implicated only as a person employing forms loosely associated with periods and geographical locations. It is pointless to inquire how far personal experiences enter into such songs as "Unter der linden" of Walther von der Vogelweide or "D'Amors, qui m'a tolu a moi" of Chrétien de Troyes, as their conventionality is proof against biographically oriented criticism.

The same easy relations of poet and audience which obtain in a fairly unified, if not homogeneous, society are hardly to be expected in a fragmented one. Conflicting interests breed competitive sets of values and therewith partisan sensitivities. While poets seem never entirely at ease with the world, the severity of tensions affecting their attitudes assuredly varies from period to period. Marked cultural heterogeneity, with its incorrigible suspicions and cross-purposes, leaves poets largely unsure of their audiences and audiences of their poets. This is in no way to suggest that poetry accurately registers current conflicts but only that poets' privileges and obligations become exceedingly problematic when general agreement fails with respect to the larger human concerns. It is doubtless impossible to discover a principle predictive of the main literary and social consequences of mutual distrust between poet and audience (including, of course, the critic), though each party will surely allege a lack of understanding and taste in the other. But perhaps the most significant possibility is that the experiences eligible for poetic work are as severely limited by a society in which most values are questioned as one in which most values are settled. Closed societies, intolerant of tolerance, limit the poet to a small number of well-defined postures; open societies, intolerant of intolerance, grant to the poet in principle the whole world of experience and yet tend to forbid him those regions which can be a source of pain to group and class consciousness. In many respects less free than Dante, Chaucer, or Milton, the modern poet may frame vague remonstrances against unfeeling institutions, but he ordinarily may not, without risk of bitter denunciation, incorporate bills of particulars offensive to articulate collectivities. This is not to argue that poetry ought to be defamatory, although it is difficult to understand how vital poetry can seem otherwise in a period of organized interest and petty sensitivities.[18] But whether committed or uncommitted to special causes, the poet is likely to be suspect, either as an apologist for or as a subverter of someone's interest. That he may be either or both and at the same time a competent artist is conceded hesitantly, for the point at which art comes to subserve prejudice is not always clear. Unfortunately, in a fragmented society the assertion even of an innocent value may strike some part of the available audience as covert ideology.

Nor can the poet assure the autonomy of his speakers and his

18. Though doubtless in good humor, the secretary of the Ice Cream Manufacturers' Association, after reading the "Emperor of Ice-Cream," wrote Stevens to inquire whether he was for ice cream or against it. See W. Y. Tindall, *Wallace Stevens* (Univ. of Minnesota Pamphlets on American Writers, No. 11; Minneapolis, 1961), p. 11.

own detachment by means of formal and grammatical objectivity; it is the character of the speaker which determines for the reader the degree of the poet's personal involvement. When the voice of the lyric is constituted of widely shared experience, the poet can be implicated only as a member of a sizable collectivity, which is as much as to say scarcely at all.[19] Thus, nothing particularly individualizing, aside from artistry, can be alleged of Herrick from the evidence of "To Daffodils" or of Donne from "Death, be not proud," although both use first-person pronouns. The explanation is that their themes are eschatological commonplaces of the Renaissance. While singularity in the speaker is no more logically predicable of the poet than banality, it can often be linked with fair plausibility to him, doubtless on the assumption that proximity tends to establish relatedness. By contrast with the Renaissance exemplars, which are superficially classifiable as subjective lyrics, the "Love Song of J. Alfred Prufrock" is dramatic—that is, objective—in form and without provable reference to the poet's personal condition. But Prufrock's confession of love-longing testifies to a deep and exceptionally gloomy view of human relations and thus to a view sufficiently singular to raise questions of its genesis. The poem assuredly evidences Eliot's insight, sensitivity, and prosodical aptness but not the similarity of Eliot and Prufrock. Eliot doubtless brought to the creation of Prufrock the same sympathetic understanding which Browning brought to Fra Lippo Lippi and his hedonistic bishop; but this circumstance gives no warrant for interchanging the data of the poem with the data of the biography. Eliot has himself remarked the risk of imputing the speaker's views to the poet: "Some poets are of so mixed a type that it is impossible to say how far they write their poetry because of what they believe, and how far they believe a thing merely because they see that they can make poetry out of it."[20] In any case,

---

19. See Hamburger, *op. cit.*, p. 163.
20. T. S. Eliot, "Poetry and Propaganda," ed. M. D. Zabel, *Literary Opinion in America* (rev. ed.; New York, 1951), p. 103.

objectivity as such has afforded poets no relief from the inspection of critics and especially from those who are disposed to separate thought from form and to award primacy to the former. It is to be suspected, moreover, that some critics study biographical data more to discover whether they can admire the poet as person than to improve their understanding of his art.

Admiration of a poet's career is not, at least for responsible critics, a precondition for admiration of his work, although some of the responses to the awarding of the Bollingen Prize to the *Pisan Cantos* approach this position.[21] But this is not to suggest that evaluations of a poet's achievement are unaffected by his supposed personal views. An uninformed reader coming to Yeats by way of a "Front" article in the *Times Literary Supplement* (June 24, 1965) might very well conclude that his poetry is somehow marred by unsanitary political and social preferences. Yeats, like every other major modern poet, has suffered from gratuitous balance sheets, which debit the privilege of independent opinion against the accomplishment of art.[22] What saves the modern lyric poet from irrelevant tests of ideological rectitude is unfortunately not objective form but banality, which, if accompanied by a show of sincerity, can sometimes win uncommon praise.

Poetry probably can be a largely innocent enterprise, consisting in the arrangement of formal components for sheer aesthetic pleasure. While such unserious contriving may disclose configurations of dark significance to *Tiefenpsychologie*, its formal surface need be nothing more than a contexture of pleasurable detail. Nonetheless, *poésie pure* seems not to earn great critical respect, whether from association with the morbidity and amorality of nineteenth-century aestheticism or from an apparent defect of concern for the human condition. To be sure, anthologists since Tottel have

21. See "The Question of the Pound Award," *Partisan Review*, XVI (May, 1949), pp. 512–22.
22. See W. H. Auden, "The Public v. the late Mr. William Butler Yeats," *Partisan Review*, VI (Spring, 1939), pp. 46–51; and J. R. Harrison, *The Reactionaries* (London, 1966).

acknowledged the occasional charm of poetic trifles and even of academic exercises, but it is chiefly the poetry of "serious purpose" which has been the object of serious criticism in recent times. Doubtless "serious purpose" pertains to art, though not entirely and perhaps not mainly; for the thrust of the phrase seems to be toward commitment of another sort. What appears to be most acceptable is commitment generally to suffering humanity conceived as victim of ritualized custom and unfeeling privilege. It is observable, however, that the poetry of the fifties, which bares a tender social conscience, consists all too frequently of unexceptional social and psychological impressions. The speakers are the dwindled voices of uncritical liberalism, disillusioned and uncertain; and despite their pretense of uniqueness, they are culturally as locatable as the stereotyped personae of the *trouvères*. Whether critics are in any way responsible for these subdued voices is probably undeterminable; but their continuing abuse of the major poets of this century can hardly be an encouragement to bold and independent expression. If it is to the credit of a majority of critics that they have acknowledged excellence no matter what its ideological resonances, they have not always done so with complete good grace. Sinister shadows have often been cast across pure artistic accomplishment, and in some cases the "true" self has been relentlessly pursued through the lyric speaker with the manifest design of convicting it of heinous crimes.

If Auden is correct and "poetry makes nothing happen," institutions stand in no real danger from it; and criticism of its ideas as instruments of good or ill is misplaced. But if poetry is as potentially influential as Arnold hoped, it doubtless requires to be certified by official guardians of the public weal. In truth, poetry cannot be considered the cause of any significant general effect; it is rather an effect, but one which stands in a largely uncertain relationship to its causes. And yet, if poetry must be allowed some influence, it is to deepen—not to increase—knowledge through the magic of language, though inevitably for a limited audience. While the poet can be responsible, he cannot at one and the same time be responsible to art and to what passes in a given historical interval as social good; indeed, he can attend to demands of the latter only by assuming the role of censor of his own work. The poet can be held responsible neither for his experience of events and conditions nor for the transaction between his imagination and language which culminates in a set of aesthetically valuable verbal signs. As artist, he is obliged to perfect his work through due regard for literary decorum and formal requirements;[23] as citizen, he is somehow responsible to his times and may feel compelled in this capacity to extinguish the products of his creative moments. Whether poets have often performed this excruciating task for other than aesthetic reasons is doubtful; rather, they are likely to claim that the freely invented and honestly contrived work of art has its own integrity and accordingly its right to public display, no matter what the response of definable groups and scattered individuals. The scientist's attitude toward discovery is no different. In any case, it is a consummate irony that the bulk of the poetry of this century which seems most likely to endure acknowledges no obligation to suit the dominant persuasions; most of it suggests either a lack of concern for noisy social passions or a profound distaste for them. In one way or another, Eliot, Yeats, Pound, Thomas, Stevens, and even Frost prove embarrassing to critics whose concern is more with causes than with art; for their verse tends to adumbrate traditional values in terms uncongenial to the times and even subversive of the hopeful new concepts of the human condition. If none of them has been denied some claim to fame, none has yet received the fulsome praise lavished, for whatever curious reasons, on Whitman; and some have endured more abuse than the Middle Ages heaped on the devil.

Nothing so effectively as high artistic achievement saves the writer from oblivion and relieves him of the animus of his detrac-

23. See Allen Tate, "To Whom Is the Poet Responsible?" *Hudson Review*, IV (1951–52), pp. 325–34.

tors. Virgil has borne a variety of good and evil reputations and never lacked an admiring audience. Dante defamed the recent dead to the discomfiture of the living, and Snorri Sturluson intrigued as cynically as a Byzantine courtier; but these circumstances seven centuries later are unconsidered footnotes to their greater accomplishment. The good and Godly John Lydgate, equally productive but unequally gifted, now languishes in the dusty volumes of the Early English Text Society, a permanent reminder that history rejudges and *sub specie aeternitatis*. Critics must know that, inasmuch as literary history forgives all save mediocrity, literary judgment complicated with contemporary issues can be little better than tendentious journalism. Yet some persist, for what to them must be considerations of the greatest weight, in thrusting poets as poets into roles which are at most relevant to their careers as proposing and disposing citizens. The fact that a critic approaches a poet's work through background data and tends to understand the biography in light of the art and the art in light of the biography does not, of course, convict him of attempting through irrelevant considerations either to diminish or to enhance what is intended, as far as can ordinarily be determined, only as art. Assuredly, allowance must be made for that class of readers who admire great literature for what it appears to reveal of great men. Nonetheless, associating the speaker closely with the poet is a means so convenient for obfuscating the purely literary issue that it must be regarded with a degree of suspicion and especially from the circumstance that the speaker can be identified with the poet only at considerable expense to probability.

The poet and the critic alike want to be admired, the one for creating monuments of the intellect, the other for recognizing their true worth. Since the poet never quite transcends human limitations and since the critic never quite achieves objectivity, which is as much as to say freedom from a passion to reconstitute and refine what others have wrought, poetry stands between the condition of universal validity and the finite order, with its implications of contemporary reference and remediableness. The critic intends to understand, to describe, and finally to evaluate; but he can hardly perform this function without disclosing what, in his opinion, poetry should and should not be. With respect to formal qualities, it is his prerogative to assume a fixed position and sometimes to err, as he certainly should if applying neoclassical criteria to romantic verse. With respect to ideological contents, his prerogatives are much less clear; for it is not evident that artistic success is contingent upon the quality of embodied ideas. Ideas may be absolutely right or absolutely wrong, but they can be excellent or not excellent only in a pragmatic sense. "A good idea" or "a bad idea" signifies a judgment about practical results; and accordingly a false idea may yet be a good idea in a literary context. Ptolemaic cosmology is surely wrong but perhaps better for Milton's purposes than Copernican; in any case, its wrongness is irrelevant to the criticism of *Paradise Lost*. Poems are perhaps limited by the order of magnitude of the ideas which they embody, though the criteria for ranking ideas are unclear; but a nonsensical idea, as the "Owl and the Pussy Cat" demonstrates, is not a bar to artistic success, at least of a limited sort. The critic as critic (and not moralist) can properly evaluate ideas only in reference to formal consequences; to evaluate them in a literary context according to degrees of supposed correctness is to commit something like a category mistake. Yet it may be too much to expect critics to avoid entirely this logical defect, for it is a means by which they can impose limitations on uncongenial poetry.

A magisterial and prophetic speaker claims for the poet simply those privileges and powers which ancient tradition granted to his kind and which the romantic period reasserted without provoking immediate demurral, but such is the conditioning of the twentieth century that critics experience some difficulty in accepting the authenticity of major voices. The modest persona, speaking from inadequacy rather than strength, finds a friendlier reception.[24]

24. Wright, *op. cit.*, p. 55.

Doubtless one explanation is that the modern intelligence acknowledges transcendent ability reluctantly and seldom without limiting it with alleged defects of body and soul.[25] Excellence can be an affront to the collective ego and to equalitarian presuppositions and accordingly a target for the rhetoric of disparagement. Another and not less plausible explanation is that the collectivities of a heterogeneous society can readily accept as true prophets only the heroes of their own persuasion and interest. Thus, a poetry which feeds the moral and spiritual concerns of one group may strike another as covert ideology or plain propaganda. Yet the poetic speaker must embody a point of view and therewith a set of preferences, which may be congenial to none or few. With older literature, there is usually no problem, as historical perspective makes possible the accommodation of disagreeable values. With contemporary literature, the situation is obviously different, and a good many critics make a rather large point of admiring a given poet's art while regretting the thought and feeling which it embodies. The difficulties of accommodation are no less evident in the attempts to claim poets of uncertain commitment for one persuasion or another.[26] This tendency, long apparent in Shakespearean studies,[27] testifies to the very real difficulty which critics face in doing complete justice to uncongenial speakers. Yet the poet's problem is the greater, for it becomes increasingly difficult for him to shape voices which are significant for the modern occasion and at the same time above the welter of social, political, and religious conflicts.

But if the poet is to be defended on principle against charges of

25. See Franz Alexander, *Our Age of Unreason: A Study of the Irrational Forces in Social Life* (Philadelphia and New York, 1942), p. 281; Lionel Trilling, "A Note on Art and Neurosis," *Partisan Review*, XII (1945), pp. 43–45.

26. See E. A. Bloom, "The Vatic Temper in Literary Criticism," *Criticism*, V (1963), pp. 297–315; N. R. Cary, "An Apologetic for Christian Criticism: A Comment on 'The Vatic Temper in Literary Criticism'," *Criticism*, VI (1964), pp. 266–72.

27. See R. W. Battenhouse, "Shakespearean Tragedy as Christian: Some Confusions in the Debate," *Centennial Review*, VIII (1964), pp. 78–87.

intending to write aught save poetry, the critic must be defended in his public intention of writing literary criticism and not something else. The question is, what constitutes malfeasance? The poet may be said to have abdicated his responsibility and accordingly to have forfeited his right to critical consideration when he exhibits in the guise of art aesthetically unrealized impressions and preferences. By the same token, the critic is discredited when, without explicitly testing the aesthetic integrity of a poem, he transfers it to a non-literary jurisdiction and proceeds to confuse the question of formal achievement with ethical judgments which are rooted in contestable grounds. This strategy ordinarily entails identification of the speaker with the poet and a survey of the latter's private affairs to establish a close relationship between poetic contents and personal inclinations. By this means the poet can be made responsible for his speaker (considered as an ideological content), and the speaker can be analyzed as an instrument of the poet's ulterior motives. Ordinarily a hostile critic need not show that the stance of the poet-speaker is against reason or against nature or that it impairs the aesthetic integrity of the poem. To suggest that it is against consensus arouses distrust, though the consensus may be no broader than the critic's own party. For whatever seems singular and antipathetical seems sinister.

Whether a poet writes in a furious Marxist passion or in a fine aristocratic pique or desires the preservation or the overthrow of institutions is, even if provable, *ipso facto* significant of nothing literary. The location of a poem is aesthetic until proved otherwise, and all the admissible evidence resides in the poem. If a poem is merely versified dogma or doctrine, both the consenting and dissenting critic must be aware of the fact; and neither can in good conscience praise or dispraise what in truth belongs to the category of practical writing. It is yet apparent that a poem may achieve an impeccable literary state of existence and at the same time inculcate and celebrate articles of sectarian faith, although this circumstance is likely to be clearly—and painfully—evident only to the critic who subscribes to other views. While no blame should attach to failures of accommodation, a critic is ethically obligated to acknowledge whatever incapacity he may have for dealing fairly with poems of disagreeable import. Damage occurs when a critic consciously or unconsciously becomes the avenging hero of his own interest and turns a legitimate assault on the intricacies of language into the conquest of what, in his self-consciousness, he has come to hear as the voice of an enemy. Although conquests of this sort can hardly be permanent, a poet's work may yet show residual effects for a generation or two. It is no exaggeration to say that by continually violating the necessary autonomy of the lyric speaker, critics have threatened the literary mode of existence of a great deal of twentieth-century poetry and that generally the most impressive.

Chapter III

Rhetoric's
Wrung Neck

The expressed distaste for rhetoric
among critics, especially of poetry, may be interpreted offhand as
a healthy, if unduly protracted, reaction to the stylistic artificiality
and pomposity of the late nineteenth century. Thundering periods
and tumid numbers, though serviceable to truth no less than to
falsehood, tend nonetheless to set feeling over thought and on that
account offend the rational faculty. It is possibly true, in any case,
that a style which matches the *Geist* of one period may falsify that
of another and accordingly that new times may require radically
new modes of expression. Nowadays, as at the outset of the romantic revolt, such artful contriving as classical rhetorics prescribe
is wholly obnoxious; and naturalness, that is, spontaneous, unpre-
meditated, though not necessarily clear, expression, everywhere
wins approval, because vouching, as it is supposed, for sincerity.[1]
For four or five decades the term *rhetoric* has signified, almost to
the exclusion of benign meanings, any more or less pretentious
style cultivated for whatever reasons. Modern critics who echo
Paul Verlaine's injunction in *Art poétique* (1882) to wring rhetoric's neck—"Prends l'éloquence et tords–lui son cou!"—seem at
first glance to have little more in mind than the florid figures and
studied orotundity with which graceless poets from antiquity to
the present have clothed their visions. Yet it is by no means unlikely
that *rhetoric* is frequently intended to suggest sinister motives, for
its reference, on close examination, seldom appears to be exclusively stylistic, and it is often uttered with a vehemence appropriate
to moral indignation.

1. M. H. Abrams, *The Mirror and the Lamp: Romantic Theory and the
Critical Tradition* (New York, 1953), p. 318, observes that sincerity "began in
the early nineteenth century its career as the primary criterion, if not the *sine
qua non*, of excellence in poetry."

T. S. Eliot once asked what those critics mean who flourish
rhetoric pejoratively but contented himself with a rather simple
answer: "And we begin to suspect that the word is merely a vague
term of abuse for any style that is bad, that is so evidently bad or
second-rate that we do not recognize the necessity for greater precision in the phrases we apply to it."[2] At another point, in connection with dramatic speech, he identified rhetoric with ornament:
"In that case we must say that rhetoric is any adornment or infla-
tion of speech which is *not done for a particular effect* but for a
general impressiveness."[3] Eliot's explanations are seriously vitiated
by the fact that a great deal of poetry which is not demonstrably
bad on account of ineptness, superficiality, or poor taste is yet
described as rhetorical. More importantly, he scarcely acknowledges
that the term can signify a defect of integrity no less than a mistaken style. Robert Graves's sophistical pronouncement about the
effect of rhetoric on the Middle Ages and about its employment in
general is ethical rather than aesthetic: "It is no business of mine
to evaluate the damage done to simple faith by the tropes, tricks,
and traductions of rhetoric; but I am convinced that poets who
rely on rhetoric rather than inspiration are behaving unprofession-
ally."[4] Oscar Williams describes the academic poet as a rhetorician
and imputes to him shameless borrowing and fraudulent pretensions: "the true academic is that literary figure who confuses his
contemporaries by displaying a mock talent wrapped in the cello-
phane of rhetoric that obeys all the rules, even to the simulation of
the faults of the best poets."[5] Whatever Graves and Williams understand by rhetoric, it is quite evidently to them a result of intent
rather than of honest error, that is, malpractice, with all the ethical
implications of the word. If not precisely sophistry—false display

2. T. S. Eliot, *Selected Essays, 1917–1932* (New York, 1932), p. 25.
3. *Ibid.,* p. 30.
4. Robert Graves, *The Crowning Privilege* (London, 1955), p. 99.
5. Oscar Williams, ed., *A Little Treasury of Modern Poetry: English and American* (rev. ed.; New York, 1952), pp. xliv f.

with intent to deceive—it is something so closely akin that Plato could not have perceived a difference.

A good deal of tact marks the discussion of particular instances, and the moral issue is not often raised, at least not formally. Herbert Read alleges Eliot's early addiction to rhetoric but emphasizes his reform: "It has been a long search for sincerity of utterance— sincerity of *poetic* utterance: a long disciplined effort to avoid the artificiality of rhetoric."[6] Speaking of a poet of the immediate past, however, Sir Herbert makes very plain that his conception of rhetoric embraces a good deal more than the superficies of style and has indeed a significant moral dimension. He describes Hardy's *Convergence of the Twain* as artificial and then adds, "It is not poetic—or rather, it is rhetorical, and like all rhetoric, a corruption of the poetic consciousness."[7] It is not usual to question Hardy's integrity or, in this instance, his craftsmanship; the most obvious cause of offense is the almost exultant fatalism of the poem and its doubtful world view. Significantly, Read is not concerned to validate the content as opposed to its expression. Randall Jarrell's discussion some years ago of W. H. Auden's development leaves the impression that the acceptable alternative to rhetoric is some sort of imagistic poetry which expresses ideas very quietly, if at all: "One sees how effective the best of the early poems are—how concrete, startling, and thoroughly realized their texture is; but one finds, on analysis, that they are astonishingly unrhetorical, that the tough magical effects that enchant one are not being accomplished by any elaborate rhetoric, but by a great variety of causes, the most noticeable of which is the language—a concrete, laconic, and eccentric variant of ordinary English." But Auden, in Jarrell's view, turned rhetorician—about the time, it should be added, that he turned Marxist: "In the late poems there is a system of rhetorical devices so elaborate that Auden might list it under *Assets*, just as

6. Herbert Read, *The True Voice of Feeling: Studies in English Romantic Poetry* (New York, 1953), p. 142.
7. Herbert Read, "The Drift of Modern Poetry," *Encounter*, IV (January, 1955), p. 4.

a firm lists its patents."[8] Yvor Winters charges Yeats with rhetoric in a not dissimilar connection. *Leda and the Swan* and *Two Songs from a Play* embody Yeats's controversial vision of the world's troubled course but are not for that outrageously inflated; yet Winters holds that they exhibit "the same sonorous rhetoric." And in connection with *A Nativity* he asserts: "The rhetorical force in the poem is close to Yeats's best—but it is purely rhetorical. What he is saying is almost as foolish as what he says in section III of *The Tower*. . . ."[9] Yeats may indeed be a rhetorical poet and a poet of foolish ideas, but it is remarkable that he should seem most rhetorical to Winters when most caught up by ideas which are at the least debatable.

Simply considered, these strictures are not entirely coherent. Modern poetry—Georgian[10] as well as imagist[11]—began with the rejection of rhetoric, however that was understood half a century ago; and a number of the accused poets have publicly deplored its use. If Yeats, Eliot, and Auden have been rhetorical, they have been so—to judge from their comments[12]—unwillingly and in the main unwittingly. Interestingly enough, Oscar Williams, who vowed to exclude the rhetorician from *A Little Treasury of Modern Poetry*, represented each of them by numerous poems which are probably rhetorical in Winters' sense. Unfortunately for the better understanding of the word in modern critical usage, he did not identify the offenders denied admission. G. S. Fraser has recently

8. Randall Jarrell, "Changes of Attitude and Rhetoric in Auden's Poetry," *Southern Review*, VII (1941–42), pp. 337–39.
9. Yvor Winters, "The Poetry of W. B. Yeats," *Twentieth Century Literature*, VI (1960), pp. 8 f.
10. Edmund Gosse, *More Books on the Table* (New York, 1923), p. 232.
11. T. E. Hulme, *Further Speculations*, ed. Sam Hynes (Minneapolis, 1955), p. 78; Ezra Pound, *Literary Essays*, ed. T. S. Eliot (London, 1954), p. 11; René Taupin, *L'influence du symbolisme français sur la poésie américaine* (de 1910 à 1920) Bibliotheque de la *Revue de Littérature Comparée*, LXII (Paris, 1929), p. 87.
12. See W. B. Yeats, *Essays and Introductions* (London, 1961), p. 497, and *Per Amica Silentia Lunae* (London, 1918), p. 21; W. H. Auden, "Making and Judging Poetry," *Atlantic Monthly*, CXCIX (January, 1957), p. 46.

questioned Read's arbitrary rejection of rhetoric, contending that "there is no critical act by which we can, as it were, strip off the rhetoric and be left with the vision." [13] The fact that no one ever attempts this problematic labor may be taken as sufficient proof that the word is, as Eliot argued, only a vague term of abuse. Indeed, it is slightly absurd to propose, even with qualifications, to extirpate what is, literally considered, inseparable from intelligible expression. Kenneth Burke has remarked: "Wherever there is persuasion, there is rhetoric. And wherever there is 'meaning,' there is 'persuasion.' " [14] Yet the persistence of the term—and long after the entombment of nineteenth-century eloquence—attests its special usefulness and meaningfulness. If its employment is with respect to style hopelessly imprecise, it may be that the primary reference is not style at all but value, more particularly, distasteful systems of value. If so, the modern objection to rhetoric is in some sense Platonic, and, insofar as this may be the case, the term can be described as a political pejorative of vague reference.

2   While traditional rhetoric has shifted its boundaries and relationships from century to century, notably with respect to logic and philosophy, it has always been, in the simplest terms, *ars bene dicendi*, in itself neither good nor ill but merely an instrument of communication. As a systematization of the capabilities of language, rhetoric of whatever sort affords a means, or choice of means, to persuasion; and the test of its *bene* is audience response. The evaluative terms appropriate to it are pragmatic, not ethical, ones; and this must be the case even though rhetorical devices can be used to excite all the lower faculties. The quality of the cause or end is the responsibility of the speaker; the rhetorical means, being neutral or innocent, cannot under ordinary circumstances be said to determine his choice. In the *Gorgias*, Socrates confused the issue by defining two sorts of rhetoric, that which is "mere flattery and

13. G. S. Fraser, *Vision and Rhetoric: Studies in Modern Poetry* (London, 1959), p. 18.
14. Kenneth Burke, *A Rhetoric of Motives* (New York, 1950), p. 172.

disgraceful declamation" and that which is "noble and aims at the training and improvement of the souls of the citizens." The second sort, he induced Callicles to admit, may hardly be said to exist.[15] Aristotle insisted on the division not of rhetoric but of speakers: "If it is argued that one who makes an unfair use of such faculty of speech may do a great deal of harm, this objection applies equally to all good things except virtue, and above all to those things which are most useful, such as strength, health, wealth, generalship; for as these, rightly used, may be of the greatest benefit, so, wrongly used, they may do an equal amount of harm" (*Rhet.*, I.i.13).[16] Just causes, in Aristotle's opinion (I.i.12), can scarcely be heard without the support of rhetoric. St. Augustine, concurring in this common-sensical view (*De doct. Chr.*, IV.ii), in effect vouched for the art in the formative period of Christianity. It is hardly necessary to illustrate the pervasive influence on Western literature of textbooks of rhetoric, from *De inventione* to George Campbell's revisions; but it may not be superfluous in view of present confusions to insist that literary achievement before the twentieth century is inextricably bound up with various sets of rhetorical prescriptions.

The rejection of rhetoric, if taken seriously, can only be interpreted as a profound distrust of traditional modes of expression and arrangement, perhaps even of conceptual discourse as such. Its rejection, as critics may or may not realize, entails the sacrifice of the sum total of methodologies and formularies which twenty-five centuries of genius and diligence shaped out of raw linguistic material, that is, out of Wordsworth's real language of men. The "tropes, tricks, and traductions" which Graves scorns are metaphors and *colores rhetorici; inventio* and *dispositio;* Shakespeare's soliloquies, Donne's cunning foolery, and Pope's mannered aphorisms.

15. The Platonic bias is apparent in Benedetto Croce, *Aesthetic as Science of Expression and General Linguistic,* trans. Douglas Ainslie (2d ed.; London, 1929), p. 423.
16. Trans. J. H. Freese, Loeb Classical Library (Cambridge, Mass., 1947). Cf. C. S. Sprigg [pseud. Christopher Caudwell], *Illusion and Reality: A Study of the Sources of Poetry* (London, 1937), p. 157.

Lacking this capital, the poet is in some sense back at the prime, with only pristine imagination and archetypal configurations to supply images and principles of organization and amplification. Apparently some critics would impose such a burden of originality as poets never before have endured and proscribe along with banalities any sort of felicitous diction which smacks of tradition. It is of course likely that not so much is actually meant, and yet the unqualified rejection of rhetoric comes to little less. Moreover, many a poet suggests by his desperate straining for disarrangement and novelty that he either deplores rhetoric on principle or fears the reproaches of critics who do. Futile as any attempt to escape rhetoric may be, the impulse is not for that without significance or indeed a kind of appropriateness. For inasmuch as the values of a culture are enshrined in linguistic formularies, a break with a culture necessitates a new departure in language. Whether this proposition is entirely true may not actually matter, for the effect must be the same if poets happen to feel that the old modes of saying, that is, of course, rhetoric, falsify their expression and impose upon them the perspectives of an unusable past.

But before so violent a reflex is charged to the twentieth century the possibility ought to be considered that critics mean only to say that poetry has its own proper movement and that, appearances rather to the contrary, this movement is not rhetorical. Aristotle appears to afford some support for this view, as he devotes separate treatises to rhetoric and poetics. Partly on the strength of this division, C. S. Baldwin was disposed to argue that antiquity perceived an essential difference: "Rhetoric and poetic connoted two fields of composition, two habits of conceiving and ordering, two typical movements. The movement of the one the ancients saw as primarily intellectual, a progress from idea to idea determined logically; that of the other, as primarily imaginative, a progress from image to image determined emotionally."[17] H. H. Hudson proposed a distinction based on ends rather than means: "For the moment,

17. C. S. Baldwin, *Ancient Rhetoric and Poetic* (New York, 1924), p. 3.

then, we shall say that poetry is for the sake of expression; the impression on others is incidental. Rhetoric is for the sake of impression; the expression is secondary—an indispensable means."[18] These pretentious generalizations contain a perfectly obvious element of truth but are nonetheless useless for purposes of discrimination. Inasmuch as traditional poetry is demonstrably rhetorical—indeed, unashamedly so—Baldwin's distinction tends to disqualify what in fact establishes the norm. Hudson's distinction necessitates a conjecture about intention and thus leads ineluctably to circularity. But if critics do conceive vaguely of a poetics definable by the absence of those features which characterize the most conspicuous displays of rhetoric, like oratory, they must need consider Hudson's conclusion that the "personal lyric, being least rhetorical, is the highest kind of poetry."[19] What is significant is not that Hudson should fail to recognize how rhetorical lyrics of all sorts have been in the past but that he should regard rhetoric as essentially an impurity in poetry. On this point Henri Brémond is singularly illuminating: "Impure, en un mot, l'éloquence, entendant par là non pas l'art de beaucoup parler pour ne rien dire, mais bien l'art de parler pour dire quelque chose."[20] The purification of poetry, by this view, entails the abandonment of rhetoric, but the abandonment of rhetoric, that is, the art of saying something, entails the loss of cognitive content; a poetry without rhetoric is a poetry without meaning and, of course, without ideology. Critics seem not to intend this consequence, even though sometimes granting with Archibald MacLeish that the function of a poem is to be rather than to mean. Yet *poésie pure,* whether according to the conceptions of Poe, Brémond, or George Moore, is the only immediately apparent alternative to rhetoric. If critics are not disposed to give up the claims of poetry to knowledge—and *poésie pure* proba-

---

18. H. H. Hudson, "Rhetoric and Poetry," ed. R. F. Howes, *Historical Studies of Rhetoric and Rhetoricians* (Ithaca, N.Y., 1961), p. 371.
    19. *Ibid.,* p. 376.
    20. Henri Brémond, *La poésie pure* (Paris, 1926), p. 22. Cf. R. P. Warren, "Pure and Impure Poetry," *Kenyon Review,* V (1943), pp. 246 f.

bly entails no less—their rejection of rhetoric can hardly be taken to imply the immediate possibility of a separate and acceptable poetics. But if the envisioned alternative to rhetoric is not a systematic poetics, it may be simply a poetry in which ideas, as opposed to states of feeling, figure so negligibly as to obviate the need for tactics of persuasion.

The proneness of critics to label rhetorical any poetry conspicuous for its ideas seems indisputable, though it is not usually evident whether their objection is primarily to the rhetoric or to the ideas. In all likelihood, most would deny that their attack on rhetoric was a covert attack on ideology; but whatever the conscious intention, the result must be much the same if, as seems not unlikely, the rhetorical is never really separable from the ideological.[21] It is reasonable to suppose that every ideology finds (or, better, originates with) terms appropriate to its expression, terms which, collectively considered, constitute a methodology or rhetoric, and, conversely, that every methodology implies an ideology, which is discoverable by analysis. Insofar as this may be the case, a given rhetoric can be held to incorporate some system of values and by that fact to exercise a degree of control over expression. It follows that rhetoric of whatever sort, because exclusive, must always be open to the charges of falsification and inadequacy, and these charges, though perhaps never quite provable, may nevertheless have a limited truth. Insofar as the twentieth century has rejected the value systems of the past, classical rhetoric, or rather the nineteenth-century modifications of it, may be said to distort reality as lately perceived and to allow insufficient discrimination of new-found experiences. Traditional rhetoric is of course plural,[22] and it ranges from the noble art of Quintilian in the first century at Rome to a debased theory of decoration in the later Middle Ages,

21. See P. A. Duhamel, "The Function of Rhetoric as Effective Expression," *Journal of the History of Ideas*, X (1949), pp. 344 f.
22. See Richard McKeon, "Rhetoric in the Middle Ages," *Speculum*, XVII (1942), pp. 3–5.

when logic claimed exclusive possession of *inventio*.[23] Notwithstanding, a rhetoric which is a product of a rationally conceived universe can be held to presuppose even in periods of misunderstanding and misapplication the integrity of reason, the accessibility of truth to rational process, and even cosmic orderliness. While the Middle Ages staked a good deal on revelation, reason, as the labors of Aquinas evidence, cannot have suffered greatly on that account; and rhetoric in any case had always a logical bias. Indeed, the relationship was altogether necessary, for rhetoric could hardly achieve a persuasive end without at least the semblance of logical structure. But poetry which depends on the commonplaces for finding matter[24] and shapes its arguments by recourse to oratorical models is in some sense a controlled art, and external controls are of course incompatible with romantic theories of inspiration. Graves opposes inspiration to rhetoric—and understandably so, by his lights; Read opposes sincerity to rhetoric—and no doubt properly, from the standpoint of expression theory. More importantly, rhetoric, by tending to enforce orderly dilatation of propositional truths, has the effect of stabilizing the flux and of course in terms of dominant value systems. Perhaps the readiest example is Renaissance poetry, which by its very excellence embarrasses any poetics based on the exclusion of rhetoric.[25] The French symbolists, who exerted a formative influence on the modernists, implicitly acknowledged the stabilizing force of rhetoric, for in setting out to shatter the orderly bourgeois world they disarranged syntax, deformed diction, and replaced syllogistic argument with symbols of conjectural reference. Whatever the aesthetic consequences, this

23. Duhamel, *op. cit.*, p. 345.
24. By the eighteenth century analysis and synthesis seemingly had replaced the commonplaces as the chief reliance of *inventio*. See W. S. Howell, "The Declaration of Independence and Eighteenth-Century Logic," *William and Mary Quarterly*, 3d Ser., XVIII (1961), pp. 467 f.
25. See C. S. Baldwin, *Renaissance Literary Theory and Practice*, ed. D. L. Clark (New York, 1939), pp. 14 f.

maneuver dethroned logic and left them free to impose irrational forms on the contents of experience. Since symbols unaccompanied by directional signals speak enigmatically, the ideological residue in French symbolist verse has a tentative, variable, and muted character.

Since it can be said with fair probability that objections to rhetoric are unlikely to be free of ideological resonances, the question arises whether objections to rhetoric can be said to entail objections to the ideology associated with it. This proposition appears to be false, for it stands to reason that good and acceptable ideas can be expressed very poorly or inadequately. Yet to maintain this contrary position necessitates the separation of form from content—and in the face of the likelihood, Eliot's doctrine of the objective correlative notwithstanding, that the poetic vision originates with the terms appropriate to its expression.[26] The original proposition can be validated if ideology is interpreted as the aspect under which ideas are presented rather than as ideas viewed singly. This amendment preserves the eternal verities, some of which are surely present in all ideologies, and focuses attention on context. The rejection of rhetoric comes then to be contingent upon the rejection of a system, though not necessarily of all the values contained therein. It follows that discourse seems rhetorical, that is, sophistical, only after skepticism has arisen concerning the value system associated with it. Conversely, the conventional expression of an ideology remains acceptable so long as the ideology commands assent. The apparent toleration of nineteenth-century oratory, with all its flamboyance and exaggeration, can be explained by the likelihood of general concurrence in a set of political, social, and religious principles; what now strikes the ear as scandalously artificial and insincere was doubtless felt to be altogether appropriate to the expansive, confident, and optimistic temper of the times. Nineteenth-century rhetoric possibly conceals as much as it reveals; but then rhetoric, inasmuch as it responds to ideological impulses, must

26. See Allen Tate, *Collected Essays* (Denver, 1959), p. 516.

be an art of concealment no less than of revealment. The rhetoric of any culture is vulnerable to the charge of concealment, but the question of falsification can hardly be raised until after skepticism has set in. And even then individual critics may remain relatively insensitive to the rhetoric of their own persuasions.[27]

3   The modernist revolt against the nineteenth century—against its rhetoric and ideology alike—was as all revolts an act of purification, but its indignation required unprecedented destruction of false emblems and rituals. Whereas Wordsworth and the romantics had been content to thrust mystical elements into the tidy cosmic mechanism of the eighteenth century and to "naturalize" poetic diction, the modernists meant, for a number of different reasons, to disorder traditional perspectives and to fracture expression commensurately. Admittedly, many a landmark reappears after revolutionary floods have subsided, and time brings to light unacknowledged debts to the past; but these commonplaces scarcely reduce the cleavage which developed in the first quarter of this century. Whatever the differences, the thought of Pope, Wordsworth, and Tennyson—to choose nicely spaced exemplars—can be viewed without undue violence under the aspect of Christian, if not scientific, optimism. Their poetry, moreover, is consciously rhetorical and accordingly marked in varying degrees by obtrusive *sententiae*, pretentious tropes, and such oratorical mannerisms as confident purposes require. Notwithstanding its irrational elements, nineteenth-century poetry, with some notable exceptions, conveys a sense of order and of a universe not in the main unfavorable to man's chances. It is possible, of course, that rhetoric to some extent falsifies the *Zeitgeist* by concealing, insofar as it does, the century's increasing perturbations, though the truth of this matter is hardly ascertainable. Falsification appears, at any rate, to have been the

27. Herbert Read observes in the foreword to Albert Camus' *The Rebel: An Essay on Man in Revolt*, trans. Anthony Bowers (New York, 1958), p. vii: "M. Camus has not delivered us [from anxiety and despair] by rhetoric, or by any of the arts of persuasion, but by the clarity of his intelligence."

ground upon which modern poets rejected the more or less traditional rhetoric of their predecessors. What their experience of the modern occasion required was evidently a movement suggestive of disorder, and this they constructed from suggestions in French symbolist exemplars and depth psychology. If not quite as radical as once supposed, their innovations can nevertheless be allowed to represent well enough the violence of their ideological reflex.

The break with the nineteenth century assuredly liberated the poetic imagination, and the absolute accomplishment of British and American poetry after 1914 probably affords justification enough for it. Yet the solutions of problems outside the realm of pure mathematics are seldom quite perfect, for they commonly entail some loss and commonly create new problems. By the long view, the alienation of the sentimental audience of Tennyson and Browning can hardly be important; in any case, new audiences may always be won. The abandonment of rhetoric, however, introduced what appear to be unresolved conflicts. If the acceptable alternative to rhetoric is not for modern poets *poésie pure* and not, as far as can be determined, a systematic poetics, then it is simply antirhetoric. Antirhetoric cannot be defined as poetic movement but only as a set of limitations on expression. It denies to poetry persuasive ends and the employment of artifices, new and old, which are conducive to persuasion. Conceptual statements must be barred on principle, for these are probably always in some sense interpretations, and interpretations implicitly appeal for concurrence. The symbol seems to offer an escape from conceptual discourse, and it is of course particularly congenial to a period which has some doubt of the power of conventional language to do justice to perceived or intuited reality. Unfortunately for this stratagem, symbols tend to cluster and gradually to adumbrate principles, which are probably sensed long before analysis plainly identifies them. If Kenneth Burke is correct, symbolism hardly affords a final escape from rhetoric: "Insofar as a poet's images are organically related, there is a formal principle behind them. The images could be said to *body forth* this principle. The principle itself could, by a properly discerning critic, be named in terms of *ideas* (or one basic idea with modifiers)."[28] The so-called constitutive symbol, it has been argued, resists the abstracting process and serves merely to synthesize experiences.[29] However useful for barricading the aesthetic domain against the competition of philosophy and science, this hypothetical construct suffers in point of plausibility. Even granted that such a centripetal symbol could be fabricated, it does not follow that practical critics would allow it to function as intended; rather, they would be inclined to dismiss it as hopelessly opaque if external references were not evident.

The practice of antirhetoric as such can hardly be considered successful, since critics manage to detect didactic purposes, accompanied by persuasive gestures, even in the symbolism of major expressionists. The simplest explanation is that poets, while disavowing the dominant value system of the nineteenth century, do not consider themselves thereby bound to prefer no value system. There may be modern poets who are content to extrude, without philosophical reflection, their impressions of a chaotic world, but a good many (and major ones in particular) appear to nourish an urge to reconstitute society and to impose upon the cosmic flux myths of their own devising or, at least, revising. Such a purpose, whether entirely conscious or not, calls up the *figurae verborum et sententiarum* and symbols which give off ideological noises. If the presence of classical artifices is not often strongly apparent in modern poetry, the explanation is that argument is entrusted to symbols rather more than to general statements. Whereas Milton very plainly announces his intention to justify the ways of God to man, Eliot is satisfied to adumbrate through symbols the formula for man's deliverance from the dark and wasted land. But Yeats and Auden mean often to be perfectly plain, and especially in their

28. Burke, *op. cit.*, p. 86.
29. See C. R. Hausman, "Art and Symbol," *Review of Metaphysics*, XV (1961), pp. 264 f.

major poems, where their earnestness leads even to broad statement. As for Auden's symbols—war, quest, Eros, city[30]—they are transparent vehicles with ideological freight. Yeats's are sometimes dense, but, when examined in different contexts and in conjunction with *A Vision*, they of course define his by now well-known value system and world view. Thus, myth, to judge from the work of these poets, entails rhetoric, and not even the method of symbolism can finally obscure from critics like Read and Winters the thrust of its persuasive ends. Whatever antirhetoric may permit, it is clearly not any sort of myth by which a poet might deliver himself from the insecurity of chronic skepticism.[31]

If to be intelligible is in some sense to be rhetorical, the question arises how any modern poets manage to avoid the charge. A part of the answer is contained in a general statement by Richard McKeon on the character of modern poetry: "A language which echoes folklore and religion has been constructed for poetry; subject matter is found in the motives and confusion of man set forth in simple unresolved oppositions; moral problems are made poetic by obscuring suggestions of resolution; and poetry may be didactic if its lessons are vague, or metaphysical if it is without commitment to a philosophy, or religious if religion furnishes a restraint to sentiment in the construction of figures."[32] In a period when the interests of poet and audience are most likely to be identical, ambiguity and irony, both symptoms of indecision and division, are protective devices; ambiguity suggests the impossibility of resolutions, and irony shatters any that may be attempted. Poetry with these qualities, because implying the unlikelihood, if not the undesirability, of integrating society according to any value system, is

30. See M. K. Spears, "The Dominant Symbols of Auden's Poetry," *Sewanee Review*, LIX (1951), pp. 392–417.
31. Herbert Read, "The Drift of Modern Poetry," p. 6, not surprisingly doubts the usefulness for poetry of modern myths.
32. Richard McKeon, "Poetry and Philosophy in the Twelfth Century, the Renaissance of Rhetoric," *Modern Philology*, XLIII (1946), pp. 233 f.

tolerable to the numerous varieties of social, political, and religious sensibility; but then it is incapable of giving absolute satisfaction in any quarter. And yet the poet who cultivates ambiguity and irony hardly deserves to escape the charge of rhetoric, for these are of course rhetorical devices mustered to the service of irresolution and ought therefore to give offense to audiences of settled belief, such as orthodox Christians and Marxists. So much considered, the uncertain reception of twentieth-century poetry cannot be owing altogether to technical difficulties. To a disintegrated culture even the noblest visions must seem partial and partisan. Time is likely to work at least for Yeats and Eliot, but only as it destroys the immediacy and perhaps the vitality of their myths and delivers them into the cool perspective of universal history.

Their concern to avoid the appearance of rhetoric seems to have made early modernists overly oblique but those since World War II overly quiet and modest. While cosmic poetry, no matter how disguised, is ultimately found out and labeled rhetoric, unambitious expression, without commitment and without technical blemishes, gathers a good deal of mild praise. Its simplicity vouches for its sincerity and, it might be added, for the equalitarianism of its authors. Its speakers look neither up to kings nor down to peasants but describe in a subdued voice those states of feeling which are more or less universal and uncontroversial. The readiest exemplars are the young "New Lines" poets of England, whose lack of large aims their spokesman, Robert Conquest, confesses with embarrassing candor: "But if we consider the poet as a generalised person of his time, perhaps we may distinguish him from earlier times in that (a) he no longer believes in grandiose political or other systems, (b) for the first time he takes for granted (and does not need to assert either of himself or others) the Freudian discoveries about his own motivation. (But he does not accept a psychological panacea either.) (c) he does not look for possibilities of absolute salvation or absolute doom. But (d) he does not shrug off the human condition and become a dilettante." [33] This is the lowered voice of the mid-twentieth century, at least in England, making no claims to speak as seer or mage but only as one of the dejected multitude. The booming rhetoric of Dylan Thomas may have produced in the "New Lines" poets a distaste for loud noises,[34] but it is a fair guess that they adopted what is in actuality a rhetoric of resignation and humility because they never felt the passionate causes and occasions which summon up the rolling periods and golden figures.

Wringing rhetoric's neck may have been fifty years ago a proper rite to purge expression of nineteenth-century influences, but its continued re-enactment testifies to a general distrust of programmatic interpretations of human affairs. The poet is barred from reordering the universe even for his own satisfaction not in actuality on account of the chronic objection to rhetoric but on account of the chronic objection to the high purposes which evoke rhetoric. The divided and skeptical state of the modern mind considered, it is probable that any poetry which in the foreseeable future bodies forth visions of resolution and reconciliation will on the right hand or on the left be labeled rhetorical, that is, ideologically repugnant.

33. Robert Conquest, "Modernity in Poetry," *departure: A Magazine of Literature and the Arts*, IV, No. 4 (1956), pp. 7 f.

34. See Geoffrey Moore, *Poetry To-day* (London and New York, 1958), p. 11.

Chapter IV

The Case for Poetic Obscurity

Difficult poetry, though nothing new to literary history, has been in the twentieth century—the century of the mass audience—an intractable anomaly and apparently for some poets in Britain and the United States a matter of conscience. Quite fittingly, all poets have affected a broad humanity, but few appear to have made concessions to popular taste and limitation. Indeed, their admitted obscurities draw the circle of qualified readers so small that contemporary verse is not even a minor topic of upper-class social discourse. If modern poetry may be said to exist for polite society, it has the name of a confusing and disturbing cultural aberration, little deserving of patronage. It goes without saying that the lower classes are wholly indifferent: their historical craving for the wisdom of their betters has seldom embraced secular verse and never that of a problematic character. But even without formal obscurities, modern poetry could hardly have general appeal, for its content neither salves the bodily and ghostly afflictions of the oppressed nor confirms the privileged in their characteristic faith in social and cosmic order. Indeed, poetry has come to express so cruelly the disorder of the modern mind that uncommon fortitude is wanted in its readers. Although reluctant to admit the exceptional exclusiveness of their art, poets in this century have spoken chiefly to persons of deep and astringent intellectual conditioning. Whether they have gained more or less honor thereby continues to be debated.

Poets have not been much inclined to accept responsibility for the general indifference to poetry but have professed to write as their *daimon* required. If the product is extraordinarily complex, it is thought to be not more so than the times which have evoked it.[1] Nevertheless, poets and critics have brooded over the problem of obscurity during the three decades since Max Eastman[2] enrolled in the "Cult of Unintelligibility" those he regarded as the worst offenders against plain sense. Whether from a bad or merely uneasy conscience, explanations and defenses in considerable number have been offered, and lately a British poet[3] has accomplished a valuable book-length study of obscurity. It is commonly maintained—and with a good deal of historical support—that a really new poetry, such as the twentieth century has undeniably wrought, presents unfamiliar idioms which challenge even adequate readers.[4] But adequate readers, it is supposed, have declined significantly on account of the loss of a common culture,[5] which classical education and social homogeneity formerly assured. The reasonableness of this simple explanation notwithstanding, the inclination has persisted to ascribe poetic obscurity, if not to intellectual arrogance, at least to insufficient concern for the common understanding. While modernist—that is, non-traditional—poets have as a group tended to deprecate the faintly bogus criterion of social utility, they can hardly have done so with the intention of alienating readers of whatever sort. Yet this stance is mildly antisocial, and perhaps in consequence of it their absolute accomplishment has not everywhere been allowed to excuse their subtle contrivances and dark colors.

The concern about obscurity should now be subsiding, for of

1. See T. S. Eliot, *The Use of Poetry and the Use of Criticism* (London, 1933) pp. 151 f, and the opposing views of Delmore Schwartz, "The Isolation of Modern Poetry," *Kenyon Review*, III (1941), p. 210; and Elder Olson, *The Poetry of Dylan Thomas* (Chicago, 1954), p. 9.

2. Max Eastman, *The Literary Mind: Its Place in an Age of Science* (New York and London, 1931), p. 57.

3. John Press, *The Chequer'd Shade: Reflections on Obscurity in Poetry* (London, 1958). I am indebted to this work for a number of references.

4. Long ago Wordsworth observed that "every author, as far as he is great and at the same time *original*, has had the task of *creating* the taste by which he is to be enjoyed"—*Essay Supplementary to Preface* (1815).

5. Marc Friedlaender, "Poetry and the Common Store," *American Scholar*, XIV (1945), p. 363; Press, *op. cit.*, p. 66.

late poetry has taken a simpler turn and is usually accessible, whether attractive or not, to moderately educated readers. The relaxation of style has been accompanied, however, by deprecation of obscurity on principle and by observations calculated to leave the impression that the modernist period—running roughly from *Prufrock* to *In the White Giant's Thigh*—perpetrated serious offenses against art, nature, and society. Robert Conquest, spokesman for the "New Lines" poets of England, has proclaimed the return of poetry to sanity and reason and the abandonment in the process of the bulk of modernist innovations.[6] Karl Shapiro, who has come to advocate clarity with increasing vehemence, has recently placed the whole modernist achievement under a heavy indictment: "Complexity and obscurity in art or poetry are always signs of the sick, enraged, frustrated artist, the nihilist, the destroyer of whatever is living in man and in nature."[7] It may be that a new style rises necessarily at some cost to the old, but it is unlikely to flourish simply for being unobscure. For the difficulty of their verse at least, modernists have honorable precedent and are unlikely in the long run to suffer from critical judgment on that account. The continuing confusion over poetic obscurity may be owing largely to the tact or negligence of modernist apologists; whatever the case, their discussions of the matter have been so incomplete and indecisive as to leave the poet's prerogatives in doubt. There is accordingly some need to set the problem of obscurity around with the considerations which anciently entered into it and with those which have arisen in this century.

1   Modernist poetry would be difficult if for no other reason than its relative independence of formal education. By contrast,

6. Robert Conquest, "Modernity in Poetry," *departure: A Magazine of Literature and the Arts*, IV, No. 4 (1956), pp. 6–9. See the same author's introduction in *New Lines: An Anthology* (London and New York, 1956).

7. Karl Shapiro, "The Farmer and the Poet," *Poetry*, XCVIII (1961), p. 180. Cf. E. B. Burgum, "The Cult of the Complex in Poetry," *Science and Society*, XV (1951), pp. 36 f.

the bulk of English verse from Chaucer to the Georgians plainly acknowledges the direct and controlling influence of the schools, and its study properly begins with the trivium. It has been asserted that conventional instruction best prepares the student for Tennyson,[8] and such is roughly the case, though, as a matter of strict fact, it accustoms him after a fashion to the poetic uses of classical grammar, rhetoric, and logic. For more than two thousand years these *artes* were essential to the composition and understanding of both prose and poetry, and changes in literary modes were accomplished within their boundaries. The Metaphysicals and romantics—to cite modern instances—purged poetic language of a great deal of overripe elegance and disclosed surprising new idioms; but they did not, for all their alterations, depart significantly from the manuals of style. In contrast, the most conspicuous of the modern revolters, with suggestions from nineteenth-century symbolists, brought startling technical innovations to poetic discourse. While not altogether forgoing the traditional arts of language, they declared their freedom from such restraints and purposes as the manuals imposed and contrived things never dreamt by the author of the *Rhetorica ad Herennium* or Puttenham. As a consequence, poetic and rhetoric decisively separated; poetry lost thereby a historic usefulness for the development of elevated prose style and by the same token an important propaedeutic. It should be recognized, however, that poetry stood to lose on any account, for by 1922, the year of the *Waste Land*, the vocational and sociological bias of modern education was rapidly emptying the classical trivium of any content particularly useful to serious literature.

To say that readers are nowadays equipped, if at all, for Tennyson is not exactly to say that they are helpless before modern verse, some of which is quite as transparent as Tennyson's, though scarcely so rhetorical. Familiarity has already dissolved a good many notorious difficulties and has even bred a measure of contempt for

8. W. Y. Tindall, *Forces in Modern British Literature, 1885–1946* (New York, 1947), p. 24.

contrivances open to suspicion of mere ingenuity. Numerous pieces which once dazzled and perplexed seem upon mature consideration to be simply unachieved. Criticism now has little patience with poets who lose their wings from flying too high and even less for those who mischievously perpetrate obscurities by means of, say, private imagery. But to dismiss the sincere failures and poetasters is not greatly to simplify matters. The reaction to the technical slovenliness and bourgeois sensibility of the nineteenth century excluded so many customary cues and admitted so many singular postures that orientation, at least to the verse of the great innovators, is likely to remain problematic. Though no modernist poets openly concur in Hugo Friedrich's opinion that obscurity has become an aesthetic principle—"Dunkelheit ist zum durchgängigen ästhetischen Prinzip geworden"[9]—the effect of their verse could hardly be different. Steady employment of ambiguity and syntactical abbreviation and omission of unifying and clarifying propositions can only result in poetry less determinate than the larger reading public is schooled to manage.

Modern poetry often omits conceptual statements and does so legitimately inasmuch as it is expressive on principle rather than rhetorical, but it thereby gives up an instrument by which coherence has been traditionally achieved. Although concrete particulars will speak for themselves, their import will vary from reader to reader and on occasion may not be unmistakably clear to anyone. Poets are perfectly aware of the risk, but far from dreading multiple (and even absurd) interpretations they are inclined to encourage independent negotiations between the reader and the voice of the poem.[10] In contrast, relatively difficult poets of the past were seldom willing to leave interpretation to chance and accordingly laced their imagery with *sententiae* sufficient, at least

9. Hugo Friedrich, *Die Struktur der modernen Lyrik von Baudelaire bis zur Gegenwart* (*Rowohlts deutsche Enzyklopädie*, XXV; Hamburg, 1956), p. 130.

10. The most generous attitude is Paul Valéry's: "Mes vers ont le sens qu'on leur prête"—"Préface à un Commentaire," *Nouvelle Revue Française*, XXXIV. (Jan.–June, 1930), p. 218.

for fit readers, to adumbrate the main lines of their arguments; on this account, their obscurity was commonly local rather than general. While explanatory and even summarizing statements have been customary from the earliest periods of European literature and cannot fairly be scorned as inorganic elements,[11] it has been evident since Poe and Baudelaire that the logic of organization may not always require them. The prevailing objection to generalizations probably sprang immediately from a distaste for blatant didacticism. More fundamentally, they may be judged undesirable because tending to be dictatorial, that is, tending to restrict meaning unduly and thus to do violence to the complexity of experience. The modern poet prefers a concourse of images which, in consequence of multiple reference, achieves maximum suggestiveness. The universe of his poetry may be bewilderingly wide and uncertain of dimensions, but the reader is free to construe to the limit of his intuitions. Unfortunately for this generous practice, readers are often more embarrassed than flattered by freedom of interpretation.

The objection to generalizing statement is probably in some part also an objection to classical rhetoric and to the rational order which it tends to impose upon poetic discourse. Rhetoric, by origin an art of persuasion, must present at least the semblance of a logical line or fail of its intention. For this purpose, statement is virtually indispensable: it functions like a general term, relating particulars to a premeditated end and by them being validated. A discipline in both the older and the newer senses of the word, rhetoric guarantees the appropriateness of the parts and the coherence of the whole—in short, a logical construct. This art was not formerly thought to be a hindrance to the imagination or to any sort of effect a poet might wish to produce; indeed, as a sys-

11. See Rosemond Tuve, *Elizabethan and Metaphysical Imagery: Renaissance Poetic and Twentieth-Century Critics* (Chicago, 1947), pp. 20, 176 f.; W. V. O'Connor, *Sense and Sensibility in Modern Poetry* (Chicago, 1948), pp. 227 f.

tematization of the capabilities of language, it was regarded as a
positive benefit to composition. Never in good repute with modernists, rhetoric has been described of late as the "curse of poetry"[12]
and a "corruption of the poetic consciousness."[13] These fierce judgments, though perhaps not closely reasoned, surely stem from a
deep conviction that rhetoric somehow falsifies the modern predicament, possibly by curtailing ambiguity[14] as much as by sanc-
tioning figures with decorative function. Whatever the merit of
this opinion, notice should be taken that the traditional arts of
language and the literature which exemplifies them were products
of a more or less rational universe. So much considered, it is appropriate that the older literature should be propositional and demonstrative and bid directly for the concurrence of readers; conversely,
it may follow that poetry spun out of the alleged disorder of the
twentieth century should be dislocated, alogical, and even private.[15]
An age so in doubt of its condition as to distrust generalization
quite understandably depreciates rhetoric, which from its logical
bias tends to force definite conclusions.[16] Poets for whom no comprehensive principle or myth is available to stabilize the flux necessarily cling to the concrete and limited actuality, by means of which
they can express the clutter of experience without committing
themselves to any sort of transcendent order. Yet even those modernist poets with a more or less workable metaphysic prefer sym-

12. Robert Graves, *The Crowning Privilege* (London, 1955), p. 99.
13. Herbert Read, "The Drift of Modern Poetry," *Encounter*, IV (Jan.,
1955), p. 4. On the loose use of rhetoric as a pejorative term, see G. S. Fraser,
Vision and Rhetoric: Studies in Modern Poetry (London, 1959), p. 18, and
T. S. Eliot, *Selected Essays, 1917–1932* (New York, 1932), pp. 25–30.
14. See I. A. Richards, *The Philosophy of Rhetoric* (New York and London,
1936), p. 40.
15. This assumption is called the "fallacy of expressive, or imitative, form"
by Yvor Winters, *Primitivism and Decadence: A Study of American Experimental Poetry* (New York, 1937), p. 49.
16. As a logical ordering of language, a rhetorical mode of whatever kind presupposes more or less firm metaphysical and epistemological principles. See
P. A. Duhamel, "The Function of Rhetoric as Effective Expression," *Journal
of the History of Ideas*, X (1949), p. 345.

bolic discourse to the discursive reason of the rhetorical mode, doubtless on the ground that their visions are not amenable to conceptual expression.

The rejection of rhetorical prescriptions, however, has not generally led to libertinism. While there may be no very strong theoretical bar even to recording the raw, unpatterned content of experience, a predisposition to tightly controlled expression has been evident since the Imagists, that is, since the beginning of modern British and American poetry. Such surrealistic work as David Gascoyne's *In Defence of Humanism* and Dylan Thomas' *Altarwise by owl-light* sonnets, which overwhelm the reader with a disorder of sense impressions and rare associations, exemplifies the allowable extreme, not the norm. Privileged in all ways respecting expression, most poets—even very minor ones—have yet acknowledged very high standards of craftsmanship and probably for that reason have relatively few poems to show for their labors.

Readers may feel that for all this meticulous artistry their understanding remains imperfect, and in fact nothing has been done to relieve them of work. In consequence of tireless experimentation, the language of poetry has become a more effective instrument, but to the confusion of the literal-minded it is calibrated for an irrational universe. Normal connectives are often dropped in order to take up slack and sometimes perhaps to deny causal relations. In place of simple predication, with its implication of rational order, substantives may stand alone, in doubt of a verb. New words are coined and old words assigned improbable grammatical functions. Mixed flocks of double-decked attributives may cluster around substantives and effect deep cognitive congestion. The syntax of English, an analytic language, is subjected to such dislocations as only a synthetic language like Latin could easily tolerate. By radically deforming language, poets have significantly energized it, though admittedly at some cost to clarity. Their achievement is of course questioned by those readers who prefer that experience be packaged in the customary manner, that is, in the relatively slack, but altogether convenient, manner of the nineteenth century.

Yet the language of modern verse, though far removed from ordinary social discourse, is unlikely to prove a permanent hindrance. Familiarity has eased the strain of reading T. S. Eliot and Dylan Thomas, to mention two radical innovators, and in time their characteristic artifices may be no more troublesome than Donne's knotty arguments or Browning's congested syntax. But after the grammatical convolutions have been unwound, massive symbols and formidable analogies will remain to embarrass even very competent readers. In traditional poetry conceptual statements usually provide a feasible, if unsporting, bridge across unlikely allusions and rare metaphors and, as needed, rescue the cognitive element from the clasp of excessive ornament. Twentieth-century poets frustrate corner-cutting simply by omitting directive statements. Their determined organicism proscribes extrapoetic aids to understanding and requires an inextricable fusion of the cognitive and emotive. Very nearly everything has been staked on the image (symbol or metaphor) by reason of its supposedly superior capability to disclose reality, but a concourse of problematic images resists the translative processes—epitomizing and paraphrasing—by which practical readers convert art to practical uses. Unless a reader can be satisfied with such fleeting impressions as *Sprachmagie* and verbal music afford, he must somehow grasp imagery that is designedly complex of meaning and improbably learned in point of reference. The poet considers himself justified in having recourse to rare and even occult pockets of knowledge, for obvious analogies, however serviceable in the past, encourage automatic accommodation and the lumping of unique experiences into intolerably crude categories of commonplace wisdom. Whatever the public impression, the search for fresh and pregnant images may be indicative of integrity rather than affectation, but until the poetry of the century is weighed down with scholia, the remote learning of its creators cannot be widely appreciated.

Finished poetry presumably speaks for itself and hardly requires an enclosed certificate of the maker's integrity. Nonetheless, readers tend to expect the poet somehow to declare himself as to character and purpose. Such a declaration furnishes an easy key to interpretation and affords some protection against imposition. "The world is too much with us" vouches for Wordsworth's piety and locates the sonnet in a familiar category of experience; what follows is not revelation but merely elaboration. Although not lacking in technical merit, the poem rather pointedly recommends itself on ethical grounds and by the same token the person of the author. Literature may be read as a reflection of a great mind or as a useful restatement of religious or secular dogma, but for reasons both ethical and aesthetic twentieth-century poets have not much encouraged either approach. The moral kernel of a typical modern poem is in point of novelty or depth seldom worth the trouble required to isolate it, and the speaker usually furnishes only very uncertain indications of the author's "real" character. The case against overt didacticism need not be restated, but something should be said about the felt need of poets to frustrate biographical inquisitiveness, which offends both author and art.

Much traditional poetry—and especially the lyrical sort—leaves an impression of personal revelation and thus satisfies the rather commonplace desire to behold the author in his work. What has not always been clearly understood is that poets from Petrarch to Browning availed themselves unashamedly of conventional masks, which to some extent protected them from morbid inquiry and yet provided their readers with an illusion of intimate personal reference. If the tired old *personae* of the dejected lover, the worldly wise cynic, the moral indignant, and the kindly sage even now speak on occasion, they are less to be trusted than before;[17] and the characteristic voices of modern poetry, though assuredly expressive

17. See Hans Jaeger, "Subjektivität und Objektivität der Lyrik," *PMLA*, XLVIII (1933), pp. 250–53; Manfred Kridl, "Observations sur les Genres de la Poésie lyrique," *Helicon*, II (1939), p. 149.

of individual will and intelligence, tend to leave very confusing material for literary biography. What is usually wanted is a poet like Robert Frost, who appears to stand close beside his speakers and to certify the common humanity of their utterances. To the general reader's satisfaction, Frost's poetry is readily, if not legitimately, convertible both to personal history and to cracker-barrel philosophy. Poetry saves its art by denying its author and resisting shredding for its memorable and usable parts, but such refractoriness often produces bewilderment and irritation in the public. Laura Riding and Robert Graves have observed, "Part of the reader's reaction to what he calls the obscurity of certain poems is really his nervous embarrassment at feeling himself left alone with the meaning of the poem itself."[18] An autonomous poem like a primitive sculpture is usually not analyzable into a set of neutral parts or reducible to a comfortable and quotable *sententia*; it is what it is and by that fact inviolable and sometimes awesome. Its enjoyment requires the relaxation of normal habits of assimilation and accordingly of customary defences against strange and disquieting experiences. To risk so much, however, calls for more than ordinary self-confidence. The inclination of the public is to neutralize portentous art by translating it to sanitary contexts and when balked of this questionable purpose to take revenge on the author, commonly by pronouncing his work obscure or even unintelligible.

The charge of obscurity doubtless comforts baffled and resentful readers, but the verse of the century is not much discriminated and sorted by it. Very nearly all the poets who have attracted serious attention since the Georgians have departed markedly in technical matters from the tradition and by that fact alone have severely limited their possible audience. Abandoning the accustomed rhetorical movement and easy rhythms of the nineteenth century cost them that numerous group which got a sentimental satisfaction from Tennyson and the pre-Raphaelites. And cultivating ambiguity

18. Laura Riding and Robert Graves, *A Survey of Modernist Poetry* (Garden City, N.Y., 1928), p. 150.

and suggestiveness beyond anything previously known in English cost them those tougher-minded readers who yet must need box in and impale a cognitive element. But the lack of popular approval cannot diminish the technical excellences which have come of their bold experiments with language. In devising new strategies of expression to replace the old rhetoric they have achieved exciting concoctions of things which have the absolute merit of affording fresh insights. Their lyrics do work reserved in the past for extended forms; if sometimes ruinously overcrowded, they are often exemplary, more concentrated and more cerebral even than Metaphysical poetry. It is possible to argue—though fatuous to do so—that the public has some sort of obligation to all this scrupulous verse; but in truth the public is ordinarily attracted to art for reasons other than its formal excellence. In any case, the characteristic poetry of the century is refined quite beyond the ordinary understanding, and to pretend otherwise is simply to exaggerate the general capability.

2   "Why is poetry no longer our daily bread?" The discreet answer is that poetry qua poetry probably never was, and assuredly not the complex secular kind which discriminating critics have chiefly respected since antiquity. Sir Herbert Read, who asked the question,[19] blamed the times—a "satanic chaos"—for the "fragmented, personal, spasmodic" character of poetry and accordingly for its lack of public appeal. Yet on this score the twentieth century seems little worse than others, for there is really not much worthwhile verse from the *Beowulf* to the *Testament of Beauty* which is known beyond doubt to have had a considerable audience or to have been written with any great expectation of one. In remote times poets doubtless addressed themselves to the whole people (as even now in some simple societies), but the status of literature

19. *Op. cit.*, p. 10. Yet in *Poetry and Anarchism* (London, 1938), p. 28, Sir Herbert doubted that higher forms of art would ever appeal to more than a minority.

among ancient tribes, whether relevant for the present situation or not, is usually much too conjectural to provide useful perspective. Some such relationship as W. H. Auden describes may have existed at one time or another in the Middle Ages: "When the things in which the poet is interested, the things which he sees about him, are much the same as those of his audience, and that audience is a fairly general one, he will not be conscious of himself as an unusual person, and his language will be straightforward and close to ordinary speech." [20] The only poets who now seem likely to have been so close to the folk were minstrels of a low order, and their work, as far as known, promises very little for art. What appears to be Auden's view, that in the Renaissance the poet first became distinct from the people in general and in consequence his diction from the language of men, has small basis in fact. The indisputably popular verse of the Middle Ages is commonly ragged and banal and so is that of the early period of printing. On the other hand, the medieval poetry which now invites attention for other than philological purposes is usually no less learned and sophisticated than the master work of later periods and no less inaccessible to the masses.

The nineteenth century may be claimed as an exception, for some serious poets did in fact speak to the generality, and Tennyson at least received honors enough. Yet the century's cultivation of poetry—by purchase of leather-bound collected works if not by study—came in considerable part of motives which were not entirely appropriate and which boded the art no ultimate good. Poets owed their seeming good fortune to a growing middle class, which since the time of Queen Anne had been increasingly prosperous and educated and increasingly concerned to acquire all the marks befitting its elevated condition. *Belles-lettres* for about two centuries had a significant connection with status, in America no less than in England; and while it would be grossly unjust to ascribe

20. W. H. Auden, ed., *The Oxford Book of Light Verse* (Oxford, 1938), p. viii.

all the literary enthusiasm of the middle class to purely social motives, it would be absurd to deny that poetry good and bad was affected quite as much out of class consciousness as out of love of literature. By a lucky chance, most of the poets, if less than sympathetic with the cultural preconceptions of their audience, were yet vaguely hopeful for the future and in any case not disposed to engage in the French intellectualist pastime of ridiculing bourgeois pretensions. Indeed, their verse was unprecedently middle class in character—moralizing, sentimental, and uplifting. It was sufficiently abstract and learned to flatter tolerably educated readers but not so difficult as to baffle them to the point of annoyance—not even Browning's, exclusive of *Sordello* and a few other pieces.

If Eliot, as Karl Shapiro suggests,[21] alienated the remnants of the Victorian audience, he performed an act which the integrity of poetry may have come to require. After 1914, right-thinking poets could no longer pretend to concur even halfheartedly in the philosophical mechanism and scientific optimism by which the nineteenth century rationalized its programs. And moral ones could not pander to the morbid side of the middle-class sensibility by speaking with what Yeats described as the "sweet insinuating feminine voice of the dwellers in that country of shadows and hollow images."[22] Society clearly deserved a glimpse of the hard-bitten face of reality if for no other end than to purge its uncritical progressivism, and Eliot, it must be admitted, raised up a Gorgon's head. But few froze to stone because few regarded. The audience for poetry was declining—most assuredly in America—and undoubtedly would have declined had Eliot and his congeners been far less ominous and far less obscure, simply because polite society no longer valued polite learning. Had the contrary been true, the public in the twenties and thirties would have patronized a number of competent poets who yet wrote in the tradition. The audience available to Eliot was an audience of his peers, and in unashamedly

21. Karl Shapiro, *In Defense of Ignorance* (New York, [1960]), p. 44.
22. *The Letters of W. B. Yeats*, ed. Allan Wade (London, 1954), p. 434.

writing difficult verse for them he had much better precedent than his detractors appear to realize.

The continuing influence of classicism from Jonson to Arnold created a strong presumption in favor of lucidity, simplicity, and euphony[23] and a corresponding disdain for obscurity, much to the disadvantage of poets possessed of remote visions. The respectable antiquity and defensible uses of obscure writing, though evident from the Scriptures, were largely discounted. Previously in the Renaissance, as in the Middle Ages, obscurity had been recognized, though not always approved, as a means of protecting esoteric truths from the vulgar. The Metaphysical style is supposed to have owed something to a desire to erect a defense against the lower classes,[24] which by the end of the sixteenth century constituted a considerable market for naive literature, whether devotional and moral or coarse and frivolous. The most outrageous expression of intellectual snobbery may be George Chapman's in the dedicatory epistle to *Ovid's Banquet of Sense*: "The profane multitude I hate, and only consecrate my strange poems to those searching spirits, whom learning hath made noble, and nobility sacred."[25] It is not to be imagined, however, that advocates of clarity were more optimistic about the capacity of the lower classes. Jonson expressed concern in *Timber: or, Discoveries* that literary language "not fly from all humanity," but his *Ode to Himself* speaks contemptuously of popular taste. The earlier Tudors wrote relatively transparent verse, though from no concern for general readers; like most court poets from the time of the troubadours they intended their work for limited circles and thus had slight reason to fear crude handling by the multitude. The obscure verse of the skalds and *trobar clus* are medieval exceptions which probably came of reckless virtuosity

23. W. S. Maugham, *The Summing Up* (Garden City, N.Y., 1938), pp. 30–33, upholds these qualities and deprecates obscurity.

24. Arnold Stein, "Donne's Obscurity and the Elizabethan Tradition," *ELH*, XIII (1946), pp. 110 f; R. L. Sharp, "Some Light on Metaphysical Obscurity and Roughness," *Studies in Philology*, XXXI (1934), p. 501.

25. George Chapman, *The Works*, ed. R. H. Shepherd (London, 1874–75), II, p. 21.

rather than social causes. However, Marcabru, the most difficult of the troubadours, seems not to have been simply mischievous; [26] like Donne [27] he had some notion of subjecting his readers to a test of fitness.

Obscurity had its most proper justification not in the alleged need to deny to the lower orders experience of pretentious literature but in the long-standing conviction that grave and weighty matter—the product of philosophical reflection or religious vision—required for decency and dignity a cloak of "cloudy fygures." [28] The villein was disqualified by ignorance no less than by reputed villainy, and the clerk was qualified by educational discipline rather than by social station. The chief end of such knowledge as the *artes liberales* and the several philosophies conferred was virtue, and it was virtue which distinguished the worthy from the swine and entitled them to pearls of wisdom. The poet, in Boccaccio's view, had need to recall the ancient and continuing dependence of art upon divine inspiration and his obligation to set forth deep truth in a "fair and fitting garment of fiction" impervious to profane scrutiny.[29] Medieval poets were generally self-effacing and could scarcely visualize themselves in so exalted a role as Boccaccio described, but the more serious of them were inclined to envelop the hard-won fruits of their meditation in dark figures. Allegory had its justification, and its long flourishing from the *Psychomachia* of

26. See Alfred Jeanroy, *La poésie lyrique des troubadours* (Toulouse and Paris, 1934), II, p. 29.

27. Stein, *op. cit.*, p. 104.

28. See Ruth Wallerstein, *Studies in Seventeenth-Century Poetic* (Madison, Wis., 1950), p. 38; E. R. Curtius, *European Literature and the Latin Middle Ages*, trans. W. R. Trask (New York, 1953), p. 205; Edgar de Bruyne, *Études d'esthétique médiévale* (Brugge, 1946), I, pp. 119 f, II, pp. 305, 317; Macrobius, *Commentary on the Dream of Scipio*, trans. W. H. Stahl (New York, 1952), p. 87; Alanus de Insulis, *De planctu Naturae*, Migne, *Pat. Lat.*, CCX, p. 445; Roger Bacon, *The Opus Majus*, trans. R. B. Burke (Philadelphia and London, 1928), Pt. I, ch. iv; Thomas Aquinas, *Summa theologica*, Pt. I, Ques. I, Art. 9; Stephen Hawes, *The Pastime of Pleasure*, ed. W. E. Mead, *Early English Text Society*, o.s., CDXXIII (London, 1928), pp. 33 f.

29. *Genealogia deorum Gentilium*, bks. 14 and 15 trans. by C. G. Osgood as *Boccaccio on Poetry* (Princeton, 1930), pp. 37–39, 58–62.

Prudentius to the *Faerie Queene* attests not only to a habit of mind but also to the settled opinion that solemn thought ought to be insulated and elevated. The desirability of heightening serious content even to the point of complexity was not disputed; indeed, the rhetorics conned most assiduously by medieval and Renaissance poets dealt with nothing if not with artifices of enhancement. Chaucer complained that "hard langage and hard matere" made a difficulty when joined,[30] but he no more than that other exemplar of clarity, Ben Jonson, used language simple enough to accommodate the generality.

In consequence of the political and social upheavals of the past two centuries, poets now affect a tenderer regard for all the lower conditions of humanity, but it is not evident that their estimate of the capacity of the masses for serious art has improved accordingly. Discussions of this matter by apologists for difficult verse understandably leave something to be desired in point of candor and comprehensiveness; to defend obscurity on the old grounds, or indeed on any grounds implying inequality of capacity, invites the charge of undemocratic intellectualism and exclusiveness. There is no remedy in disclaiming antisocial notions, for the marked contrast between nineteenth-century clarity and twentieth-century obliquity conserves the suspicion that modernists lack a proper regard for the social body. The content of their poetry is often humane to a fault, but its obscurity presumably confesses their unwillingness to perform agreeable public service. E. E. Stoll's complaint rests on the assumption that obscurity is *prima facie* evidence of antidemocratic sentiment: "Since ancient times society has, in the long run, become more democratic; but art, whether auditory or visual (strangely enough) decidedly less so; in the most democratic countries, least of all."[31] Stoll misconceives at least the literary history of Europe, and his use of *democratic* assuredly

---

30. *The House of Fame*, pp. 861–63.
31. E. E. Stoll, "The Downfall of Oratory: Our Undemocratic Arts," *Journal of the History of Ideas*, VII (1946), p. 9.

begs a question; yet such a rhetorical fling menaces poetry because leaving the suggestion that it ought to assume secular obligations. Traditionally, serious poets have thought to serve humanity by serving truth, often esoteric truth; and they have considered themselves answerable, if at all, to divine, not temporal powers.[32] To deprecate this posture is in some measure to detract from much of the greatest literary accomplishment. Yet a period which has an overdeveloped social conscience but little faith in transcendent values is scarcely to be expected to acknowledge the legitimacy of poetry which bodies forth the eternal verities in figures too cloudy for popular use.

Whatever the case against difficult poetry, there is no warrant nowadays for resembling it to delectable viands reserved for a refined elite and enjoyed in secret places, though some such observation could be made with proximate justice about a very great many of the world's literary monuments before the twentieth century. Literacy and letterpress have delivered the poet wholly into the hands of the masses; they have the means to construe and judge his work and the privilege of dismissing it utterly. As it turns out, George Chapman had not so much to fear; for the new literates rushing out of the free schools in this century have not paused to show vulgar interest even in poetry of an open and public character. The very evident disposition of general readers considered, detractors of obscurity can scarcely believe that a considerable audience is to be won just now by any means; their real concern may be less to bring art down to the level of the common understanding than to abolish a symbol of intellectual superiority. Even granted that modern poetry is in some part a calculated affront to philistinism and dullness, society is ultimately responsible for the poet's experience of it, and a free society is bound to respect his right to reservations of whatever kind. To insist that the poet make stylistic concessions and lay before the generality clear and in the

32. Cf. Allen Tate, "To Whom Is the Poet Responsible?" *Hudson Review*, IV (1951–52), p. 333.

main positive responses to the prevailing ethos, if that can be determined, is to insist that he substitute public service for vision and thus give up the service of truth in the interest of fluctuating social and political exigencies. Of course, no one in English-speaking lands seriously threatens to impose this awkward function on the poet, but he must realize that his similar in the communist world has accepted it.[33] The modernist cannot be unaware, moreover, that free societies increasingly seek to integrate opinions as well as men and may one day notice his embarrassing autonomy. If his social function ever comes seriously in question, the evident availability of his verse to all who would read will not be a sufficient defense.

It is certainly a painful reproach to modernists, many of whom profess very liberal sympathies, that not even aristocratic poets of the past so far surpassed the common understanding. They would gladly be more serviceable were any means available to reconcile the requirements of art and the common taste. Whether Karl Shapiro has found a legitimate means or not, he has lately deplored the divorce of poetry from social action and called upon poets to adopt a more responsible public attitude. To what kind of poetry his change of heart[34] commits him is far from clear, though something obviously of general appeal: "The true audience, when it is allowed to grow, may of course reach all levels of appreciation from the lowest to the highest; it is ever the job of the poet to address himself to the present *condition* of the audience and to the language of that audience."[35] Whatever Shapiro has in mind, Randall Jarrell's comments on a similar impulse in Auden are instructive: "Auden has been successful in making his poetry more accessible; but the success has been entirely too expensive. Realiz-

33. Margaret Schlauch, *Modern English and American Poetry: Techniques and Ideologies* (London, 1956), p. 21, reports from Warsaw that the Soviet poet has achieved a "vital and dynamic position in society."

34. Cf. "I shall deprecate the idea of a great audience, mass culture, and the esthetic of the American middle class."—"What is Anti-Criticism?" *Poetry*, LXXV (1949–50), p. 339.

35. *In Defense of Ignorance*, p. 44.

ing that the best poetry of the '20's was too inaccessible, we can will our poetry into accessibility—but how much poetry will be left when we finish? Our political or humanitarian interests may make us wish to make our poetry accessible to large groups; it is better to try to make the groups accessible to the poetry, to translate the interests into political or humanitarian activity."[36] Jarrell's statement may be taken as an oblique answer to the question, whether poetry ought in consequence of society's ameliorated conception of its nature and destiny to take a more popular form even at the risk of falsifying experience.

It should be axiomatic by now that the poet who speaks in the language of men to immediate public concerns is unlikely in the long run to be honored either by society or by critics. Verse of mainly sociological and political import seldom outruns the circumstances which bring it forth; and the common idiom, besides tending to banality, imposes a ruinous limitation on the expression of subtle and elusive concepts. The neglected state of poetry is an understandable vexation both to poets filled with social passions and to those with no more than ordinary self-esteem, but to judge from the past there is no remedy whatever in conceding to popular taste. John Peale Bishop apprehended two shards of ancient wisdom which deserve the notice of any poet with visions of immortality—"Concepts clearly and explicitly expressed are thereby condemned to death," and "The poet is explicit at his peril."[37] The notion is as old as Boccaccio that difficulty enhances the value of poetry,[38] and at least until the Romantic Movement there was nothing particularly reprehensible in setting tests worthy of deep readers.[39]

36. Randall Jarrell, "Changes of Attitude and Rhetoric in Auden's Poetry," *Southern Review*, VII (1941–42), pp. 348 f. Cf. Jarrell's "The Obscurity of the Poet," *Partisan Review*, XVIII (1951), pp. 66 ff.

37. John Peale Bishop, *Collected Essays*, ed. Edmund Wilson (New York and London, 1948), pp. 369, 371.

38. *Genealogia*, p. 60.

39. It should be recalled, however, that Shelley depreciated the taste of the masses in a letter to Charles Ollier, ed. Roger Ingpen and W. E. Peck, *The Complete Works* (new ed.; New York and London, 1965), X, p. 236; and that

Chapman put the matter bluntly: "There is no confection made
to last, but it is admitted more cost and skill than presently-to-be-
used simples; and in my opinion, that which being with a little
endeavour searched, adds a kind of majesty to Poesy, it better than
that which every cobbler may sing to his patch."[40] This observation
smacks of cunning and insincerity, but it recognizes the continuing
attractiveness of that verse which reserves its wisdom and delights
for perseverance.

3   What probably disturbs the poet above all is his isolation not
from the semiliterate elements of society but from that considerable
minority which through capacity and position tends to define cultural values. There was never any legitimate hope that serious art
would become, by whatever educational stratagem, identical with
kitsch or even compete successfully with it.[41] If for no other reason
than their undistinguished and therefore unflattering condition
the masses prefer palliatives; and no amount of uplifting could
induce them to stain their leisure with the artist's special insights
into the dread reality they know all too well. While difficult art and
music have yet their affluential patrons, poetry can count few ad-
mirers among the reputed great and perhaps none to whom a poet
might address himself as confidently as Dante to Can Grande
della Scala.

The obscurity of poetry is not the main cause, if cause at all, but
its seeming unreliability and inapplicability in a scientific age.[42]
The poet's models of the world of human experience, that is, his

---

Blake in a letter to Dr. John Trusler (1799), ed. Geoffrey Keynes, *The Complete
Writings* (new ed.; London, 1966), p. 793, invoked classical arguments for
obscurity and further remarked, "That which can be made Explicit to the
Idiot is not worth my care."

40. *Loc. cit.*

41. See Dwight MacDonald, "A Theory of Mass Culture," in *Mass Culture:
The Popular Arts in America*, ed. Bernard Rosenberg and D. M. White (Glencoe, Ill., 1957), pp. 59–73.

42. See H. H. Waggoner, *The Heel of Elohim: Science and Values in Modern
American Poetry* (Norman, Okla., 1950), pp. 5–9, 208; Murray Krieger, *The
New Apologists for Poetry* (Minneapolis, 1956), p. 5.

myths, are largely discounted because not achieved by any sort of respectable methodology. The *furor poeticus* which even Plato thought productive of deep truths, is more likely to be ascribed to psychic disorders than to any kind of decent inspiration. What the poet accomplishes is in no respect valuable to the age; he cannot put in a reasonable claim to exact description or to exact prediction, and probably not to knowledge in the narrow sense. Under the circumstances there is no remedy in declaring that history somehow certifies the larger significance of poetry, for it is obviously set around by theoretical disabilities. Yet poets have obstinately affirmed their traditional powers and have asserted against the times that some truths are accessible only to imagination and intuition and that these truths are often not directly expressible. To hold this position has been to invite ridicule, and there is no disputing the fact that poets, unprovided as they are with statistical vouchers, are the least regarded of the several categories of intellectuals who speak under various disguises as sages.

Were there a strong presumption that poetry contains "words of the wise," its "dark sayings" would be considered altogether necessary and a fitting challenge to deep thinkers. The scientist, his wisdom conceded, uses cryptic notation with the complete approval of the learned and by means of it creates in the mass-mind an impression of magical powers. Since the age has come to respect so exceedingly logical inferences from sense data and therefore cannot conveniently recognize another and apparently irreconcilable mode of knowing, poetic obscurity can only be regarded as a superfluous integument of what in any case is unsubstantial, or, more bluntly, nonsensical. Knowledgeable men discount poetry because of its defect of evidence and suspect it of imposition because of its obscurity. Unfortunately, arguments put forward to establish a respectable status for it commonly fail to satisfy positivist or other presently accepted criteria and on occasion terminate in logical dilemmas. For instance, to claim knowledge for poetry—without which it may be no more than verbal objects addressed to the emotions[43]—is possibly to cast it into the dominion of science or philosophy and to expose its conceptual part to insensitive analysis.[44] Perhaps poetry cannot also be science or philosophy without suffering partial eclipse as poetry, but nothing is gained from insisting so far on its autonomy as to sever its relations to these disciplines and to place it beyond defining in rational terms. Declaring that the function of a poem is to be rather than to mean, though useful for pointing up its mode of existence, does not in fact create a sanctuary for it or protect its cognitive elements from piecemeal evaluation.[45] The inclination to insulate poetry is of course understandable; logical analysis, while sometimes useful for uncovering imprecisions, becomes a menace when leaving the impression that what a poem overtly states is substantially all that it means. Reductive measures injure modernist poetry in particular, for its obscurity is in part justified by the assumption that experience is complex and most adequately rendered by suggestion and ambiguity rather than by direct statement.

What nowadays sustains the poet is not the Arnoldian hope that poetry will save the world and that he will be its singing master, but an impudent suspicion that the rationale of science is far from impeccable and, despite what I. A. Richards describes as "the transference from the Magical View of the world to the scientific,"[46] that man's experiences yet run in the primordial grooves. If science in general has intimidated him, depth psychology and cultural anthropology have suggested better reasons than Blake and Shelley knew for evoking the archetypes and speaking with an oracular voice. Doubtless obscurity is sometimes to be set

43. W. M. Urban, *Language and Reality: The Philosophy of Language and the Principles of Symbolism* (New York, 1939), pp. 476–502, systematically defends the poet's revelatory powers and the truth status of poetry.

44. Cf. Allen Tate's claim for literature in *On the Limits of Poetry: Selected Essays, 1928–1948* (New York, 1948), p. 15, with the remonstrance of F. X. Roellinger, Jr., "Two Theories of Poetry as Knowledge," *Southern Review*, VII (1941–42), p. 693.

45. R. W. Hepburn, "Literary and Logical Analysis," *Philosophical Quarterly*, VIII (1958), pp. 352–54.

46. I. A. Richards, *Science and Poetry* (2d ed.; London, 1935), p. 52.

down merely as a failure of construction, a retreat from the common reader, or a psychopathic manifestation,[47] but in the modernists it seems more often to be an implicit claim to speak those remote truths which lie beyond experimental method and deductive reason and which rise to the meditation of seers and mages. Although the times on principle allow less and less scope to individuals and at most leave only a small egocentric role to the poet, modernists, with the exception of T. E. Hulme,[48] have admitted no limitations. Yeats, Eliot, and Auden, indeed Dylan Thomas, have taken as seriously as the French symbolists the traditional pretensions of poets to penetrate, in Carlyle's words, "into the sacred mystery of the Universe." While by no means all in this century have aspired to cosmic and apocalyptic expression, most have set themselves to very solemn issues and have been little inclined to occasional and frivolous verse. Their attachment to symbolic formulations, probably the major source of obscurity, may owe something to admiration of a French grace, but it is mainly significant of faith in the power of the symbol to create and contain reality.[49] To demand that for the sake of clarity they translate their symbols to general terms is to demand that they blunt the fine point of their perceptions and divest their visions of the materials which give them substance and force.[50] That they have made no concessions to public bewilderment probably ought not to be ascribed in the main to arrogance but to recognition of the impossibility of revealing the shape of things unseen and un-

47. See Kenneth Burke, *A Rhetoric of Motives* (New York, 1950), p. 280; John Caffrey, "The Critic as Interlocutor," *ETC.*, VIII (1950–51), p. 270.

48. T. E. Hulme, *Speculations: Essays on Humanism and the Philosophy of Art*, ed. Herbert Read (London, 1936), p. 131.

49. W. K. Wimsatt, Jr., "Two Meanings of Symbolism: A Grammatical Exercise," *Catholic Renascence*, VIII (1955), pp. 12–25, discusses the complex function of symbols in some modern theories.

50. See Jolande Jacobi, *Complex / Archetype / Symbol in the Psychology of C. G. Jung*, trans. Ralph Manheim (New York, 1959), p. 123; John Senior, *The Way Down and Out: The Occult in Symbolist Literature* (Ithaca, N.Y., 1959), p. 95.

seeable to the common understanding.[51] And in this matter the
scientist and philosopher are no less helpless. The difference is
that the obscure formulations of the poet are widely regarded as
a social abuse rather than as a worthy effort to comprehend the
complexities of the modern experience in the limits of form.

If poets have been little inclined to conciliate even those seg-
ments of society which offer fair promise of an audience, the explanation may be their obsession with the notion of the world's
confusion and accordingly with the need to get things straight
for themselves and for their soul's good. They speak, it is true, to
all who will hear, but particularly to themselves; and their verse
appears to be most importantly a record of the triumph of the spirit
over the forces of disintegration. Although the spiritual travail of
poets is a commonplace of literary history, it is presumably greater
in this century because of the decay of traditional values. Whereas
Dante, despite the political turmoil of his times, was assured of
an audience receptive to his vision of the soul's progress from darkness into light, modern poets stand in doubt and perhaps unconsciously seek through opaqueness to avoid the flings of skeptics.
If their poetry is a claim to see the world whole, it is also a private
labor to reorganize an unsatisfying universe. In the latter regard
it is offered neither for public instruction nor for public approval;
it is something of a declaration of belief and as such not subject
to correction and refinement. While modernists are usually critics
and probably on that account the more tolerant of searching exam-
inations of their own work, they can hardly be agreeable to criticism
which commits trespass on their privacy or calls in question the
authenticity of their visions. If alienated, they are hardly more so
on account of the state of the world and the indifference of serious
readers than of the depredations of well-meaning critics who are
in one way or another affected by scientific methods. Rationalistic

51. See Martin Foss, *Symbol and Metaphor in Human Experience* (Princeton, 1949), p. 124.

criticism lays bare the cognitive bones of their constructs, Freudian analysis degrades their essentially creative distortions of language, and source-hunting tends to dispel their magic.[52] However deplorable in the modern view, obscurity affords a measure of protection, as it always has for seers, against those who would abuse the truth and against those who would void its shape by seeking its causes. To "sing high and aloofe" *in contemptu mundi* inflames the social passions of the times, but, as Jonson observed, in his "Ode to Himself," it is a means to avoid the "wolves black jaw, and the dull Asses hoofe."[53]

Modernists, of course, give better reasons for writing obscurely than confusing the multitudes and heavy-handed critics, and in the long run they may perform more valuable public service than poets who strive—and inevitably fail—to speak to all humanity. If reduction of whatever kind poses a special threat to their verse, then obscurity can be a means of securing its integrity and accordingly its relative permanency. Moreover, obscurity, as St. Augustine explained,[54] may be a means of unexpected enrichment: the reader who sets himself to difficult poetry may or may not divine the original meanings, but he is likely to be led by his excogitations to the discovery of others no less valuable. Whatever its present social implications, obscurity has a long-standing justification as a delight in the mind and as an instrument to deepen the understanding; and whoever holds it to be necessarily a fault sets himself against an impressive tradition.

52. See the protests of T. S. Eliot, "The Frontiers of Criticism," *Sewanee Review,* LXIV (1956), pp. 525–43; Karl Shapiro, "A Farewell to Criticism," *Poetry,* LXXI (1947–48), pp. 196 f; and Randall Jarrell, "Poets, Critics, and Readers," *Vanderbilt Alumnus,* XLVI (July–Aug., 1961), pp. 12 f.

53. Cf. Lionel Trilling, *The Liberal Imagination* (New York, 1950), pp. 101 f.

54. *De civitate Dei,* XI.xix.

Chapter V

The Literary Status
of the English
Popular Ballad
Scholars have generally been inclined to view the English popular ballad not as an aesthetic object but as a relic of an early and primitive state of society, in which the literary process was governed more by instinct than by convention. They have implicitly denied the existence of a purely literary problem, and their speculations about the ballad matrix have had the effect of discouraging criticism of any but an appreciative sort. Yet excellences appropriate to learned literature have been incidentally claimed for the ballad, and, in contrast to other forms of popular art (e.g., lyrical folk song, folk tale, broadside), it has received extensive notice in anthologies and literary histories. This is not to argue that it deserves less but only to remark the impropriety of assuming value for what, beyond an occasional explication, has escaped close critical scrutiny.

The ballad doubtless owes its relative immunity from value judgments to the naturalistic explanation of its origin. Most of the older scholars probably felt that standards derived from literature of the main cultural stream were largely inapplicable to songs which, in the best opinion, came ultimately from the illiterate throng. For some time now, the theory of communal composition has been in the discard, but discussions of the ballad continue to be colored by romantic attitudes toward the ill-defined folk and their creative activity. In important respects the ballad has not been wrenched free of the context in which the eighteenth century placed it by reason of an unconscionably narrow view of literary form. It is my opinion that literature even of the humblest order is completely accessible to criticism and that, accordingly, the ballad, whatever its degree of sophistication, is susceptible to systematic analysis. With the object of clarifying the literary status of the

English ballad, I propose to test the obstacles to critical study which by general agreement have been set around it and to consider the achievement of some of those specimens which seem to have very significantly shaped scholarly thinking.

1   The word *ballad* derives from OF *balade*, which in Chaucer's usage as in the French denoted a courtly lyric of fixed form. During the fifteenth century the term was loosely employed and afterward applied somewhat indiscriminately, though perhaps more often than not to more or less popular narrative songs.[1] There is no very ancient authority for the specialized sense standardized by F. J. Child, nor is there any evidence that the Child ballad was ever regarded outside of scholarly circles as *sui generis*.[2] The contents of his monumental *English and Scottish Popular Ballads* (1882–98) —305 ballads with variants—remained after a long and uncertain sifting process, some notion of which can be gained from an examination of his earlier collections.[3] He did not live to write an introduction, and the criteria by which the corpus was assembled can only be conjectured. Scholars in this century have commonly agreed (often without independent investigation) that the term "popular ballad," covering Child's exemplars and a few subsequently reported, properly designates a distinct genre.[4] It can hardly be maintained, however, that a ballad genre has been validated, for nowhere are the principles set forth by which these

1. Louise Pound, *Poetic Origins and the Ballad* (New York, 1921), pp. 39–46; G. H. Gerould, *The Ballad of Tradition* (Oxford, 1932), pp. 235–38; E. K. Chambers, *English Literature at the Close of the Middle Ages* (Oxford, 1945), pp. 137–39.

2. William Shenstone in two letters to Percy in 1761 seems first to have insisted on limiting the term "ballad" to narrative songs. Quoted by S. B. Hustvedt, *Ballad Criticism in Scandinavia and Great Britain during the Eighteenth Century* (New York, 1916), pp. 160 f.

3. According to the calculations of Thelma G. James, "The English and Scottish Popular Ballads of Francis J. Child," *Journal of American Folk-Lore*, XLVI (1933), pp. 51–53, the third and definitive edition of 1882–98 rejects 115 pieces from the first, published under the title *English and Scottish Ballads* (Boston, 1857), and adds 90 pieces, of which 37 were not previously available.

4. See Gerould, *op. cit.*, pp. 84–86.

pieces are ordered and contrived and thereby discriminated from other popular narrative song.[5] In short, this reputed genre yet lacks a serviceably exclusive definition and an unambiguous description of its peculiar art.

The impression is sometimes created that Child might have been able to resolve some of the doubts about the ballad, but what he wrote after a good many years of reflection encourages no such view. His article under "Ballad Poetry"[6] in the *Universal Cyclopaedia* (1900) is with respect to the major issues more intuitional than evidential, and it is wavering besides.[7] His discussion is affected by romantic notions of ancient literature, and the ballad never emerges from the medieval shadowland as conceived by the nineteenth century. For him it appears to have been essentially a relic, beautiful but without literary pretensions:

The popular ballad, for which our language has no unequivocal name, is a distinct and very important species of poetry. Its historical and natural place is anterior to the appearance of the poetry of art, to which it has formed a step, and by which it has been regularly displaced, and, in some cases, all but extinguished. Whenever a people in the course of its development reaches a certain intellectual and moral stage, it will feel an impulse to express itself, and the form of expression to which it is first impelled is, as is well known, not prose, but verse, and in fact narrative verse.

Child postulated as the matrix of the ballad a homogeneous community in which "the whole people form an individual." Since the "author counts for nothing" under these conjectured circumstances, the ballad is necessarily distinguished by the "absence of subjectivity and of self-consciousness." Yet he was unwilling to

5. In the loosest sense of the term, subsuming many specimens besides Child's, the ballad may possibly be considered a genre; but it has not been shown to constitute a genre in the sense of the classical epic, the Italian sonnet, and other forms controlled more or less by formula. James, op. cit., pp. 57–59, raised the legitimate doubt that a definition could be devised to comprehend all the Child pieces.

6. Published originally in *Johnson's Cyclopaedia* (1874).

7. For an attempt to clarify Child's position, see W. M. Hart, "Professor Child and the Ballad," *PMLA*, XXI (1906), pp. 755–807.

abandon the ballad to a community of illiterates—"the lower orders of a people"—and out of his sense of the fitness of things he contrived an agreeable cultural situation which, unfortunately for his argument, has no demonstrable historical reality: "Nothing, in fact, is more obvious than that many of the ballads of the now most refined nations had their origin in that class whose acts and fortunes they depict—the upper class—though the growth of civilization has driven them from the memory of the highly polished and instructed, and has left them as an exclusive possession to the uneducated. The genuine popular ballad had its rise in a time when the distinctions since brought about by education and other circumstances had practically no existence."

Child's indecisive statement is highly significant; it expresses a measure of allegiance to the old theory of communal composition, which F. B. Gummere was later to elaborate with special reference to the ballad,[8] and at the same time a doubt that ballads could have originated in a throng of dancing and singing illiterates. He apparently recognized the danger of an upper-class origin to the concept of the ballad as an artless form and almost in the same breath reaffirmed the classless, homogeneous setting. Child's work was in a sense completed by Kittredge, who wrote the introduction to the Cambridge abridgement of the *English and Scottish Popular Ballads* (1904). Kittredge apparently felt nothing of his master's misgivings but spoke strongly for the communal principle, though, to be sure, not for group authorship of extant specimens.

The rise and fall of this theory is not of principal concern here; suffice it to say that Louise Pound among others exposed its ab-

8. Gummere's exposition of the theory is spread through "The Ballad and Communal Poetry," *Studies and Notes in Philology and Literature*, V (1896), pp. 41–56; *Old English Ballads* (Boston, 1904); *The Popular Ballad* (Boston and New York, 1907); *The Beginnings of Poetry* (New York, 1908). The theory had been largely discredited before Gummere picked it up from German sources, which, in the opinion of Phillips Barry ("Das Volk dichtet nichts," *Bulletin of the Folk-Song Society of the Northeast*, No. 7 [1934], p. 4), he wrenched in order to support his argument.

surdities,[9] in the end forcing it out of serious consideration—but, oddly enough, not freeing scholarship of its influence. The important questions were reargued by Gerould, who said all that could be said in defense of Gummere's views against Pound's attack. While finding much to blame in the anticommunalists, he nonetheless executed a perceptible retreat from the more extreme positions maintained by the communalists. His concessions appear, however, to jeopardize the traditional concept of the ballad without much clarifying its origin and status.

Acceptance of the principle of single authorship has meant something less than a complete turnabout. The folk, collectively considered, is a more important factor than the original author, if, as it is widely believed, all of the ballads have been significantly altered in oral tradition by a supposedly beneficial process called communal re-creation.[10] By this view, every ballad is multiple and mutable, consisting of an unascertainable number of versions, all of which may be undergoing change. It is thus futile to speak of an author and impossible to establish a text. Even judgments about individual versions are not entirely feasible, since the ballad is not simply text but a joint product of words, music, and singer which varies with each performance. In this vein Evelyn Kendrick Wells has recently observed: "It is the product of no one time or person; its author, if ever known, has been lost in the obscurity of the past and in the processes of oral tradition. Its medium is word of mouth rather than print. It goes its way independent of literary influences, carrying for a while the accretions of this or that day and singer,

9. A. K. Davis, Jr., ed., *Traditional Ballads of Virginia* (Cambridge, Mass., 1929) pp. 4–9, provides a summary account of the controversy.

10. Fully stated by Phillips Barry, "Communal Re-Creation," *Bulletin of the Folk-Song Society of the Northeast*, No. 5 (1933), pp. 4–6, and approved by Gerould, *op. cit.*, pp. 168 f, who, however, used an earlier article by Barry, "An American Homiletic Ballad," *MLN*, XXVIII (1913), pp. 4 f. On the question of the handling of the ballads by the folk, see the very full discussion of Sergio Baldi, *Studi sulla poesia popolare d'Inghilterra e di Scozia* (Rome, 1949), pp. 42–65.

but sloughing them off as it passes to the next. It has no one original text, being freshly created by each successive singer as he makes his own version."[11] Behind this modified communalism probably lies Gerould's remarkable statement of the ballad's mode of existence, which tends to invalidate the title of the original author to his work: "The popular ballad . . . has no real existence save when held in memory and sung by those who have learned it from the lips of others. In saying this I am not ignoring the difficult question of its origin . . . but merely emphasizing the primary condition of its being. Strictly speaking, the ballad as it exists is not a ballad save when it is in oral circulation, and certainly not until it has been in oral circulation."[12]

Gerould intended, of course, to support the claims of the folk, but the dense metaphysical integument which he fashioned for that purpose would, if accepted, effectively insulate the ballad against all literary inquiry and indeed against all efforts at understanding. If it cannot be essentially represented in print, it can hardly be apprehended for critical examination. Gerould probably did not mean quite so much, for on occasion he dealt with the ballad as if it belonged to the province of literature and could be discriminated accordingly. He was nonetheless inclined to deny the applicability of any standard save what might be called "balladness," signifying a norm presumed to be implicit in the irrefutable instances.[13]

The confused status of the ballad today can be explained by reference to the cultural and literary biases of the period which officially discovered it. Percy was in most things a man of his century, with a characteristic tenderness for the past and for the peasant, but also with a view of literature founded in neoclassical theory and practice. A century which revised Shakespeare and rejected Donne could hardly be expected to regard inartificial song

11. Evelyn Kendrick Wells, *The Ballad Tree* (New York, 1950), p. 5.
12. *Op. cit.*, pp. 2 f.
13. *Ibid.*, p. 35.

seriously as literature, and Percy carefully refrained from making
any such claim; yet the primitivism and antiquarianism of the
times permitted unbounded enthusiasm for whatever related to
ancient men living close to nature. His dedicatory epistle to the
Countess of Northumberland presents the ballads "not as labours
of art, but as effusions of nature, showing the first efforts of ancient
genius";[14] and his "Preface," while invoking the taste of ballad
lovers like Addison,[15] avoids their critical indiscretions: "In a
polished age, like the present, I am sensible that many of these
reliques of antiquity will require great allowances to be made for
them. Yet have they, for the most part, a pleasing simplicity, and
many artless graces, which in the opinion of no mean critics have
been thought to compensate for the want of higher beauties, and,
if they do not dazzle the imagination, are frequently found to
interest the heart."[16]

Later scholars much abused Percy for taking editorial liberties,
but none denied that the ballads considered as literature left a
great deal to be desired. If less apologetic than Percy, Child actually
claimed no more, nor did Kittredge. The latter concluded his introduction to the Cambridge edition with an infelicitous discussion
which evidences a firm intent to claim value for the ballads without
stating precisely wherein value resides:

Of the merit of the English and Scottish ballads nothing need be said.
It is unhesitatingly admitted by all persons who care for ballads at all.
There is no occasion to make comparisons as to excellence between
these pieces and the poetry of art. Such comparisons are misleading;
they tend only to confound the distinctions between two very different
categories of literature. The ballads must stand or fall by themselves,
not by reason of their likeness or unlikeness to Dante or Shakspere
or Milton or Browning. Above all things, they should not be judged
indiscriminately or in the lump. . . . Finally, the popular ballad, though

14. Thomas Percy, *Reliques of Ancient English Poetry*, ed. H. B. Wheatley
(London, 1887), I, p. 1.
15. For praising *Chevy Chase* (*Spectator*, Nos. 70, 74) Addison endured
considerable ridicule.
16. Percy, *op. cit.*, I, p. 8.

it may be despised, cannot be ignored by the student of literature. Whatever may be thought of the importance of such verse in its bearing on the origin of poetry in general . . . the ballad, like other forms of popular material, has in the last two centuries exercised a powerful influence on artistic literature, and it will always have to be reckoned with by the literary historian.[17]

This melancholy argument confesses the lack of a sufficient rationale, an original defect of ballad scholarship which to this day has not been repaired.

The followers of Child and Kittredge have not considered the possibility of dissolving Percy's distinction between art poetry and natural poetry, which the critical inflexibility of the eighteenth century dictated,[18] but rather have felt a need to reaffirm it as an integral part of the ballad concept. To allow art to the ballad is to invite troublesome questions about its origin and form, though to deny art is not quite reasonable. Gerould argued that the difference was a matter of consciousness of aesthetic principles. While not denying the existence of principles somewhere in the background of the ballads, he yet minimized to the vanishing point their influence on the composers. His defense of Percy's dichotomy, it must be said, entails an explanation of the creative process in the folk milieu which is highly intuitional, if not mystical.[19] Leach accepted Gerould's distinction and then pressed on to the logical but nonetheless absurd conclusion that the ballads were products of dabbling by the collective illiteracy: "The musician and storyteller on the conscious level intellectualizes his material and method by trying them against aesthetic principles already codified and drawn up for him. The folk, on the other hand, accept, reject, modify, augment their songs and stories through unconscious subjective processes; and what one generation accepts, another may

17. H. C. Sargent and G. L. Kittredge, eds., *English and Scottish Popular Ballads* (Boston, 1904), pp. xxx f.
18. See René Wellek, *A History of Modern Criticism: 1750–1950* (New Haven, 1955), I, pp. 126 ff; M. J. C. Hodgart, *The Ballads* (London, 1950), pp. 159–61.
19. *Op. cit.*, pp. 13 f.

change or reject entirely. So we hit on beauty, or pathos, or sense of tragedy not exactly by chance but nearly so."[20] In the end Leach states, as he must, that the makers of folk song are without art.[21]

Whatever the full explanation of the creative process, there is no reason for thinking it differs fundamentally according to time, place, or social circumstance. It is not evident that learned poets have ever followed rule books slavishly or that unlearned ones have worked without conscious regard for convention. A good deal has been staked on artlessness, which has yet to be plausibly explained. Indeed, the question arises whether this crucial concept is very clear to those who insist upon its validity. For instance, a comment by Wells on a passage of dialogue in *Young Hunting* is something less than coherent: "It is the simplicity of great art, as well as of great artlessness."[22] It is perhaps just as well for the traditional view that artlessness, implying at most an unconscious critical sense in the folk, cannot be substantiated; for the absence of definite critical controls is incompatible with a ballad genre.

The old idea of natural poetry, which psychologically considered has little to recommend it, is rendered even less tenable in the case of the ballad by a concession made by Gerould and affirmed with damaging elaborations by Leach. They agree, against the opinion of Kittredge and others, that ballads may have been composed on social levels somewhat above the illiterate commonalty and even by minstrels. Percy, it may be recalled, ascribed the ballads to the "ancient English bards and minstrels,"[23] though without much supporting evidence. Kittredge argued that minstrels could not have composed them because their repertoires, as fas as known, consisted of very different matter.[24] Gerould rather cautiously granted that the makers of ballads may somtimes have been "middle-class folk," even professional minstrels of a rude and illiterate

---

20. MacEdward Leach, ed., *The Ballad Book* (New York, 1955), p. 10.
21. *Ibid.*, p. 33.
22. *Op. cit.*, p. 91.
23. *Op. cit.*, I, 7.
24. Sargent and Kittredge, *op. cit.*, p. xxiii.

order.[25] Leach expressed the same view, though apparently without Gerould's concern about its implications: "Who are the ballad folk? There is a general impression that they are illiterate hillbillies, wandering around barefoot and smoking corncob pipes. The evidence from numerous records as far back as the Middle Ages points rather to the middle class: small farmers, shoemakers, village schoolteachers, nursemaids, tinkers, wives of small tradesmen, innkeepers, drovers. Among these too are the itinerant singers of songs who go from village to village plying a small trade but concerning themselves largely with singing their stores of songs."[26] Some of these categories must be reckoned lower class; but, if Leach means what he says, he has fathered the ballads upon a class which produced the bulk of medieval literature, including the *Roman de la Rose* and the *Canterbury Tales*, and which from the fourteenth century on was increasingly literate. Not even on the lower side could the middle class be described as artless. Indeed, it may be doubted that any section of medieval society was innocent of artificial literature, since knowledge of it depended simply on auditory receptiveness,[27] not literacy. The middle class may have composed ballads, but neither in the Middle Ages nor in the Renaissance was it demonstrably free of the literary taint which has been thought ruinous to balladry. If actually middle class in origin, the ballad can hardly be regarded as a special case, implying an unusual cultural situation and mode of composition.

The inordinate concern from Percy to the present with the ballad matrix has been largely owing to the simple conviction that the ballad, while often pleasing, differs in fundamental ways from the verse of more or less learned poets and cannot stand comparison with it. Encumbered by this preconception, scholars have supposed that the ballad could be legitimately prized only as a product of a cultural situation separate and apart from the main

25. Gerould, *op. cit.*, pp. 185, 225 f.
26. *Op. cit.*, pp. 8 f.
27. Ruth Crosby, "Oral Delivery in the Middle Ages," *Speculum*, XI (1936), p. 100.

stream. This is not to say, of course, that they have had to make excuses to themselves for taking unqualified pleasure in favorite pieces. But it is quite another matter to claim absolute excellence for poetry which appears to fall far below the norms established by major writers. By means of rather shaky inferences a home was found for the ballad in the vast wastes of the Middle Ages, though not in a location that scholarship might visit. The search for origins is not in itself reprehensible, but it has been carried out with something less than scientific objectivity and to the neglect of the ballad as art. The cause was sought before the effect was rightly understood; and perhaps necessarily the supposed matrix, besides lacking historical probability, precluded the possibility of conscious artistry and thus of high achievement. It is not a reproach to Percy that he made no attempt to demonstrate the aesthetic integrity of the ballads; but literary scholars in this century, which in criticism is flexible if anything, cannot pretend to be hampered by neoclassical standards. Criticism was never freer or better equipped than now to determine whether the ballads individually and collectively have value as literature as well as *for* literature.

2   Most things relating to the ballad have been violently disputed, but there has been unusual agreement about those specimens especially worthy of inclusion in the golden treasuries of literature. That this should be the case is rather surprising, since literary standards have not been thought applicable to the ballad.[28] It is of course possible that the preference of anthologists has been altogether determined by nonaesthetic criteria. This supposition fails, however, to account for the narrow range of their choices among scores of ballads which demand equal consideration by virtue of metrical arrangement, subject matter, use of authentic conventions, impersonality, and freedom from elegance. The con-

28. Gerould, *op. cit.*, p. 85, insisted that "we must . . . look with unprejudiced eyes at everything that has the warrant of tradition behind it, whether or not it seems to us 'good' according to any theory of origins or our sophisticated standards of aesthetic taste."

clusion is hard to resist that in some way literary quality rather than typicalness has recommended them. This inconsistency would perhaps be of little significance except for the likelihood that the influence of the preferred pieces on scholarly thinking has been far out of proportion to their number. In that event, they would invite close study for their central importance to the very concept of the ballad as well as for their probable literary excellence.

It is evident from the anthologies of English literature intended for undergraduate use that scholars have a marked preference for eight of Child's 305 ballads, and in the same versions.[29] *Sir Patrick Spens* (A) seems never to be omitted and *Edward* (B) almost never. *Barbara Allan* (A) and the *Wife of Usher's Well* (A) appear four times in five. The incidence of the *Twa Corbies, Lord Randal* (A), *Johnie Armstrong* (A), and the *Daemon Lover* (A) is about 50 percent. Others selected with significant frequency—about once in three times—are the *Three Ravens, Mary Hamilton* (A), *Young Waters, Lord Thomas and Fair Annet* (A), *Thomas Rymer* (A), *Kemp Owyne* (A), and the *Twa Sisters* (A). The interest in the last three pieces of this group is perhaps chiefly folkloristic. The *Hunting of the Cheviot* (*Chevy Chase*) and the *Maid Freed from the Gallows* figure importantly in ballad scholarship but for one reason or another do not often appear in anthologies.

While the validity of any useful grouping is likely to be vitiated by marginal instances, the claim can be made with considerable justice that the more famous of these pieces stand somewhat apart in point of internal form. Since none is rich in narrative detail and most are positively deficient, the definition of the ballad as a folk song that tells a story is for this group assuredly inadequate, if not misleading. Telling a story is not the only concern and probably not even the major one. The claim of the ballad to literary

29. I have based my estimates on thirteen well-known textbooks (e.g., Woods-Watt-Anderson, *The Literature of England*) which are now in print or have been until recently.

merit thus depends to a large extent on pieces which are not, with minor exceptions, pre-eminently narrative. Rather interestingly, in view of the standard definition, no one has argued that they would be the better for telling completer stories; it is perhaps evident that, whatever the method, they do their work well.

Yet the relative sketchiness of the anthology ballads is the source of a difficulty which, though perhaps more apparent than real, requires attention. Inasmuch as time and transmission work substantial and, by the common view, usually unfortunate alterations in the ballad,[30] there is some antecedent probability that even the earliest recorded versions, which anthologists almost always prefer, differ markedly from their originals. It stands to reason that a ballad caught up after a century or two of oral transmission will register a loss of detail, if of nothing more serious, and in any case will have suffered as art. Accordingly, the ballads in question here may represent varying degrees of deterioration from originals which, if available, would provoke contempt for their derivatives. Although there is not much concrete evidence to oppose this view, it rests ultimately on the unwarranted assumption that most extant ballads traveled far—some even from the Middle Ages—before lodging in print. But, however ancient their story content, the ballads themselves are not, except in a small handful of instances, demonstrably medieval, and very few antedate the seventeenth century.[31] Most of the favored anthology pieces cannot be dated earlier than the eighteenth century, and none recalls extant medieval song in style. Indeed, the authentic medieval specimens, which might be expected to show balladry at its best, are as a group neither rich in detail nor remarkable as literature. While the most admired ballads as now known probably differ from their originals, it would be absurd to postulate for them a long and generally

30. See J. R. Moore, "The Influence of Transmission on the English Ballads," *Modern Language Review*, XI (1916), p. 408.

31. Louise Pound, "On the Dating of the English and Scottish Ballads," *PMLA*, XLVII (1932), p. 15, argues persuasively that the great period of ballad making was after the Renaissance.

deleterious oral career prior to the earliest recordings. In any event, the literary value of a ballad is properly measured only by its aesthetic achievement; how it reached its available state or states, though important for cultural history, is ultimately of no concern to criticism. Close analysis tends to show that in the main the anthology versions require no literary allowances to be made for them and thus provide no basis for assuming superior, or even longer, originals.

It is possible to describe the method of the popular ballads as narrative, dramatic, or even lyrical, but none of these terms or any combination of them (e.g., dramatic narrative, lyrical-dramatic narrative)[32] is of much use to criticism. Some years ago M. J. C. Hodgart proposed to supply the lack of a serviceable term with "montage."[33] Whether generally applicable to the ballads or not, the term permits a valuable insight into the method of the ones at issue here. At the center of most of these pieces is a commonplace (and usually tragic) predicament set around by scenes sufficient to define it and at the same time to outline, often very vaguely, a story of considerable magnitude. The matter, shaped up from various angles of representation, tends to point away from the particular situation and toward a general meaning, and it is upon the higher level that these ballads have their greatest interest. They are most significantly symbolic structures; and to speak of them as narrative, dramatic, or lyrical is to call to mind poetry of different management. W. K. Wimsatt, Jr., has written, "But the best story poems may be analyzed, I believe, as metaphors without expressed tenors, as symbols which speak for themselves."[34] His example—La Belle Dame Sans Merci—is incontrovertible, though its aesthetic appears to differ from that of the symbolistic popular ballads. Wimsatt does not state the criteria by which the

32. Leach, op. cit., p. 5; W. J. Entwistle, European Balladry (Oxford, 1939), p. 18.
33. Hodgart, op. cit., p. 27, acknowledges his debt to S. Eisenstein's The Film Sense (1943), in which parts of Paradise Lost are studied as montage.
34. W. K. Wimsatt, Jr., The Verbal Icon (Lexington, Ky., 1954), p. 80.

best story poems are to be sorted out, but he would probably agree
that little is to be gained by analyzing as symbolic structures those
fairly long and detailed ballads in which the story seems to be everything or nearly so. Child's collection assuredly abounds in innocent
narratives (e.g., *Young Beichan*) and dramatic exchanges (e.g.,
Riddles Wisely Expounded), and possibly only a minority actually
demanded metaphoric extension. This is not to imply, however,
that only the popular anthology pieces are eligible for such treatment or that others are any the less the products of conscious and
individual artistry.

The most famous version of *Sir Patrick Spens*, though decidedly
fragmentary as narrative, leaves a distinct impression of achieved
art. The literary result considered, it can hardly be thought accidental that the spectacular circumstances surrounding the foun-
dering of the ship are neglected and that acts and scenes of an
unessential order are held up to view. The very poverty of local detail sets a limit on narrative interest, while the obviously symbolic
import of much of the content points the whole experience ineluctably toward an abstract level of meaning. Indeed, *Sir Patrick
Spens* insists so powerfully on being something more than a story
of death at sea that its otherness densely overspreads the simple
relation. At the center of the ballad is an ironic situation—the
king sitting "in Dumferling toune" appears to honor Sir Patrick
by choosing him to undertake an important voyage which, on
account of the season, is unlikely to turn out well. The poet exploits the mixed feelings with which the sailor quite naturally
reads his orders from the king:

The first line that Sir Patrick red,
   A loud lauch lauched he;
The next line that Sir Patrick red,
   The teir blinded his ee.

Spens must need laugh and weep at a command which is, the conditions for sailing considered, utterly absurd and yet full of dark

fatality for him. An ominous weather forecast spoken by a crewman supports his pessimistic appraisal of the situation and removes all doubt about the result:

'Late late yestreen I saw the new moone,
  Wi the auld moone in hir arme,
And I feir, I feir, my deir master,
  That we will cum to harme.'

With his poem largely secured by this exciting symbol, the poet might have been expected to proceed in a conventional way to the tragic conclusion, but he elected to risk a novel tactic. What follows is then, not a step-by-step narration culminating in the sinking of the ship, but a series of scenes which ironically announce the outcome and cast shadow after shadow across the experience:

O our Scots nobles were richt laith
  To weet their cork-heild schoone;
Bot lang owre a' the play wer playd,
  Thair hats they swam aboone.
O lang, lang may their ladies sit,
  Wi thair fans into their hand,
Or eir they se Sir Patrick Spence
  Cum sailing to the land.
O lang, lang may the ladies stand,
  Wi thair gold kems in thair hair,
Waiting for thair ain deir lords,
  For they'll se thame na mair.
Haf owre, haf owre to Aberdour,
  It's fiftie fadom deip,
And thair lies guid Sir Patrick Spence,
  Wi the Scots lords at his feit.

The effect of the poet's shift is to lower the pitch and to generalize the tragedy; the particular disaster, which is of a sort most poignantly meaningful to seafaring people, tends to merge with the multitude of other fatal misadventures dogging the footsteps of mankind. The scenes contemplated by the poet, besides fleshing out the narrative slightly, reveal human beings taking pathetic and somewhat irrelevant postures in the face of circumstances beyond their power to control. The Scottish nobles are said to be concerned with emblems of rank and wealth—their cork-heeled shoes—when life itself is in jeopardy. The wives, waiting helplessly on shore with fans and gold combs in their hands, recreate and suffer the last agonies of their men. And "guid" Sir Patrick, arranged at the bottom of the sea with the Scottish lords at his feet, receives such honor as position confers but an honor which no man would rush to claim. Several questions about the tragedy remain unanswered but make no demand for answers, since larger considerations overshadow the particular event. By using an ironical angle of vision, and avoiding detail closely related to the calamitous moment, the poet blocks off the pathetic level of experiencing the tragedy and compels his audience to brood over the fatal forces which in one form or another overtake all men.

The achievement of *Sir Patrick Spens* is approached, though hardly equaled, by some other ballads which use much the same formula. In *Young Waters* the observations are relevant and moving but not overwhelmingly portentous; their focus is rather the particular tragic instance than the moral design of a world in which a young man can be executed for no other offense than his own handsomeness. It is significant of little more than personal distress for the victim to remark:

'Aft I have ridden thro Stirling town
    In the wind bot and the weit;
Bot I neir rade thro Stirling town
    Wi fetters at my feet.'

Such a statement, obvious and even trivial, is of course two-layered; but it makes no large demands and folds quietly into the story. *Mary Hamilton* tends in the opposite direction despite a series of sentimental gestures toward the close. In its best part the ballad has as much tension as *Sir Patrick Spens* and as much symbolic force. There are few passages in Child's collection more powerful

than Mary's reply to the "auld queen," who has accused her of
murdering the infant got on her by the "hichest Stewart of a' ":

'I winna put on my robes o black,
    Nor yet my robes o brown;
But I'll put on my robes o white,
    To shine through Edinbro town.'

Although weakened by the concluding matter—Mary's drinking
healths to her "weil-wishers" and her unexceptional reflections on
her parents—the ballad refuses to be taken at either the literal or
the moral level and constantly intimates the hopeless struggle of
a valiant spirit against a universe of evil consequences.

The fragmentary *Wife of Usher's Well* bears certain formal resemblances to the ballads previously discussed, but it is less obviously manipulated than any of them. Whereas the scenes sifted
out by the author of *Sir Patrick Spens* betray very artful discrimination and ironic twisting, those of the *Wife of Usher's Well*
have a central importance and, moreover, seem to speak pretty
much for themselves. Since the tragic situation is basically ironical,
the poet has only to report the circumstances in order to create a
powerful impression. It is noteworthy, however, that his extreme
detachment tends to call attention to the cruel universe which
surrounds the hapless wife. Word comes to the woman of the
death of her sons, presumably by drowning, and in her distress she
pronounces a terrible curse:

'I wish the wind may never cease,
    Nor fashes in the flood,
Till my three sons come hame to me,
    In earthly flesh and blood.'

The curse appears to effectuate the return of the sons, but the
audience learns a grim fact unknown to the mother, that the birch
of which their hats were made grew "at the gates o Paradise." The
Prodigal Son was not more cordially entertained than the unsubstantial sons of the deluded wife:

'Blow up the fire, my maidens,
  Bring water from the well;
For a' my house shall feast this night,
  Since my three sons are well.'

And she has made to them a bed,
  She's made it large and wide,
And she's taen her mantle her about,
  Sat down at the bed-side.

Cock's crow brings the inevitable revelation; as usual in such cases the revenants must return to the grave or abide a "sair pain." The distress of the mother is not reported and need not be. The ballad finally speaks most significantly not of a woman whose cursing earned a terrible punishment but of the vanity of human wishes. Its success is owing to an attitude so remote and restrained as to create a positive deficit of compassion and accordingly a very naked symbolization of the human predicament. The achievement of the *Wife of Usher's Well* can be measured by the *Daemon Lover*, which, though involving a revenant and an even more sensational action, is nothing more than a sentimentalized ghost story.

Laying stress on strategy, as I have done, supposes conscious authorship and thus affronts the notion that the ballads evolved without expert guidance. If every ballad, as in the standard view, registers the impress of several hands, the question of the author's attitude is very nearly an impertinence. Understandably, older scholars often felt impelled to doubt the authenticity of specimens strongly intimating a sophisticated point of view, though admitting the most attractive of these to the canon on the assumption that they were originally honest folk songs. Apparently from principle, the importance of the ballad speaker has been implicitly denied, and his varying angles of representation have been lumped without much discrimination under objectivity. While the ballads are of course objective, they are not for that naive reportage; indeed, the anthology pieces are patently artificial structures, evidencing conscious shaping from definable angles. The simple-seeming *Wife* of *Usher's Well* is no less a work of conscious art than *Sir Patrick Spens*, which has been suspected of learned handling. Although *Barbara Allan* has not been questioned on this count, it is instinct with compassion and selective of detail to the point of serious incompleteness. What may have originated as a grim account of malefic image making or similar witchery[35] has been culled for tender moments, and these have been organized to obtain a sentimental response. Although telling a poor story, this ballad unmistakably commemorates tragic love and thus by contrivance succeeds at an abstract level. The same general theme is embodied much more fully in *Lord Thomas and Fair Annet* and *Fair Margaret and Sweet William*; but in contrast to *Barbara Allan* these insist strongly on a higher meaning only in versions embellished with that widely used symbol of true love, the intertwined briar and rose.

The *Three Ravens* with its speaking birds and dense symbolism also suggests rather more contriving than natural poetry would allow, while its superlative congener, the *Twa Corbies*, indisputably declares the hand of a conscious artist. Child could not bring himself to accept the latter, though he had evidence that it was every bit as traditional as the other, if not so old. He printed it with the inconclusive remark that it sounded "something like a cynical variation of the tender little English ballad"—meaning the *Three Ravens*. "Cynical variation" is apparently intended to leave the impression that some version of the *Three Ravens* suffered, at least in ballad quality, from sophisticated handling.

What led Child to reject the *Twa Corbies* was probably not so much its tone as its sheer perfection; such metrical felicity and freedom from irrelevancy were hardly to be expected in folk song. The older ballad is no less artificial, and it ends with a frank intrusion, "God send euery gentleman, / Such haukes, such hounds, and such a leman"; but a certain roughness and incoherency ap-

35. A mere conjecture. There is some suggestion of a causal connection between the man's illness and Barbara Allan's resentment of the slight.

pear to vouch for its subliterary origin and career. The *Twa Corbies*
is less detailed and less exciting in content but more complex in
meaning. Literally considered, it announces the practical interest
of a pair of scavengers in a dead and deserted knight. Most significantly, it is a kind of *Earth Song*, grimmer for lacking Christian
reference and more plausible for being a symbolic structure rather
than a rhetorical and dialectical exercise. Much of the power of
the ballad comes through its evaluation of the knight from a scav-
enger's angle of vision and thus in nonhuman terms. The victim's
desertion by hawk, hound, and lady—all emblematic of worldly
felicity—is immediately significant of faithlessness and perhaps in
the last instance of treachery, but the scene is thereby symbolically
emptied of civilized values. Accordingly, the social amenities which
tend to soften the fact of death are precluded, and the knight is
seen simply—and terrifyingly—as an article of consumption, a mere
incident in cosmic process which by various means returns all
organic matter to that state whence it came. This commonplace
of nature becomes excruciatingly evident when one of the corbies
specifies the "bonny blue een" and the "gowden hair" as the first
parts to be utilized. The same bird concludes the poem with a
solemn observation, which is, the situation considered, positively
bizarre:

'Mony a one for him makes mane,
But nane sall ken where he is gane;
Oer his white banes, when they are bare,
The wind sall blaw for evermair.'

The speaker of the poem—the "I" of the first line—does not return
and need not; for the experience finds its significant level of meaning in the last stanza.

Edward and Lord Randal leave as strong an impression of conscious art as the *Twa Corbies*, but probably have been saved from
suspicion because of the conspicuous use of incremental repeti-

tion. Gummere professed to see in this device an archetypal feature and staked a good deal on it.[36] Yet in both of these ballads incremental repetition plainly subserves a structural principle which cannot be accounted for by an improvising throng—namely, the climactic ordering of parts. In *Edward* the mother's questions about the victim of her son's bloody sword elicit increasingly grave responses—hawk, horse, and then father. Lord Randal's meeting with his "true-love," his eating fried eels, and his mortal illness gradually show a causal relationship, and each new disclosure casts a deeper shadow across the central experience. When the principal has at last made known his predicament (patricide in *Edward*, poisoning in *Lord Randal*), he proclaims the extent of his temporal loss in a last testament, the parts of which are arranged in an ascending scale of interest culminating in a terrible curse. These symmetrical ballads cannot be easily faulted, nor can their excellence be plausibly explained by the process of communal creation or even re-creation.

The foregoing discussion permits the observation that the best of the ballads show some significant resemblances. They appear to share a moral universe which is not certainly Christian and probably not primitive. Though of uncertain design, it vaguely recalls the world of *King Lear*, in which evil circumstances harass the just and the unjust alike. The characters appear to be resigned to their fate; and, if they allow themselves a comment, it is commonly irony born of hopelessness. At the center in each case is a rather simple tragic situation which can be known essentially from a very sketchy relation. Ordinarily, a good deal of the story is left to inference, and not all the information directly provided is of first importance to it. Only a slight impression of linear movement is created because the circumstances held up to view tend to work centripetally on an anguished moment, which is, strictly considered, only a short dramatic interval in the narrative continuum. Concrete

36. *The Popular Ballad*, pp. 117–34. For dissenting arguments, see Pound, *Poetic Origins*, pp. 121–35, and Gerould, *op. cit.*, pp. 105–107.

particulars are chosen for their logical relevance to the central predicament and somewhat too for their symbolic force, as, for example, the "cork-heild schoone" which the Scottish nobles of *Sir Patrick Spens* were reluctant to wet. The contracted focus is regulated by the angle of representation and finally validated by the symbol which evolves. The measure of success is not story interest—indeed, most of the good ballads fail signally on this count—but abstract meaning or meanings. It is fair to say, I believe, that the quality of the experience developed by these ballads is more appropriate to lyrics of an objective kind than to narratives.

My examination of the anthology ballads points to the conclusion that their art is conscious and successful. To claim so much for them is not, however, to imply that they are equally successful or that even the very best deserve the status of monuments. Kittredge obfuscated the issue of achievement by invoking some of the greatest names in literature,[37] whose major work obviously lies several degrees of magnitude beyond any of the ballads. Their proper place is with the shorter, more or less narrative poems, of which the language affords a multitude between *Robene and Makyne* and *Sister Helen*; and in this broad category they appear to no disadvantage. These ballads are admittedly conspicuous for their lack of elegance and for their freedom from the influence of the schools. Their rhetoric is not classical, and their diction, though hardly colloquial, is assuredly not Latinate. But they are not on that account inartificial or inferior. So much formal contriving evidences an art which, though as yet imperfectly understood, is assuredly highly disciplined.[38]

37. Sargent and Kittredge, *op. cit.*, p. xxxi.
38. I have left music out of account from a conviction that the ballads, though unquestionably written to be sung, exist primarily as poems. This is in no way to deny that a given ballad benefits from a melody which unobtrusively confirms its tone or that the music has technical interest, if not much independent value. The fact that ballads have remained fairly intact and coherent in oral tradition is strong evidence that their accompaniment has always been sufficiently subdued to allow easy communication. Yet most of the ballads invite musical utterance; and, while not literally writing their own music, they suggest it, within broad

3   A moment's reflection will show that to claim distinctive form and superior excellence for the anthology ballads is to create a number of difficulties. Unless highly unlikely results are to be ascribed to communal re-creation, the existence of single and successful craftsmanship must be recognized for them and at no great distance from the earliest dates of record. An alternative is to consider as sophisticated adaptations the specimens which have been thought most worthy of notice; but ineptness would then become a test of genuineness. If the authenticity of the anthology pieces is granted and at the same time their exceptional ordering, the definition of a popular ballad as a folk song which tells a story has very limited usefulness. If the ballad is by origin medieval and if, as Wells states, the Robin Hood exemplars provide a "norm of style by which we may judge other ballads,"[39] the anthology pieces clearly belong elsewhere; for neither in idiom nor in internal form do they recall indisputably early ballads. To be sure, the quality ballads are not *sui generis*, however similar some of them may be, but in their exceptionalness they suggest reasonable objections to viewing Child's collection as a genre in any useful sense of the word.

It is unlikely that the term "popular ballad' can be validated even for very general use. The cultural circumstances under which Child's exemplars and others thought comparable[40] were produced cannot be known with any certainty and thus cannot warrant the attributive "popular" with respect to origins. Though doubtless

---

limits, by rhythm and tone. *Barbara Allan*, for example, has attracted several dolefully romantic tunes. It would be absurd to discount the power of music to deepen the kind of tragic experience which ballads most successfully communicate, but it would be equally absurd to argue that music is necessary to their success. Many a valued ballad survives without music, while the music which attaches to some others of quality, including *Sir Patrick Spens*, is unimpressive, if not unworthy.

39. *Op. cit.*, p. 11.
40. Gerould, *op. cit.*, pp. 28–31, denied the inclusiveness of Child's collection and Leach, *op. cit.*, has anthologized specimens rejected by Child.

popular by destination, they are not by that fact distinguishable from numerous other story poems.[41] It is not even feasible to limit "popular" to those pieces which have been transmuted in oral tradition, since this distinction assumes a restricted form. Unqualified "ballad," ringed though it is with sociological connotations, must be retained, in the absence of a better term, to designate the whole class of short story poems in common measure and variations thereof.

If the popular ballad is then nothing definable, what principles of selection could have guided Child? A definite answer is of course impossible,[42] but it is a fair guess that he cast a net wide enough to include all but the most elegant story poems in common measure and couplets and then thinned his catch by imposing rather vague socioliterary requirements. He was apparently disposed to accept any specimen which recalled by its meter and stylistic devices[43] the more famous ballads in the early collections, whether or not there was much structural similarity. He was apparently disposed to reject whatever evidenced learning or the more objectionable features of the broadsides, especially sentimentality and intimacy of presentation. But he seems never to have settled upon the minimum requirements of a popular ballad, and there is no rational principle by which all of his selections can be associated. Critically considered, his collection is a mélange, diverse both as to matter and as to method. Although a model of editorial reliability and a storehouse of valuable information, it is not as a unit significant for literature.

Judged by the poems which wear the label, the ballad is an external form hospitable to narrative matter of any sort and indif-

41. Baldi, *op. cit.*, p. 42, asserts: "Non credo che sia possibile documentare per quegli anni altro senso della parola 'popolare' se non quello di 'rinvenuto fra il popolo'; né dimostrare che il popolo fosse allora visto altrimenti che il fedele e passivo depositario di un'arte dimenticata dalle classi colte."

42. See Gerould, *op. cit.*, pp. 27 f.

43. E.g., understatement, questions and answers, alliterative formulas, incremental repetition.

ferent to its management. This is not a very satisfactory definition, but further delimitation, whether by sociological or literary criteria, invites vitiating exceptions. Yet the ballad loses nothing by being at once more numerous and less definite than Child imagined; it is a form of social expression highly interesting in many of its exemplars for folklore and social anthropology, and nonetheless literature of intrinsic merit. Systematic study remains as feasible as ever, for numerous groupings are logically justified with respect to social use and structure.[44] It is perhaps needful to remark, however, that what is no more precisely definable than the ballad form cannot reasonably be traced back to the French *carole*[45] and the eleventh-century dances of Kölbigk.[46] Furthermore, sociological data, though often necessary to the understanding of the ballads, cannot properly be invoked for purposes of classifying or evaluating them as literature.

Critical analysis appears just now to be the most useful approach to the ballads. More definite answers to questions relating to origin, age, priority of competing versions, and transmission seemingly cannot be given, and purely historical scholarship in any case is not competent to deliver the ultimate value judgments needed to decide their literary status. The brief explications attempted in the preceding section suggest that attention to internal form, besides demonstrating the achievement of individual ballads, can lead to the recognition of new and less ambiguous groupings. Traditional classifications, usually according to subject and rhetorical furniture, have tended to create false impressions of uniformity and thus have had the effect of closing up lines of questioning most likely to reveal the intricacies of ballad structure. The art of the

44. Many poems loosely classifiable as ballads are most properly to be considered under other headings, e.g., romance, *chanson d'adventure*, epic.
45. W. P. Ker, *Collected Essays*, ed. Charles Whibley (London, 1925), II, pp. 101–104; Chambers, *op. cit.*, p. 184.
46. See Gerould, *op. cit.*, pp. 207–10; Wells, *op. cit.*, p. 203; Edward Schröder, "Die Tänzer von Kölbigk," *Zeitschrift für Kirchengeschichte*, XVII (1896–97), p. 151.

ballads is often of a respectably high order and accordingly deserving of serious critical study unfettered either by genetic fallacies or by historical relativism. This view appears to be shared by a number of recent anthologists, who in their discussions of individual ballads simply ignore the theoretical restraints on criticism which this article has considered and, as I believe, substantially removed.

Chapter VI
Medieval English Literature and the Question of Unity

of Unity Whether in consequence of the depletion of prime philological materials or an increasing general interest in aesthetic values, medieval English studies have taken a pronounced critical turn since World War II. All things considered, this has been a fortunate development; for two or three preceding generations of medievalists left the question of artistic achievement embarrassed, either by their silence or by their impressionism and affectivity. Perhaps a majority, conditioned by classical criteria and nineteenth-century exemplars, took mainly an antiquarian and historical interest in what was very often literature seemingly careless of formal requirements. While the works of Dante and Chaucer, after more than five centuries of steady approval, were regarded as proper objects of critical scrutiny, medieval literature was for the most part secured from objective evaluation by suspicions and reservations engendered by the *Liedertheorie*, literary evolutionism, and the romantic concept of *das dichtende Volk*. Filled nonetheless with high regard for the contents of manuscripts dating from before 1500, older scholars often accorded the same careful attention to literature of a commonplace character as to that which made serious pretensions to excellence; and the feeling lingers that considerable importance somehow attaches to whatever material copyists elected, for whatever pious or practical reasons, to preserve. While scholars hereafter are likely to be less concerned with the trivia contained in the medieval legacy and more attentive to the formal achievement of those works which suggest lasting value, rigorous description and evaluation seem not to be an immediate prospect. The apologetic tone evident in earlier studies persists in some degree; but even more disconcerting is the disposition which accompanies the new critical interest to wrench moderately successful works so far as to satisfy alien canons. While the consequences of this bias cannot be entirely foreseen, it is no risk to say that tendentious and unlikely analyses are not the means to increase understanding and not the means to demonstrate unobvious merit.

The rather loose and even disorderly appearance of much medieval literature considered, it is altogether proper that the bulk of critical work should at first relate to questions of organization. While their constructive skills seem usually not to have been of the first order, medieval writers were very likely constrained by some considerations which are as yet poorly understood. In any case, scholars are completely justified in seeking out the presuppositions, if not the rules, to which this literature is amenable. Whether necessarily or not, but certainly unfortunately, most discussions of individual specimens stake a good deal on demonstrating unity and, to judge from the arguments, unity conceived rather too vaguely for firm critical work. This is not, of course, to question the usefulness of the concept of unity for criticism or even its applicability to medieval verse and prose. Nonetheless, the term is a philosophical puzzle and a logical pitfall. Predicable in one sense of almost nothing and in another of perhaps everything, it is a will-o'-the-wisp which can seldom be apprehended without some expense to probability. Not all attempts to demonstrate the unity of medieval works are unbelievable, but perhaps none applies a defensible definition of unity so rigorously as to preclude alternative proposals. Taken in the lump (and the lump now embraces most monuments and a number of lesser pieces), the unity studies illustrate the divergent and often laughable results to which the unreflecting use of a problematic general term must lead. Unity cannot be a significant predicate unless defined in terms of the conditions of its achievement, and this theoretical labor medievalists have conspicuously neglected.

It is a matter of some importance, though unacknowledged, that theories of unity serviceable to literature are necessarily special. A completely general theory, such as that implicit in the proposition of Dionysius the Areopagite, "Nothing is devoid of oneness,"[1] furnishes no useful distinctions. To state that an object of perception is unified means, without qualification, that it is located in space and time; and in this general sense unity is predicable of a scattering of odds and ends no less than of the *Oedipus Rex* of Sophocles. A useful theory of unity states the necessary relations of parts to each other and to the whole, and a work of literary art may be said to exhibit unity (or disunity) according as it satisfies (or fails to satisfy) the necessary and sufficient conditions which constitute the theory adopted for the occasion.[2] Whatever the unity of the vernacular literature of the Middle Ages may consist in, it is obviously neither the elegant balance and symmetry of classical verse nor the relentless causality of, say, modern detective fiction; but there is no reason for doubting that on this score medieval writers somehow satisfied the expectations of their audiences. They may, of course, have contented themselves with concepts of unity which, pragmatically considered, were not entirely efficacious, though, for reasons that will appear, the warrant for asserting so much cannot be easily established.

Ineptness or plain ignorance of the aesthetic advantages of orderliness may explain the intolerable looseness of some medieval specimens,[3] but neither circumstance can be plausibly generalized. There is no sufficient reason for believing medieval art significantly

1. *De divinis nominibus* XIII. ii (*Patrologiae cursus completus, Series Graeca* [Paris, 1857], III, p. 977).
2. The ultimate location of unity—in the audience or in the aesthetic object—is not at this point in question; but see C. A. McLaughlin, "Two Views of Poetic Unity," *University of Kansas City Review*, XXII (1955–56), pp. 309–16, and Ernst Cassirer, *The Philosophy of Symbolic Forms*, trans. Ralph Manheim (New Haven, Conn., 1953–57, I, p. 104.
3. Cf. J. S. P. Tatlock, *The Mind and Art of Chaucer* (Syracuse, N.Y., 1950), p. 58. Kenneth Sisam, *The Structure of Beowulf* (New York, 1965), p. 66, doubts that the Anglo-Saxons had a "keen sense of form."

less conscious or assured than that of later periods, and there is
reason for believing that classical theory was readily available in
one form or another to literate composers. Moreover, a considerable
number of writers of the High Middle Ages and after must have
been perfectly aware of such Horatian notions of unity as Geoffroi
de Vinsauf promulgated in the *Poetria nova* (ll. 60–69):

> Mentis in arcano cum rem digesserit ordo,
> Materiam verbis veniat vestire poesis.
> Quando tamen servire venit, se praeparet aptam
> Obsequio dominae: caveat sibi, ne caput hirtis
> Crinibus, aut corpus pannosa veste, vel ulla
> Ultima displiceant, alicunde nec inquinet illud
> Hanc poliens partem: pars si qua sedebit inepte,
> Tota trahet series ex illa parte pudorem:
> Fel modicum totum mel amaricat; unica menda
> Totalem faciem difformat.[4]

(When order arranges itself secretly in the mind with the thing, let the
art of poetry come to dress the matter with words. Since, however, poetry
comes to serve, let it prepare itself fittingly in obedience to its mistress:
let it take care lest a head with shaggy hairs, or a body with ragged dress,
or anything at all should be displeasing; nor in polishing one part let it
corrupt another: if any part sits unsuitably, the whole series of parts
draws disgrace from this part: a small amount of gall makes all the
honey bitter; a single blemish deforms the whole face.)

The uncongeniality of strict formalism may of course account for
the negligible influence of prescriptions such as these,[5] but the
neglect of them also suggests that for medieval writers there was
a rational alternative. Edmond Faral thought that their slight concern with unity and the larger aspects of composition was to be
explained by the special circumstances of performance: "On se
l'explique si l'on considère qu'ils n'ont pas été faits, en général,
pour soutenir l'examen d'un public qui lisait et pouvait com-

---

4. In Edmond Faral, ed., *Les arts poétiques du XIIe et du XIIIe siècle* (Paris,
1924), p. 199. Cf. Geoffroi's *Documentum de arte versificandi* II. iii. 154.
   5. The influence of textbooks of rhetoric on the superficies of style is, of
course, widely observable.

modément juger de l'ensemble, mais pour être entendus par des auditeurs auxquels on les lisait épisode par épisode."[6] While leaving out of account works of small compass, he clearly recognized that the ordering of literature is affected by the mode of its existence. Inasmuch as the reception of vernacular literature—though probably not scholarly work in Latin—was auditory rather than visual,[7] its condition was essentially oral rather than written. The scarcity of manuscripts considered, it cannot be doubted that much of what even the literate knew came by way of the singing or reciting voice. The likelihood of high auditory receptiveness granted, the medieval audience could hardly have discriminated nicely in many small matters which figured importantly after literature came to the printed page. It is accordingly a doubtful demonstration of unity which presupposes an audience's close recall of antecedent detail or its ready comprehension of verbal complexities. Nor is this altogether an a priori limitation on criticism, for it is a matter of observation that attempts to demonstrate the unity of medieval literature without due regard for the oral mode commonly encounter intractable elements.

Historical critics stake a good deal on reconstructing the milieu and describing the cultural context of the literature which occupies them. That they can by means of this labor become as citizens of remote periods may be doubted, but presumably they are able to set a given literature around with historical probabilities and thus with reasonable limitations on interpretation. While the relationship of theories of art to the times which foster them is far from clear, it is worthwhile under the circumstances to consider whether the medieval experience of this world and intimations of the next sort well with theories of unity which stipulate balanced structures

6. Faral, ed., op. cit., p. 60. Cf. A. C. Spearing, Criticism and Medieval Poetry (New York, 1964), pp. 24–25.

7. Ruth Crosby, "Chaucer and the Custom of Oral Delivery," Speculum, XIII (1938), pp. 430–32, and "Oral Delivery in the Middle Ages," Speculum, XI (1936), p. 100.

and neat juxtapositions.[8] The medieval world is assuredly not like
the Greek, rational and symmetrical, or like the modern, with a
unified scientific basis. It is nonetheless unified: history is in some
sense a closed book, predetermined from Creation to Doomsday,
and all things stand in an intelligible relationship to the Creator.
Even so, the surface of experience is ruffled by indeterminacy,
discontinuity, irrationality, and mutability; by the interpenetration
of the real and the unreal, the mundane and the supermundane.
Nothing is quite as it seems, but all objects of perception are potentially signific—signs of things past and to come. It is indeed
a world of potentiality, of miracles of deliverance and miracles of
material advantage. If Providence descends low, it is yet hindered
in the finite order by Destiny and the stars. Vertically considered,
the medieval view is doubtless coherent and complete; but no such
unity can be said to supervene on the curious impressions which
stuff the medieval experience of the temporal realm. It is fair to
say that if people do in fact order their art in conformity with their
universe, then medieval literature is no more formally wayward
than it should be. Plausible or not, this conclusion at least chal-
lenges the probability that medieval works should be informed by
such firm concepts of unity as have arisen in more rationalistic
periods. Whatever the opinion of critical absolutists, literary historians can only agree that claims of unity ought to take some
account of historical probabilities.

Yet the medievalist turned critic may decline—and not without
reason—to accept such limitations on the achievement of unity
as may be inferred from the mode of existence of the literature or
the perplexities of the medieval mind. Unity, as any other supervening attribute, should be evident simply to objective scrutiny.
It is well to recall, however, that unity is predicable a priori of
any object, literary or other, for it is in fact a necessary condition

8. For evidence of confusion on this score, see C. L. Wrenn, ed., *Beowulf
with the Finnesburg Fragment* (Boston, [1953]), p. 66.

of being perceived.[9] A nontautological—that is, discriminating—predication of unity requires to be covered by a special theory, which defines the relations obtaining between parts and wholes and thus the conditions required to project the subject literature in a form congenial to customary focus, that is, to the audience's manner of attending to concrete particulars and structural components. If the necessary and sufficient conditions of unity vary and vary according to the exigencies of time and place, focus may not be a self-evident constant but a variable ordering of percepts according to acquired angles of vision. This is not to suggest that every work achieves significant unity if regarded in contemporary focus but only that it may be hazardous to speak of unity without regard for contemporary focus. While focus can scarcely be said to dictate the conditions of unity, it assuredly sets limits to the kinds of relations which may be supposed to operate in a literary work. Minute correspondences, for example, cannot reasonably be adduced in support of a claim of unity for oral literature and if adduced, should fail of plausibility.[10] Nonetheless, the possibility must be accepted that a work of literary art may satisfy the conditions embodied in more than one theory and thus appear unified to later audiences, though for different reasons. It yet can be only from the rarest accident or plain imitation that the literature of one cultural location should present to perception the same hierarchy of relations as another. So much considered, the ordering of medieval literature may be assumed, without proof to the contrary, to require a special covering theory. If so, claims of unity unaccompanied by statements of necessary and sufficient conditions

9. See D. N. Morgan, "Art Pure and Simple," *Journal of Aesthetics and Art Criticism*, XX (1961–62), p. 188, and Harold Osborne, "Artistic Unity and Gestalt," *Philosophical Quarterly*, XIV (1964), p. 224.

10. Eugène Vinaver, "On Art and Nature: A Letter to C. S. Lewis," in J. A. W. Bennett, ed., *Essays on Malory* (New York, 1963), pp. 38–39, argues that the audience of the French Vulgate Cycle was capable of holding in mind a multitude of cross-references, but he supposes that this was a reading audience.

are just so many subjective perceptual judgments, which may be instructive but hardly compelling.

It is a fair guess that recent unity studies have been significantly affected by Aristotelian and Coleridgean theories, though neither system has been fully acknowledged[11] or rigorously applied. The point should be made, therefore, that these theories seem not to have been a priori conceptions but products of logical induction from literary materials of ordering different from the medieval. Whereas the older philologists, whose conception of unity was frankly classical,[12] conceded the organizational defects of medieval literature, more recent scholars have apparently commenced with the assumption that much of it possesses unity, though perhaps of a special kind, and then, by invoking principles of doubtful relevance, have risked distorting what in vague focus leaves an impression of passable cohesiveness. In this connection, an attempt some years ago by H. W. Wells to unify *Piers Plowman* is particularly interesting, for he confessed the want of a model adequate to his subject but in the end could not divorce the poem from alien systems of perception:

Undoubtedly the author or authors enjoyed the effect of violent transitions and surprises and definitely sought this effect in the poem. This is merely to recognize it as a dream poem, composed in the same spirit that dominates gothic architecture. The poem undoubtedly has a rough surface. To read it is like riding over a bad road; we are jerked and bounced and tossed. But so we may be at the hands of the most rigorous logician. That the poem has a rough surface should by no means prejudice us as to its fundamental coherence or incoherence.

.   .   .   .

That a poem is of the gothic spirit really tells us nothing of its essential organization or disorganization. The latter qualities cannot be felt by mere surface touch, such as we employ for style. An alligator's skin may

11. While demonstration of "organic unity" is the declared purpose of a good many studies, none actually takes account of the conditions which constitute the theory.

12. E.g., W. P. Ker, *Epic and Romance* (2d ed.; London, 1908), pp. 158–75.

be rougher than the surface of a pile of sand, but one covers an exquisite organism and the other is merely a confused heap.[13]

Instead of ascribing roughness to the poet's intention, which is unknowable, Wells could have argued with better warrant for the smoothing effect of vague focus. Yet his desperate search for apt metaphor describes the process by which usable models are discovered. None of his analogies, unfortunately, resulted in a model —and therewith a special theory—capable of encompassing imprecision and unevenness, which, according to classical and organic theory, frustrate unity.

Fabricating a model which somehow accommodates irregularities and irrelevances perceived as such may very well overtax ingenuity. Although it is customary to speak of more or less unity, the term narrowly interpreted admits of no degrees of attainment and accordingly of no disharmonies, incongruencies, or discrepancies. So regarded, unity seems well beyond the capability of any writer, and yet Aristotle prescribes nothing less in the *Poetics* (viii): "so too the plot being a representation of a piece of action must represent a single piece of action and the whole of it; and the component incidents must be so arranged that if one of them be transposed or removed, the unity of the whole is dislocated and destroyed. For if the presence or absence of a thing makes no visible difference, then it is not an integral part of the whole."[14] The model for this conception appears to be geometrical, for instance, a sphere, with all points on the surface equidistant from a center, or a triangle, exhibiting interdependence of parts. Disunity follows necessarily from ruffling or chipping the surface of the sphere or unpropping the triangle. Aristotle was probably concerned only with plot, although his final sentence appears to include other parts of compo-

13. H. W. Wells, "The Construction of *Piers Plowman*," PMLA, XLIV (1929), p. 124. Cf. Eugène Vinaver, ed., *The Works of Sir Thomas Malory* (New York, 1948), I, p. 1, who, following Ferdinand Lot, resembles the structure of the French Vulgate Cycle to a tapestry.
14. Trans. W. H. Fyfe, Loeb Classical Library (Cambridge, Mass., 1953).

sition. In any case, his paradigm makes insufficient provision for accidents and for the varying importance of structural elements.[15] If he yet must be allowed to have accounted for the integrity of Greek dramatic plots and neoclassical imitations thereof, his theory is nonetheless special and doubtfully applicable to literature of less rigid ordering, such as that of the Middle Ages.

If existence, as Dionysius, implies, is the only necessary condition of unity generally considered, then interdependence of parts can be necessary only for a special theory like Aristotle's; for some others, it may be merely a sufficient condition. While interrelatedness of parts is a necessary consequence of their interdependence, interrelatedness seems not to entail interdependence. This circumstance offers literature considerable advantage, inasmuch as it permits the whole to be viewed as a continuum of reconcilable components rather than as a rigid complex of interdependences. There may be, of course, some question whether interrelatedness is a sufficient condition of literary unity, but its sufficiency appears to be assumed in some notable discussions. Although Plato may have conceived unity no less firmly than Aristotle, at least one passage in the *Phaedrus* (264C) employs a biological model and, whether in consequence or not, stresses interrelatedness rather than interdependence: "But I do think you will agree to this, that every discourse must be organised, like a living being, with a body of its own, as it were, so as not to be headless or footless, but to have a middle and members, composed in fitting relation to each other and to the whole."[16] What is particularly to be remarked is that Plato, while insisting upon completeness and harmony, does not in fact maintain that the parts of an organic whole, whether structural components or concrete particulars, are in all instances logically (or aesthetically) inviolable. By the strictest view of

15. Catherine Lord, "Organic Unity Reconsidered," *Journal of Aesthetics and Art Criticism*, XXII (1963–64), pp. 264–66.
16. Trans. H. N. Fowler, Loeb Classical Library (Cambridge, Mass., 1914).

organic unity, no part may be added or subtracted or relocated without substantial impairment of the whole.[17] So considered, the theory has demonstrable logical defects; and, indeed, only a computer could be counted on to hold in "mind" the totality of parts constitutive of a whole.

Plato's paradigm, by incorporating motion, does justice to an important aspect of the literary phenomenon; at the same time, it suggests an inner dynamic and probably invites hypostasis. This danger is plainly evident in Coleridge's employment of another biological figure to expound the concept of organic, as opposed to Aristotelian, unity: "The form is mechanic when on any given material we impress a pre-determined form, not necessarily arising out of the properties of the material, as when to a mass of wet clay we give whatever shape we wish it to retain when hardened. The organic form, on the other hand, is innate; it shapes as it develops itself from within, and the fullness of its development is one and the same with the perfection of its outward form."[18] Coleridge's rather mystical statement slights the author's rational control over composition and to that small extent anticipates psychological theories of literature and what might be called the theory of linguistic determinism. That he did not mean so much appears from a well-known passage in the *Biographia Literaria* (chap. xiv), which acknowledges the power of the artist to order the discordant and disparate contents of experience: "This power, first put in action by the will and understanding and retained under their irremissive, though gentle and unnoticed, controul (*laxis effertur habenis*) reveals itself in the balance or reconciliation of opposite or dis-

17. Lord, op. cit., pp. 263–64; I. C. Hungerland, *Poetic Discourse* (University of California Publications in Philosophy, XXXIII [Berkeley, 1958]), p. 76.

18. *Coleridge's Shakespearean Criticism*, ed. T. M. Raysor (Cambridge, Mass., 1930), I, p. 224. Cf. A. W. Schlegel, *A Course of Lectures on Dramatic Art and Literature*, trans. John Black (London, 1846), p. 340. See also the discussions by W. K. Wimsatt, Jr., and Cleanth Brooks, *Literary Criticism: A Short History* (New York, 1957), p. 377, and Morris Weitz, *Hamlet and the Philosophy of Literary Criticism* (Chicago, 1964), pp. 171–73. Herbert Read, *Collected Essays in Literary Criticism* (London, 1938), pp. 19–20, restates and elaborates Coleridge's theory.

cordant qualities: of sameness, with difference; of the general, with
the concrete; the idea, with the image; the individual, with the
representative; the sense of novelty and freshness, with old and
familiar objects; a more than usual state of emotion, with more
than usual order." Thus the romantic alternative to neoclassical
formalism proposes the reconciliation of opposites as the necessary
and sufficient condition of unity; and it presupposes, therefore,
an audience alert to analogies and polarities. Whereas Aristotle's
theory suits a stylized drama like the Greek, with its traditional
narrative content, the organic theory suits literature which exploits
the ironies, ambiguities, and paradoxes of existence in language
densely imaginal.[19] Organic theory may, of course, have more
extensive validity, but only from pure chance could it afford an
apt model for medieval literature.

Nowhere better than in *Beowulf* studies can the practical consequences of inadequate theory be observed. Since the decline of the
Liedertheorie the unity of the poem has been repeatedly proclaimed,[20] but on the basis of very different relations. The seeming
agreement between such statements as "The unity of *Beowulf*
has long been taken for granted"[21] and "this question of artistic
unity need no longer be debated"[22] is small agreement indeed,
for these affirmations refer to different and doubtfully compatible
readings. It was perhaps Friedrich Klaeber who first raised the
question of unity in such form as to threaten the absolute value
of the work and accordingly to provoke demurrals: "The poem of
Beowulf consists of two distinct parts joined in a very loose manner

19. Cf. Cleanth Brooks, *The Well Wrought Urn* (New York, 1947),
pp. 178–79.
20. Rather early, Enrico Pizzo, "Zur Frage der ästhetischen Einheit des Beowulf," *Anglia*, XXXIX (1916), pp. 1–15, debated the question of interpolations
and concluded that the poem was "ein konkretes geisteserzeugnis seiner zeit,
der einheitliche ausdruck des frühen angelsächsisch-christlichen ideals."
21. Joan Blomfield, "The Style and Structure of Beowulf," *Review of English
Studies*, XIV (1938), p. 396.
22. M. E. Goldsmith, "The Christian Perspective in Beowulf," *Comparative
Literature*, XIV (1962), p. 72.

and held together only by the person of the hero."[23] His subsequent references to the lack of causal connections suggest classical presuppositions,[24] and in all likelihood he had in mind as well Aristotle's judgment, "A plot does not have unity, as some people think, simply because it deals with a single hero." It is, of course, arguable that in vague focus a work may achieve unity simply through the continuity of the hero—at least to the satisfaction of an unlearned audience—but the focus for modern scholars is not vague, nor does the poem exist for them in the oral mode. Moreover, denying organizational integrity to Beowulf by whatever standard faults an obvious monument and tends to associate it indirectly with the scores of disorderly narratives—and especially romances—which have survived from the Middle Ages. Attempts by latter-day medievalists to vindicate the constructive skill of the Beowulf poet against Klaeber's imputations have met with some success, though not without questionable adjustments of perspective.

Simply considered, Beowulf belongs to the category of heroic literature, and heroic literature involves by common understanding heroic struggles between ethically polarized parties. While some confusion of roles may be observed in so sophisticated a work as the Nibelungenlied, the protagonist perforce symbolizes good as opposed to the evil of the assorted antagonists who confront him. Unity no less than interest inheres in the archetypal struggles. Minimally, a heroic exemplar, whether epic or romance, consists of a series of more or less discrete confrontations terminating in

23. Friedrich Klaeber, ed., Beowulf and the Fight at Finnsburg (3d ed.; Boston, 1941), p. li. In this connection it is significant that Jan de Vries, Heroic Song and Heroic Legend, trans. B. J. Timmer (London, 1963), p. 68, denies unity of whatever kind to the Nibelungenlied and that Sister Mary Frances, S.N.D., "Architectonic Symmetry in the Nibelungenlied," Germanic Review, XLI (1966), p. 169, discovers that the poet "has achieved an 'ultimate reconciliation' of opposites."

24. For a defense of the poem against classically oriented criticism see J. R. Hulbert, "Beowulf and the Classical Epic," Modern Philology, XLIV (1946), pp. 65–75.

death or marriage; maximally, the confrontations exhibit logical progression and constitute a network of varyingly complex interdependences or interrelations. Since heroic literature exists primarily in overt oppositions, to state that an epic is unified through the conflict of good and evil is merely to state a condition which obtains necessarily of an epic, and no implications for artistic achievement follow. One task of the critic is to consider in what less general terms the conflict may be plausibly stated, for the success of an archetypal theme is contingent upon its embodiment in actions and feelings of immediate interest. Between the most general level and the literal, however, description manifests a strong affinity for interpretation;[25] and attempts to demonstrate unity by recourse to supposed political, social, theological, or other concerns tend to be interpretive and often prove mutually exclusive. The test of interpretation is reasonableness or, in other words, the application of relevant principles to a particular case. Unless it can be demonstrated, however, that unity is a principal objective of the creative act, the reasonableness of an interpretation is neither increased nor decreased by its capability for providing an all-encompassing order. While all literary works tend toward a unified state and in some focus achieve it, a work cannot be said to exist for the sake of achieving unity. Complex unity—that is, unity consisting in many interconnections—may be accounted a consequence, though not a necessary one, of complex purpose; but the interconnections exist to represent experience and not to produce unity.[26] The achievement of local meaning—that is, meaning in significant contemporary terms—is not contingent upon the achievement of unity at the same level, which is as much as to say that a work may have political or theological implications without being entirely explicable in such terms. But the question remains whether a work can be convincingly unified by interpreta-

25. See Arthur Child, *Interpretation: A General Theory* (University of California Publications in Philosophy, XXXVI [Berkeley, 1965]), pp. 49–50.
26. See R. B. Perry, *General Theory of Value: Its Meaning and Basic Principles Construed in Terms of Interest* (New York, 1926), pp. 63–65.

tion as contrasted with description, and the answer is in part that interpretation requires inferences and that inferences, at least from literary materials, are often contestable. The problem of the critic who seeks to unify medieval literature by this means is further complicated by the circumstance that interpretation is logically limited to demonstrations only of such unifying relations as may be reasonably supposed to exist in contemporary focus. Thus, a perfectly brilliant demonstration of unity may encounter skepticism for positing relations which assume unlikely habits of perception.

Klaeber's account of the ordering of *Beowulf* resists rebuttal because it is essentially descriptive and therefore verifiable. Nor have dissenting critics been inclined to deny that the poem, literally considered, is a series of encounters loosely connected by the person of the hero. Instead, they have maintained that rightly—which is to say symbolically—perceived it is an organic whole with only negligible imperfections. Their claims, of course, entail interpretation and the assignment of local or abstract meanings to the various actions. This methodology may in given instances produce quite impressive results, but logically it is less than impeccable. If unity consists in relations and all parts of composition are potentially relatable by reason of location or posited significance, it is theoretically possible by means of interpretation to unify any literary work and according to any concept of unity not inapplicable to the genre involved. While various criteria can be invoked to test, though not to determine conclusively, the truth status of an interpretation, the long-standing privilege of intuitive reading largely protects the critic from strict accounting. Indeed, the inventor of even the most preposterous scheme commonly escapes censure if he does not flagrantly claim that his is an objective empirical judgment and therefore correct beyond cavil. The objective validity of the several *Beowulf* schemes is in no case explicitly claimed, and yet each is presented as if a close approximation of the truth. A. E. Du Bois, perhaps the first to attempt the unification of *Beowulf* by interpretation, invokes historical circumstances of uncertain import to forge such formal relations as what he terms "organic unity" requires: "The fact that it was written by a Christian, presumably, in the eighth century, that it survived, and that linguistic evidence points to its having been popular in Wessex, Northumbria, Mercia, and Kent at times when the Danes were certainly not popular—these facts seem to indicate that *Beowulf* had a meaning and a structural self-sufficiency that made it vitally appealing to its original audiences and that amount to an organic unity."[27] It is one thing to suppose that a poem achieves unity in contemporary focus and quite another to claim that interrelations and symbolic values which are no longer self-evident confer on it a kind of unity prescribed by theory of later origination and in any case doubtfully applicable to oral literature. Political and moral concerns quite obviously intermingle in *Beowulf,* and the eighth century was assuredly more acutely aware of them than the twentieth. But in the absence of positive internal cues and thrusts, to identify Beowulf with "national integrity, resulting from internal harmony"; Grendel and his dam with the "Danes's liability to punishment for weakness, pride, and treachery"; and the dragon with "internal discord"[28] is as arbitrary as Karl Victor Müllenhoff's mythological assignments. The poem doubtless commemorates after some fashion the rise and fall of Danes and Geats, but tribal histories cannot be shown to provide the reconcilable oppositions required by organic theory.

Whereas Du Bois is schematic to the point of absurdity, J. R. R. Tolkien is general to the point of banality. The latter views the poem in such vague focus as to blur the intractable irrelevances and in order to unify it invokes thematic resonances which are familiar to heroic literature as a class. Klaeber should not have quarreled with the statement that the unifying theme of *Beowulf* is "man at

27. A. E. Du Bois, "The Unity of *Beowulf,*" PMLA, XLIX (1934), p. 376.
28. *Ibid.,* p. 391.

war with the hostile world, and his inevitable overthrow in Time,"[29] but this description merely qualifies it as an epic[30] and in no way smoothes the movement, which in sharp focus appears quite jagged. To bridge the awkward chronological gap, Tolkien reclassifies the poem from heroic narrative to "heroic elegy"—a genre otherwise unknown—and sets the two main parts in symbolic opposition: "But the poem was not meant to advance, steadily or unsteadily. It is essentially a balance, an opposition of ends and beginnings. In its simplest terms it is a contrasted description of two moments in a great life, rising and setting; an elaboration of the ancient and intensely moving contrast between youth and age, first achievement and final death."[31] These relations are self-evident; but to claim that they effect the unification of Beowulf is to assume that the poem exists in a focus which subordinates a considerable narrative content to the interplay of abstractions. The interpretation is so far partial as to suggest that it owes its inception less to objective consideration of empirical data than to the demands of a special theory of unity—probably organic, to judge from Tolkien's language. Subsequent scholarship demonstrates that a critical canon can be served equally well by a plurality of interpretations.[32] The unifying schemes proposed since Tolkien depend on

29. J. R. R. Tolkien, "Beowulf: The Monsters and the Critics," *Proceedings of the British Academy*, 1936, XXII (1936), p. 260.

30. See Sisam, *op. cit.*, pp. 24–25.

31. Tolkien, *op. cit.*, p. 271. Tolkien's view has been approved enthusiastically by, among others, Adrien Bonjour, "Grendel's Dam and the Composition of Beowulf," *English Studies*, XXX (1949), pp. 113–24, and opposed by T. M. Gang, "Approaches to Beowulf," *Review of English Studies*, N.S., III (1952), p. 6; H. L. Rogers, "Beowulf's Three Great Fights," *Review of English Studies*, N.S., VI (1955), p. 341; and J. C. van Meurs, "Beowulf and Literary Criticism," *Neophilologus*, XXXIX (1955), pp. 115–29.

32. See Kemp Malone, "Beowulf," *English Studies*, XXIX (1948), pp. 161–72; J. L. N. O'Loughlin, "Beowulf—Its Unity and Purpose," *Medium Ævum*, XXI (1952), pp. 1–13; A. G. Brodeur, "The Structure and Unity of Beowulf," *PMLA*, LXVIII (1953), p. 1195; and P. F. Fisher, "The Trials of the Epic Hero in Beowulf," *PMLA*, LXXIII (1958), p. 171. H. G. Wright, "Good and Evil; Light and Darkness; Joy and Sorrow in Beowulf," *Review of English Studies*, N.S., VIII (1957), p. 11, recognizes sets of opposites but concedes that they do not effect the unification of the poem.

the same principle of paired opposites and differ largely with respect to the varyingly abstract titles assigned to persons and events. Regarded as instruments of critical intention to reconstitute *Beowulf* in accordance with organic theory, they can hardly be discriminated in point of value; regarded as overviews which take account of the oral mode and at the same time assimilate a clutter of moral and historical reflections to a simple epic story, they leave much to be desired. Their very plurality suggests, moreover, that none of them is a convincing alternative to Klaeber's simple, though deprecatory, model of the noncausative continuum.

The failure of *Beowulf* scholars to agree on the formal cause of the unity which most profess to perceive underscores the liabilities of interpretation. Interpretation, while privileged, is not privileged beyond reason. If all the unifying schemes are presented quite persuasively, all yet posit symbolic titles and interconnections which lack the firm support of internal evidence and which finally locate *Beowulf* in unbelievable perspectives. It is altogether possible that a work may be rather confused as perceived on the literal level and yet unified on the symbolic, but the warrant for claiming as much consists in unmistakable internal thrusts. Accordingly, to suppose that thrusts toward the symbolic level exist in a work but so confusedly as to raise doubts about their character is to admit a defect of integrity in the work itself. This problem arises conspicuously in the case of *Piers Plowman*, which, like *Beowulf*, has been declared unified and on a variety of grounds. D. W. Robertson, Jr., and B. F. Huppé hold that *Piers Plowman* is not "chaotic and formless" as sometimes thought but "no less perfect structurally" than the *Divine Comedy*—that is, if perceived "on the level of the *sentence*."[33] Whether the passages of scripture distributed through the poem constitute, when glossed by biblical

33. D. W. Robertson, Jr., and B. F. Huppé, *Piers Plowman and Scriptural Tradition* (Princeton Studies in English, No. 31; Princeton, N.J., 1951), p. 247. Other attempts to use the method of patristic exegesis include Goldsmith, pp. 71–90, and F. J. Thompson, "Unity in the *Second Shepherds' Tale*," *MLN*, LXIV (1949), pp. 302–306.

commentaries, thrusts sufficient to justify application of the fourfold method has been vigorously disputed and, the quality of the inferences considered, quite properly.[34] But the question of immediate concern is whether a poem which presupposes an audience's capability for attending simultaneously to topological, allegorical, and anagogical significances can be said to have a real existence in the oral mode. If unity is a condition of popular success, than assuredly the unity of *Piers Plowman* occurs farther down the scale of complexity. Indeed, the Robertson-Huppé exposition is so complicated of astonishing references as to raise the question, if only superficially, whether unity may not vary inversely with complexity. But if "there is not the slightest excuse for decking out a personification-allegory [i.e., *Piers Plowman*] in the mystic garments of medieval scriptural exegesis," as R. W. Frank, Jr., maintains,[35] then Robertson and Huppé have carried interpretation to the point of *allegoresis*. While all critical commentary is in some sense allegory,[36] there is an important difference between interpretation consisting of defensible inferences from empirical data and interpretation which takes leave of probabilities and fabricates a model from merely possible relations. Yet unbridled interpretation has seldom galloped so far as the allegorization of allegory. Describing the wonderfully ingenious glossing of Robertson and Huppé as *allegoresis* may be something less than just; but the title is apt insofar as they have reconstituted *Piers Plowman* in a form congenial to a priori conceptions. The fourfold method enables them not merely to integrate the poem but to integrate it at a high level of significancy and finally to claim that it is not inferior to the *Divine Comedy*. A wonderfully flexible instrument, *allegoresis*

34. See E. T. Donaldson, "Patristic Exegesis in the Criticism of Medieval Literature: The Opposition," in Dorothy Bethurum, ed., *Selected Papers from the English Institute, 1958–59* (New York, 1960), pp. 1–26.

35. R. W. Frank, Jr., *Piers Plowman and the Scheme of Salvation* (New Haven, Conn., 1957), p. 8. See also J. A. Mazzeo, "Dante's Conception of Poetic Expression," *Romanic Review*, XLVII (1956), pp. 241–58.

36. Northrop Frye, *Anatomy of Criticism: Four Essays* (Princeton, N.J., 1957), pp. 89–91.

can wash the tincture of blasphemy from the Homeric poems and serve critical canons no less well; but it is always liable to contradiction by disinterested observers.

Patristic exegesis confers complex unity on *Piers Plowman* and thus appears to enhance its absolute value, but the gain is nullified if, as seems likely, this model calls for habits of perception appropriate to theological treatises. While a poem may be accounted all the deeper for being translatable into theological or philosophical terms, its real existence is literary and not otherwise. The *Divine Comedy*, for example, may yield to inference a systematic theology; nonetheless, it exists essentially as an intuition, narrative—not discursive—in form, of the condition of souls after death, and nothing in the Can Grande letter alters this circumstance. Such unity as can be properly claimed for *Piers Plowman* is only such unity as it possesses as a literary work, and John Lawlor leaves the impression that this is little more than the noncausative continuum: "Perhaps, too, our modern practice of concentrating upon the *Vita de Dowel, Dobet, et Dobest* increases the difficulty of apprehending the whole work serially, experiencing its crises as they occur and not as they may be extracted from their setting for the purposes of cross-reference and detailed comparison. It is the merit of Langland's poem that we share the sense of confusion and apparent repetition of experience: for how otherwise shall we see that man must be brought to simple practice?"[37] By this view *Piers Plowman* is obviously of a lower order of excellence than the *Divine Comedy*, but it is unmistakably a poem, not a treatise, and a poem existing, furthermore, within the perceptual field of a listening and not exclusively literate audience.

It is by now a matter of observation that the indeterminacy of medieval literature increases with sharpening focus and that so-called close reading, far from resolving perplexities, actually pro-

37. John Lawlor, "The Imaginative Unity of *Piers Plowman*," *Review of English Studies*, N.S., VIII (1957), pp. 125–26. The author afterward modifies his conclusion so as to avoid what has been called the fallacy of imitative form.

duces a bewildering variety of interpretations. Critics who begin
with the assumption that a poem is more than it seems and more
interconnected than supposed can often on the level of posited
symbolic significances confirm their a priori judgments, though
usually to the complete satisfaction of no one but themselves. Tendentious reading—that is, manipulation of meanings and relations
in the interest of a priori conceptions—commonly outrages probability and relocates the subject literature in a nonaesthetic dimension; and it almost invariably entails the claim that the whole very
much exceeds the sum of its parts. A good deal of solemn interpretation has been devoted to translating the *Parlement of Foules*, for
example, from a condition commensurate with the lightheartedness
of St. Valentine's Day to a grave commentary on politics or love or
felicity, and a number of these reconstructions have been presented,
at least by implication, as the price of unity. Granted that an occasion does not strictly define the form and content of an occasional poem, substantial evidence should accompany claims that a
given work greatly transcends, in point of significance or reference,
the requirements of the occasion. Only by exaggerating the significance of medieval commonplaces and ignoring obvious tonal
qualities can R. M. Lumiansky describe the *Parlement* as a philosophical treatise "unified by Chaucer's statement of his philosophical dilemma ['the reconciliation of true and false felicity'] at both
the beginning and the end of the poem and by his frequent references to that dilemma throughout."[38] Like earlier critics who
sought to convert the *Parlement* to political and social satire,
Lumiansky has mistaken passing references for structural and
thematic components. Many medieval poems contain reflections
on felicity—and faith, hope, and charity, too—without for that
being treatises. Since literature is concerned by definition with the
human condition, it is possible to read a given work in terms of
any one of several aspects thereof; but refractory data plainly con-

38. R. M. Lumiansky, "Chaucer's *Parlement of Foules*: A Philosophical
Interpretation," *Review of English Studies*, XXIV (1948), pp. 88–89.

tradict at least the extreme instances of tendentiousness. It is as it
should be that critics who have steadily regarded the *Parlement*
as a poem celebrating love and related affections in a tone appropriate to St. Valentine's Day have vindicated its aesthetic integrity.[39]
If they have not sought to satisfy organic theory, they have yet
demonstrated cohesiveness without invoking unlikely relations.

The interpretive strategies employed in the bulk of unity studies
tend to obscure the central question of necessary and sufficient
conditions. Perhaps most rest on the assumption that, whatever
the problem of digressive matter, the fact of unity is established
if major persons and actions can be caught up in an over-spreading
symbolic order. But the symbolism of much medieval literature
is merely conventional and not constitutive of unifying principles.
The romances, for example, usually have no significant existence
beyond the literal level, and their unity is demonstrable, if at all,
in description of self-evident relations. So limited, arguments for
the unity of romances ought to be particularly revealing of the
conditions which medievalists accept as necessary and sufficient.
Unfortunately, arguments have not been so limited, and literalness
is obviously no bar to the fabrication of symbolic titles. Whether
altogether representative or not, the exchanges provoked by
Eugène Vinaver's denial of unity to the *Morte Darthur* first of all
demonstrate the sheer fatuousness of affirming or denying unity
without reference to the conditions of its achievement. Further,
these exhibit in exaggerated form weaknesses to which the unification enterprise as a whole is prone—most notably, confusion of
matters of opinion and of fact, critical intentionalism, and abuse
of rules of evidence. Influenced—and unduly so—by explicits
occurring in the Winchester manuscript of the *Morte* (though
not in Caxton's edition), Vinaver concludes that Malory's "con-

39. See especially B. H. Bronson, "*The Parlement of Foules* Revisited," *ELH*,
XV (1948), pp. 252–60; Gardiner Stillwell, "Unity and Comedy in Chaucer's
Parlement of Foules," *Journal of English and Germanic Philology*, XLIX
(1950), pp. 470–95; and R. W. Frank, Jr., "Structure and Meaning in the
Parlement of Foules," *PMLA*, LXXI (1956), pp. 530–39.

tribution would seem to consist not in making one story out of a 'vast assemblage' of stories, but in breaking up the complicated structure of earlier fiction and in using its fragments for smaller narrative patterns."[40] Against this view Lumiansky maintains that "the Morte Darthur possesses historical as well as critical unity, and that Malory from the beginning of his writing meant to produce a unified treatment of the Arthurian legend."[41] Charles Moorman declares even for organic unity but omits from his general discussion Coleridge's stipulation concerning the reconciliation of opposites and, in addition, the interdiction implicit in organicism of unassimilable contents.[42] Yet Vinaver can hold after long study that a very large section (pp. 289–787 in his edition, cited in n. 40) is "unrelated to any of the themes which occur before or after."[43] And D. S. Brewer, who at Vinaver's suggestion grants a measure of "cohesion" to the Morte, admits to perceiving so much confusion as to absolutely preclude organic unity.[44] Nor can medievalists of contrary opinion take much comfort from Brewer's observation that the work achieves unity of tone and atmosphere,[45] for this concession relates only to the speaker's attitude and to the cultural matrix. The controversy is further complicated by scattered admissions from the proponents of unity that incon-

40. Eugène Vinaver, ed., The Works of Sir Thomas Malory (New York, 1947), I, p. lvii.

41. R. M. Lumiansky, "The Question of Unity in Malory's Morte Darthur," Tulane Studies in English, V (1955), p. 33. By "historical" unity Lumiansky seems to mean the acceptance over the centuries, as far as known, of Caxton's edition as a unified work and, in addition, of Malory's intention to produce such a work.

42. Charles Moorman, The Book of Kyng Arthur: The Unity of Malory's Morte Darthur (Lexington, Ky., 1965), pp. xxiii–xxx. The relevance of the theory of organic unity for the Morte is specifically denied by Eugène Vinaver in "Form and Meaning in Medieval Romance" (Presidential Address of the Modern Humanities Research Association, 1966), p. 13.

43. Eugène Vinaver, "Sir Thomas Malory," in R. S. Loomis, ed., Arthurian Literature in the Middle Ages (New York, 1959), p. 544.

44. D. S. Brewer, "the hoole book," in J. A. W. Bennett, ed., Essays on Malory (New York, 1963), p. 41.

45. Ibid., p. 45.

sistencies do in fact occur and of such magnitude as to mar the *Morte*; but these, it is supposed, would have been smoothed in revision, as Malory most assuredly meant to accomplish an organic whole.[46] It is commonly by circular reasoning—and necessarily so—that the responses to Vinaver have developed; for the unity of the *Morte Darthur* on the level of complex interrelations is not self-evident and cannot be asserted without reference to Malory's intention, which is unknowable save as it is made manifest in his work.

The recurring figure of Arthur, the Round Table brotherhood, courtly love, and chivalry are glue enough to stick the adventures of the *Morte Darthur* together and to produce a unified impression, at least in vague focus; and the problematic explicits make little difference to perception. The question is whether the interrelations —those inherent in the material and those presumably fashioned by the author—do in fact produce unity at a significantly high level of complexity. Vinaver, who takes the work as it stands and not as it might appear after revision, in effect denies that adventure by adventure the *Morte* recalls beginning and end and thrusts relentlessly toward a conclusion logically determined by antecedent circumstances. The opposition contends that, inconsistencies and irrelevances notwithstanding, the dissolution of the Round Table is forecast at the outset and largely determined by the cumulative ab-errations of the actors. Moorman perceives in the intersection of three large actions—"the intrigues of Lancelot and Guinevere, the challenge and failure of the Grail quest, and the feud between the houses of King Lot and King Pellinore"—the instrumentality of organic unity.[47] Since there is no substantial disagreement about Malory's use of French sources, his ordering of adventures, and

46. See T. C. Rumble, " 'The Tale of Tristam': Development by Analogy," in R. M. Lumiansky, ed., *Malory's Originality: A Critical Study of Le Morte Darthur* (Baltimore, 1964), p. 120; Rumble, "Malory's Balin and the Question of Unity in the *Morte Darthur*," *Speculum*, XLI (1966), p. 75; Moorman, op. cit., pp. xxvii; and Lumiansky, ed., "Introduction," *Malory's Originality*, p. 7.
47. Moorman, loc. cit.

his addition of links and cross-references, Vinaver's and Moorman's opposing conclusions seem unaccountable. Nor can the controversy be resolved into a mere difference of theories, for Moorman does not appear to accept weaker conditions of unity than Vinaver. The most likely explanation is that they have in view two different literary objects—the objectively describable book which Malory actually wrote and the book which he somehow meant to write. The admitted failures of execution considered, organic unity can be predicated, if at all, only of an unrealized intention; and the intention can be known only from such evidence as failure affords. Moorman's is the familiar error of fabricating an inclusive symbolic order—"the rise, flowering, and downfall of a well-nigh perfect civilization"[48]—from scattered discursive matter and interpreting the parts accordingly. Such strategy entails unlikely perspectives and inevitably leaves a residue of undisposed contents.

Did the *Morte Darthur* achieve such thematic grandeur as Moorman perceives, it would indeed be "a highly original literary work," as Lumiansky asserts,[49] and scarcely classifiable as romance. As a matter of fact, the word *tragedy* occurs with significant frequency in the contributions to *Malory's Originality*. What this term might mean appears from Moorman's statement: "Yet it seems to me that although Malory was totally ignorant of the Greek tragedies, his book is in many ways closer to them in emphasis and depth than to the simpler concepts of the Monk's hundred tragedies."[50] If Malory wrought so magnificently, he probably exceeded his expectations; for the apparent task of romance writers was to recapitulate traditional narratives in contemporary terms. This entailed excising matter become mysterious or gross, recostuming the cast, and adjusting contexts and motives in accordance with current ideals. Such work may achieve great artistry but hardly

48. *Ibid.*, p. xi.
49. *Malory's Originality*, p. 7.
50. Moorman, *op. cit.*, p. 68.

originality as understood since the eighteenth century. Moreover,
for reasons pointed out long ago by N. E. Griffin,[51] the uses of
romance, as contrasted with epic, have never been very serious.
The integration of the *Morte Darthur* at a high level of significancy is antecedently improbable; and attempts to demonstrate
so much in the face of Vinaver's argument and Malory's casual
and not always meticulous chronicling seem little more than
tendentious glossing in the service of enhancement.

The *Morte Darthur* reconstituted may be a more perfect work
than the existential *Morte Darthur*, but there is yet some question
whether an aesthetic object is necessarily better for fulfilling the
conditions of unity prescribed by strict, symmetrical theory. R. M.
Jordan has recently argued that the form of unity commonly accepted of the *Merchant's Tale* does not in fact exist, and he creates
the impression that the poem is none the worse for this seeming
failure.[52] The problem arises in an interesting form in connection
with narrative sequences, for in such cases the aesthetic integrity
of the parts seems to vary inversely with the integration of the
whole. Organic unity, could it be demonstrated, would assuredly
deprive the separate narratives of the *Morte Darthur* of considerable autonomy and thus of independent interest. Each part would
become in perception an embodiment of a unifying principle and
take its value from the perfection of the whole. The *Canterbury
Tales*, of even looser weave than Malory's book, has been subjected
from time to time to tightening strategies. Frederick Tupper long
ago attempted to demonstrate Chaucer's "architectonic use of

---

51. N. E. Griffin, "The Definition of Romance," *PMLA*, XXXVIII (1923),
pp. 50–70.
52. R. M. Jordan, "The Non-Dramatic Disunity of the *Merchant's Tale*,"
PMLA, LXXVIII (1963), pp. 293–99. For doubts that unity is an unquestion-
able ground of excellence, see A. G. Pleydell-Pearce, "On the Limits and Use of
'Aesthetic Criteria,' " *Philosophical Quarterly*, IX (1959), pp. 29–45; Michael
Scriven, "The Objectivity of Aesthetic Evaluation," *Monist*, L (1966), pp.
178–80; and H. Morris-Jones, "The Logic of Criticism," *Monist*, L (1966),
p. 219.

the *motif*" of the Deadly Sins.[53] Soon after, G. L. Kittredge described the collection in dramatic terms and accordingly insisted: "From this point of view, which surely accords with Chaucer's intention, the Pilgrims do not exist for the sake of the stories, but *vice versa*. Structurally regarded, the stories are merely long speeches expressing, directly or indirectly, the characters of the several persons."[54] Lumiansky endeavored to correct Kittredge's bias by introducing the principle of reciprocal relations: "The crowning genius of Chaucer's enveloping plan for the *Canterbury Tales* derives from the fact that the Pilgrims and their stories exist for the sake of themselves and, at the same time, for the sake of each other."[55] Intentionalism aside, this opinion seems unexceptional and in any case imposes no strain on historical probabilities. But the claim that the tales are "complementary to the portraits"[56] and thus peculiarly suited to the tellers, whether generally true or not (and its truth has been denied), imposes a doubtful perspective on what is objectively describable as a sequence of stories framed by a pilgrimage and a contest and causally interconnected only occasionally. By Lumiansky's unifying scheme, the tales become extensions of character or fulfillments of obligatory personal exchanges and no longer exist in perception as independent aesthetic entities. So considered, the parts ought to stand in a necessary relationship to each other and to the whole, but it is a matter of observation that few teller-tale combinations are indispensable or tale assignments inevitable. This is not to say that a listening audience would be unaware of the compatibility of teller and tale or of connecting links between tales but only that the *Canterbury Tales*, objectively considered, exists primarily in dis-

53. Frederick Tupper, "Chaucer and the Seven Deadly Sins," *PMLA*, XXIX (1914), p. 97. J. L. Lowes, "Chaucer and the Seven Deadly Sins," *PMLA*, XXX (1915), pp. 237–371, discredited Tupper's notion.

54. G. L. Kittredge, *Chaucer and His Poetry* (Cambridge, Mass., 1915), p. 155.

55. R. M. Lumiansky, *Of Sondry Folk: The Dramatic Principle in the Canterbury Tales* (Austin, Tex., 1955), p. 7.

56. *Ibid.*, p. 4.

crete narratives. Indeed, the very terms of the contest tend to separate the tales in perception. A dramatic model is inappropriate to a very long serial production, and it is doubtful in any case that twice-told tales could be so far deprived of autonomy in contemporary focus as to permit integration at the level of complex relations.

Were medieval unity studies based on reasoned theory and elaborated systematically, fundamental questions would be in order concerning the logic of correlation and parallelism, causality and anticipation, and other grounds for unity claims. Their very evident defect of methodology renders such questions superfluous. Impeccable unity studies require to be inclusive of contents and formal elements and exclusive of alternative constructions; but most schemes proposed have encountered a plethora of amendments and revisions. If some of these studies are unquestionably perceptive, few take systematic form; and most are essentially summations glossed at intervals according to preconceived notions. To be sure, criticism need not achieve scientific rigor, but a thesis propounded obligates the author to orderly procedures. While a large enterprise ought not to be judged mainly from eccentric productions, it is yet significant of vast confusion that attempts should have been made to unify a fragment of uncertain direction (the *House of Fame*),[57] a set of *thulas* (*Widsith*),[58] and an entry in the *Anglo-Saxon Chronicle*.[59] Demonstrations of unity are inherently difficult, and the problems are complicated for the medievalist by the lack of applicable models. Applying organic theory to medieval literature is much like looking at the "Mona Lisa" through a magnifying glass; unsuspected relations become visible and unsuspected irrelevances, too. Through the wrong end

57. P. G. Ruggiers, "The Unity of Chaucer's *House of Fame*," *Studies in Philology*, L (1953), pp. 16–29.

58. R. J. Meindl, "The Artistic Unity of *Widsith*," *Xavier University Studies*, III (1964), pp. 19–28.

59. T. H. Towers, "Thematic Unity in the Story of Cynewulf and Cyneheard," *Journal of English and Germanic Philology*, LXII (1963), pp. 310–16.

of a telescope all medieval literature appears unified, but it is hardly necessary to proclaim what is self-evident. Rare perception may discover a previously unsuspected formal cause of unity, which, when announced, gains universal acceptance; but the path between banality and absurdity is narrow indeed.

The unchecked flow of unity studies is perhaps ascribable to the instinct for wholeness, which, as R. B. Perry observed long ago, sometimes "creates its own object."[60] And yet the liabilities of the enterprise are so great that it is to be wondered if unity is actually the principal concern. That it may be a pretext for a larger claim is suggested by several circumstances: (1) the almost invariable implication of enhanced value through claims of complex unity (and hence complexity) and therewith deeper significancy; (2) the mingling of encomiastic rhetoric with interpretive statements; (3) the preference for the term *unity* over more accurate, though less pretentious, terms, for example, *cohesion*; (4) the tendency to relax the requirements implicit in the concept of unity by means of qualifiers, for example, structural, thematic, artistic, dramatic, tonal, religious. So much considered, together with the relative imprecision of the expositions, it can only be concluded that the use of the term *unity* is essentially valuational rather than descriptive. In short, it is a means of enhancing the value of numerous medieval poems and prose works well beyond previous estimations. However meritorious the impulse to show value, unity is an acceptable ground only if demonstrated in significant and plausible relations. Hence, to claim that a literary object is unified and at a level of significancy which is neither provable nor rendered probable by contemporary circumstances is to evoke skepticism rather than increased appreciation. Several nice questions arise in connection with this unexceptional observation, but they may be comprehended briefly in one platitudinous answer: criticism exists to serve art through making its excellences known and no less to serve the truth through judicious appraisals of cultural objects.

60. *Op. cit.*, p. 64.

Chapter VII

Formalist Criticism
and
Literary Form

Formalists over the past several decades
have had considerable success in purging criticism of irrelevances
and, ironically, no less success in exposing theoretical defects in
their own claims to provide valid accounts of literary productions.
Their sophisticated arguments against methodologies incorporating
genetic and teleological assumptions secure for literature a respectable aesthetic location but leave in doubt whether the aesthetic
object can be objectively determined for critical purposes. Regarded
as an effect produced by cultural causes, including, of course, circumstances relating to the author, the poem or prose work exists
mainly in the condition of a gloss to human culture, or, more
narrowly, to the biography of the author; regarded as a monument
to human culture, it has a different mode of existence and hence
of integrity. While not in the latter condition explicable in terms
of its external references or, indeed, answerable to them, literature
is yet supposed by formalists to be accessible to plausible criticism,
in particular part-whole analysis. What disturbs formalist criticism
profoundly is the circumstance that its descriptive statements are
often and necessarily formal statements, which in some measure
constitute the very object of description. Though a necessary
condition of the existence of any object, verbal or other, form is
yet nothing self-evident in objects which are not antecedently
determined and, as assumed in criticism, may be unwarrantable.
Whatever its perplexities, the problem of form is logically prior to
all other critical problems, for formal assumptions govern the allocation of literary properties in critical description, and hence in
interpretation, and ultimately rationalize value judgments.

Some years ago René Wellek and Austin Warren proposed to
substitute in critical discourse the terms *materials* and *structure*

for *content* and *form* in order to avoid what has always been a troublesome dichotomy.[1] More recently, Wellek has urged that both form and structure be abandoned and for the reason that definitions of the terms spread through contemporary scholarship are "radically and basically" contradictory.[2] The following examples, whether entirely supporting Wellek's contention or not, underscore the confusion to which the term *form* is peculiarly liable:

The word "form" has many meanings, such as shape, configuration, structure, pattern, organisation, and system of relations.[3]
the form of an aesthetic object is the total web of relation[s] among its parts. . . .[4]
Form in poetry, simply defined, is the manner in which a poem is composed as distinct from what the poem is about.[5]
And by "form" here we mean to locate that pattern which works on the reader and is recognized by him, no matter how unconsciously or irrationally, to constitute a significant abstract repetitive frame. . . .[6]
Or seen from another angle, form is the creation of an appetite in the mind of the auditor, and the adequate satisfying of that appetite.[7]
Form may then be defined as the operation of forces that carry the experience of an event, object, scene, and situation to its own integral fulfillment.[8]
Der Geist des Stoffes heisst Form.[9]

1. René Wellek and Austin Warren, *Theory of Literature* (New York, 1942), pp. 140 f.
2. René Wellek, "Concepts of Form and Structure in Twentieth Century Criticism," *Neophilologus*, XLII (1958), p. 2.
3. L. L. Whyte, ed., *Aspects of Form: A Symposium on Form in Nature and Art* (Bloomington, 1951), p. 2.
4. M. C. Beardsley, *Aesthetics: Problems in the Philosophy of Criticism* (New York and Burlingame, 1958), p. 168.
5. "Form," q.v., *Encyclopedia of Poetry and Poetics*, ed. Alex Preminger et al. (Princeton, 1965).
6. Paul Fussell, Jr., *Poetic Meter and Poetic Form* (New York, 1965), p. 164.
7. Kenneth Burke, *Counter-Statement* (2d ed.; Los Altos, Calif., 1953), p. 31.
8. John Dewey, *Art as Experience* (New York, 1934), p. 137.
9. Oskar Loerke, "Formprobleme der Lyrik," *Neue Rundschau*, XL (Jan., 1929), p. 114.

For all their inability to define form with dictionary precision, critics have not often doubted that the concept is meaningful and useful. Benedetto Croce proclaimed, "The aesthetic fact, therefore, is form, and nothing but form." [10] "Form alone exists," [11] Paul Valéry wrote, and elsewhere quoted approvingly Mistral's cryptic observation, "What is 'form' for anyone else is 'content' for me." [12] Such asseverations considered, it can only be supposed that the term, though loosely conceived, figures significantly in much critical thinking. What occasions wonderment is that the felt need for a concept of form has not been accompanied by equal concern for its inherent perplexities, though these must create doubts about the whole critical enterprise. To speak of the form of an object is to lay implicit claim to knowledge of its very quiddity and, moreover, to possession of a rationale which in effect warrants critical investigation. A claim to know that which is not self-evident is always a claim to the possession of good and sufficient reasons or to special powers of divination. While the latter, interpreted as extraordinary perceptiveness, ought not to be discounted, insights yet have grounds, and these are usually statable. However obtained, knowledge of the form of an aesthetic object necessarily falls short of "the thing in itself." This limitation is directly owing to the circumstance that form, even if theoretically singular, cannot be known absolutely but only under one or another aspect which entails some transformation, if not deformation, of the object of perception. For this reason, unqualified claims to knowledge of form are at best unwarrantable and at worst nonsensical.

Form confronts the critic (as critic rather than as philosopher) under at least three mutually refractory aspects: (a) as author's intended disposition of particulars and allocation of properties, which cannot, however, impose logically certain effects on aes-

10. Benedetto Croce, *Aesthetic as Science of Expression and General Linguistic*, trans. Douglas Ainslie (2d ed.; London, 1929), p. 16.
11. Paul Valéry, *The Art of Poetry*, trans. Denise Folliot, Bollingen Series, 45. 7 (New York, 1958), p. 253.
12. *Ibid.*, p. 183.

thetic production; (b) as his own intuition which somehow comprehends the flux of actual perception; and (c) as model which rationalizes description in critical discourse. While these different aspects of form can probably be reconciled in the object of perception, they are yet separated by logical barriers. These, it is fair to observe, critics cross and recross without so much as acknowledging shifts of reference and perhaps sometimes without full awareness. The author's form, interpreted as scheme or set of relations, may be assumed a priori, but usable knowledge of it entails the imposing task of discovering, sorting, and weighing the multitudinous factors which enter into composition. This line of inquiry in any case could not be fruitful and for all the reasons that militate against intentionalism. The critic in the very act of experiencing the literary work approaches what might be called, for the lack of an unambiguous term, essential form, but his resources are surely inadequate for representing in critical discourse the temporal character of experiences of this sort.[13] Experience of a literary event is experience of moments, which, because subtracting from and adding to preceding moments, create an impression of what Henri Bergson called "the fluid continuity of the real." [14] Form must change as one moment succeeds another, but memory rebels at storing the minute constituents of flux. Indeed, it is a miraculous deficiency that enables mind to smooth the moments of the literary continuum and to recapitulate the whole in a single act of apprehension.[15] So transformed, the literary work is objectively describable, but it is important to recognize that the form by means of which the critic rationalizes description differs

13. It may be that literature is inevitably spatialized in description, but see J. H. Miller, "The Antitheses of Criticism: Reflections on the Yale Colloquium," *MLN*, LXXXI (1966), p. 570; Susan Sontag, *Against Interpretation and Other Essays* (New York, 1966), p. 12; and William Holtz, "Field Theory and Literature," *Centennial Review*, XI (1967), p. 540.

14. Henri Bergson, *Creative Evolution*, trans. Arthur Mitchell (New York, 1944), p. 328.

15. Cf. S. C. Pepper, *The Basis of Criticism in the Arts* (Cambridge, Mass., 1949), p. 71.

necessarily from his intuition of form and, as far as could ever be determined, from the author's form.

Literature consists of series of verbal signs which physically imitate nothing but encode information in accordance with the conventions of language. The sum total of the signs of an original literary work constitutes a necessarily unique verbal system which testifies to real or vicarious experience and stands in a causal relation to it. The system as literature is, however, a ground and not a product of experience. What the critic as reader experiences is language, and it is by means of intuition that he encompasses its potentialities for thought and feeling. Intuition is shaped out of a congeries of assumptions which gather unpredictably as the successive moments of the continuum are experienced. The premised assumptions of intuition doubtless comprise a coherent relational system from the beginning of the literary experience or there could be no apprehension; but further reading leads to the addition and subtraction of premises on grounds of relevance (and doubtless of preference) and thus to the refinement of intuition. While the reading process may be said to perfect intuition, the perfected intuition relates necessarily to the whole and accordingly falsifies in some measure the discrete moments of the continuum. This consequence is entailed by the averaging and summarizing which make intuition of the whole possible. When rationalized in reflection, intuition of the whole becomes a model and thus a frame of reference for descriptive, interpretive, and evaluative statements. Literary form, under the only aspect available to critical discourse, is a collocation of premises conceived in the interaction of the presupposing mind with language of ostensibly aesthetic character. The arrangement of premises both causes and constitutes the relational system which content may sometimes be thought to manifest absolutely. If a cognitive content presupposes form with or without a perceiver, the actual conception of form is an intellectual feat compounded of both invention and discovery. Doubtless scientific hypotheses are similarly constituted. Conceptions of literary form, however, ordinarily take account of the unique as well as the typical and by reason of this circumstance can win only such verification as consensus confers.

The formal assumptions of even exemplary analysis are so often contestable as to discountenance criticism as a discipline, and there is accordingly some need to consider what theoretical remedies are available. Genre theory, inasmuch as it describes (and prescribes) the metes and bounds of literary kinds, provides for determinate and therefore verifiable forms. Like most theories, it works passably well with that material it was originally designed to account for, but classical models are not universally valid, and their applicability to modern literature is assuredly limited. Tragedy since Ibsen, for instance, largely disappoints the expectations incorporated in classical form. While the old genre terms persist, they are chiefly useful for designating, without prescriptive force, broad literary categories. The vaguest is doubtless *lyric*, which best comprehends the surpassing variety of modern poetry. Antiquity provided no theoretical basis for the lyric and may not even have recognized it as a genre; [16] nor has the term subsequently acquired positive formal implications. Partial exceptions are those fixed forms (e.g., sonnet, ballade, villanelle) which may be subsumed under lyric, for certain well-defined correspondences are conditions of their achievement. These are particularly instructive for suggesting, in the first place, limitations inherent in criticism according to kinds and, in the second place, the grounds for variation in critical judgment. *Sonnet form*, for instance, is a perfectly comprehensible class term, but it implies very little for the form of any sonnet. It designates formal components which are largely fixated and do not interact. Though theoretically all parts of composition influence intuition of the whole, the models which serve explication cannot—and for reasons that will appear—provide for total

16. Irene Behrens, *Die Lehre von der Einteilung der Dichtkunst vornehmlich von 16. bis 19. Jahrhundert: Studien zur Geschichte der poetischen Gattungen.* Beihefte zur Zeitschrift für romanische Philologie, XCII (Halle, 1940), pp. 202–21.

interaction. While the critic recognizes a sonnet by virtue of features which sonnets possess in common, he is usually not concerned to show that these features—chiefly prosodic—are significant of anything in relation to the whole. For modern criticism, what determines a poem as a type does not determine it as a poem. Though genre theory can perhaps be defended against Croce's strictures,[17] it provides slight assistance to the understanding of literature which acknowledges no models or to criticism which celebrates novelty rather than conformity to type.

Without a theory of genres, practical criticism has no apparent use for a concept of form as an isolable entity in the sense either of Platonic essence or of Aristotelian determinant of kinds. Although much critical writing appears to assume, against the protest of aestheticians,[18] the separability of form and content, not a great deal is actually staked on this hypothetical disjunction. If genre titles signify little more than boundaries and standard models are nonexistent, then form, when predicated meaningfully of a literary object, is at most an ad hoc hypothesis without necessary implications for other productions. So considered, form has contestable credentials as a basis for descriptive and interpretive statements. Critics may contend that the very intelligibility of a verbal system guarantees the real existence of form and that it is accessible to scrutiny. Nonetheless, language manifests only potentialities for intelligibility and thus for form; nothing appears to guarantee the objective validity of the intuition of form which originates in the experience of the literary continuum or of the rationalization of that intuition as model. Nor can common sense be invoked to vouch for form: if form is self-evident and the premises of which it is constituted determine critical judgments, then the radically variant and yet plausible impressions so frequently offered of the same work are unaccountable. In fact, form

17. See Luciano Anceschi, "A Debate on 'Literary Types,'" trans. Creighton Gilbert, *Journal of Aesthetics and Art Criticism*, XIV (1955–56), pp. 324–32.
18. See Richard Kell, "Content and Form in Poetry," *British Journal of Aesthetics*, V (1965), p. 382.

is not self-evident, nor do critics ordinarily assert the objective validity of the forms which they affect knowledge of. Variations in critical opinion are primarily understandable as variations in working models, which originate as subjective perceptual judgments.

The probable unverifiability of form seems on first thought an insufficient excuse for the inexplicitness of critics, as ad hoc hypotheses can be evaluated according to plausibility, inclusiveness, and elegance. In truth, the immediate problem is not verifying but simply stating the relational systems presupposed by the partitions and allocations of analysis. Since contents, considered as particulars, are not per se significant but become so by virtue of opinions about causal or other relations, it seems possible to translate such opinions about a given work into general propositions and thus to separate out the premises which constitute its form. The form of a specific work, however, is not the mere sum of premises about literary causes and effects but a complex in which premises are modified in relation to each other and to the object of perception. While every semantic, grammatical, rhetorical, and acoustical feature predicable of a literary work can be generalized in the first term of a hypothetical or conditional, no single effect is certain unless all other things are equal, that is, fixated. In actuality, other things are seldom equal, and the production of specific effects is conditional upon the interaction of a plurality of features. Sublime language and thus its usual consequences may be muted by successions of trochees, pathetic details by irony, metrical virtuosity by banality. While the critic is likely to cover such melancholy contingencies as these with appropriate modifications of formal premises, he can hardly pretend to represent all the premises and modifications thereof which constitute his intuition of the whole. His model of the whole, however, is a product of reflection and as such seemingly amenable to exposition. And yet models, as assumed in analysis of even the simplest literary events, are so complicated of tenuous relations that their exposition poses enormous difficulties. Under the circumstances, it is not so strange that critics should speak indecisively even of what is a necessary condition of their "knowing" literature at all.

False analogies and obvious omissions so far impair most expositions of form that it is to be wondered if critics undertake them with full awareness of their implications for subsequent judgments. The frequently encountered geometrical and organic metaphors tend to falsify not only what is given in experience but also the models of experience.[19] Perhaps more importantly, critics leave unacknowledged many, if not most, of the premises which seem to constitute their models and effect the polarization of contents for purposes of analysis. It is perhaps supposed that very general indications of organization, argument, recurring rhetorical and acoustical features, and tonal qualities suffice as expositions of form; but until interrelated and generalized in covering premises, these are parts of composition and only inferentially formal components. The tone of a work may be described as ironical, the diction inflated, the argument syllogistic, the imagery mainly visual or aural; but these commonly ascribed properties are significant of nothing unless covered by formal premises which invest them with consequences for the whole. Now, it may be that, whatever the theoretical obligations of criticism, providing complete exposition of form is no more feasible than justifying intuition, which somehow sorts and sifts the myriads of properties and partitions present in perception.[20] Nor, perhaps, would so much elaborate structuring even be desirable, for a good many premises are so far incontestable as to be safely taken for granted. Others, however, and often those most significant for analysis, are so far contestable that the critic cannot state them without provoking

19. On the relation of image to form, see Neil Cooper, "The Importance of △IANOIA in Plato's Theory of Forms," *Classical Quarterly*, N.S., XVI (1966), pp. 65–69.

20. See K. Z. Lorenz, "The Role of Gestalt Perception in Animal and Human Behaviour," ed. L. L. Whyte, *Aspects of Form: A Symposium on Form in Nature and Art* (Bloomington, 1951), p. 177.

demurrals. Thus, such premises as "sea images evoke suggestions of death and rebirth" and "prosodic irregularity produces conversational effects," while perhaps more likely than not, are yet more conveniently assumed than stated. Granted that insights outrun their warrants and that critics in any case cannot be expected to defend all of them, it is important to recognize the precarious state of many undisclosed formal premises.

If literary models are often falsifiable for embodying unlikely formal assumptions, they are not less so for excluding more or less significant areas of potential experience. This last limitation is owing not only to human incapacity for discovering and weighing all conceivable features of an event but also to the circumstance that any angle of vision entails exclusions. To look at an object in one way is to miss seeing it in other ways. The content of simple description, interpreted as random identification and enumeration of parts, can never be comprehensively modeled, that is, interrelated and covered by formal premises. It is, of course, observable that description is never random but, indeed, so far ordered as to presuppose smoothing of intractable features. This is to suggest that coherent description necessarily bears the impress of form, though not that form exists prior to or separate from content; description presupposes perception and therewith sorting of sense-data from a specific angle of vision. If form is a necessary condition of the existence of an object abstractly considered, no object is fully determined without specific form, which sieves, and accordingly subtracts from, the conglomerate. Critics do not actually pretend to exhaust the potentialities of verbal systems but rather claim implicitly that their models embody all significant relations, that is, take account of everything which may be supposed to cause observable effects. Scientific models are not less selective and exclusive; the difference is that in science effects are measurable and hence a means of testing the integrity of models, while in literature they are endlessly disputable. If the question of excluded features is not directly raised in criticism, it is yet acknowledged in claims for the efficacy of models. Such claims often materialize as demonstrations of unity, which pretend to order the parts of wholes according to self-evident principles. These demonstrations, simply considered, are otiose, as unity is predicable of any object of perception; they are best understood as critics' vindications of their models against alternative constructions. Capability for unifying a sequence of verbal signs assuredly recommends a model, but its exclusive validity is not thereby established.

A sequence of verbal signs is essentially "seeable" and hence describable in virtue of form; but form, in overcoming the indeterminacy of language, imposes such limitations on seeing that description is inevitably partial and tendentious. If coherent description must need be skewed, it follows that criticism cannot make a warrantable beginning. While consistent with the argument that form is accessible to critical discourse under a limited aspect only, this proposition yet seems readily falsifiable, for it leaves out of account an author's capability for achieving coherency and therewith perceptible form. The accomplishment of an author is not, however, self-evident, as witness the wide divergence of critical opinion. And even if the aspect of form under which a specific work was achieved were accessible from likely inference, the critic would not from this circumstance necessarily have a usable model, that is, a model consistent with his experience of the work. The form required by the critic to bring verbal signs into intelligible focus could conceivably coincide with the author's only on the absurd supposition that creator and perceiver are substantially identical. This is not to insist that critics, out of temperamental differences and dissimilar resources of knowledge, radically reconstitute what authors suppose they have accomplished, though this may sometimes be the case. This is to insist that critics have no reason to suppose that the forms by which they recreate works of literature for purposes of analysis can claim any sort of warrant from the original creative processes. Admittedly, literature comes provided with incontestable evidence of authors' formal commitments—with chapters and stanzas and with scarcely less obvious strategies of development and recurrent features of presumable significance. But these indications are minimal; intelligibility and hence communication could only be fortuitous without them. Critical description largely passes over self-evident partitions and seemingly neutral detail; attention is focused on decisive properties which may reasonably be supposed to define thematically significant curves and thus to provide plausible locations for particulars. At this level, the author's form is commonly unobvious; description, if coherent, conforms to the critic's model and is, in fact, a covert defense of it. A firmer warrant could be adduced for description were literature conceivable as sets of declarative sentences conforming to semantic and grammatical conventions and referring to recurrent events in the phenomenal world. Scientific reports are of this character; the question of their integrity is a question of their one-to-one relation to what is objectively verifiable. Autotelic, at least by formalist assumption, and accordingly lacking in explicit ends, literature, perhaps with some didactic exceptions, cannot be described as the agency of any determining consequence. If literature is broadly referable to experience, its language and relations are commonly oblique; and neither context nor function can ordinarily be empirically established for it. Critical description, it is true, answers directly to language and is falsifiable for taking leave of linguistic convention. At the same time, description is description of something determined; and literature is determined not by pre-existing relational systems but by formal premises which gather in perception. Common sense may prefer one description of a literary work over another, but all descriptions are liable to embarrassment in consequence of the partialities entailed by form itself.

Literary description is in some sense explanatory and interpretive and at the same time a ground for explanation and interpretation; yet analysts, who are, of course, descriptionists, do not ordinarily profess to explain or interpret, and interpreters do not profess to

analyze. While criticism seems to permit—indeed, to require—
these cognitive functions in concert, the perplexities of form tend
to disjoin them. Analysts mark the partitions of verbal conglomerates, conjecture their controlling properties, and reintegrate the
parts—all in accordance with formal premises. For this work the
term *explication* is commonly used, but not *explanation*. Whereas
explication has become a conventional term for more or less formal
analysis, *explanation* recalls scientific expositions and the hard
criteria thereof. Few if any critics would undertake to explain
literature on C. G. Hempel's and Paul Oppenheim's terms: "The
decisive requirement for every sound explanation remains that it
subsume the explanandum [descriptive statement] under general
laws [explanans]."[21] While Hempel and Oppenheim make no
exceptions, their condition is clearly intolerable to disciplines
deficient in general laws and lacking substantial agreement about
primary data. The descriptive statements of criticism are subsumed
under formal premises which are as often as not contestable; and
the indeterminacy of literary language considered, an entirely
satisfactory solution for this methodological problem is not to be
expected. By contrast, interpretation, less afflicted than explanation
with the perplexities of causality and warranted in some degree
by a long and generally respectable history, may not appear to
encounter serious difficulties. Difficulties there are, however, not
the least of which is the possible indistinguishability of interpretation from either explanation[22] or description.[23] If in fact neither
of these but a discrete function designed to elicit meaning, interpretation appears to dispense with form and therewith the agency
which determines any verbal system. Actually, form is a necessary

21. C. G. Hempel and Paul Oppenheim, "Studies in the Logic of Explanation," *Philosophy of Science*, XV (1948), p. 146. But see A. W. Collins,
"Explanation and Causality," *Mind*, LXXV (1966), pp. 482–500.
22. Morris Weitz, *Hamlet and the Philosophy of Literary Criticism* (Chicago
and London, 1964), pp. 245 f.
23. Arthur Child, *Interpretation: A General Theory* (University of California
Publications in Philosophy, XXXVI [Berkeley and Los Angeles, 1965]), pp. 49
f, and F. E. Sparshott, *The Concept of Criticism* (Oxford, 1967), pp. 132 f.

assumption of all interpretive exposition, but the very concept of form is an unresolved embarrassment to interpretation considered as an autonomous critical function.

The concept of the aesthetic object involves literary interpretation crucially with form and at the same time creates doubts about both its grounds and its ends. Interpretation, whatever it may be, is not a methodology for discovering the essential character of an entity but, indeed, commences with an entity determined—by its supposed purpose, consequence, or specific kind. The initial assumptions necessary to determine a sequence of verbal signs for purposes of interpretation are not inevitably risky: the determining properties of practical writing, for example, are usually self-evident; and disagreements are of the character of semantic quibbles. That most familiar of ancient forms of interpretation, biblical exegesis, encounters difficulties enough with figural relations and with the metaphorical integument of religious mysteries; the Bible is nonetheless fully determined as a revelation and a communication, as a spiritual history and a guide to righteous living. Exegetes have perhaps always valued unity and harmony and other formal excellences but only as effective means of enshrining divine wisdom, which they have been concerned to unearth and make manifest in *sententiae* and abstract titles. Profane literature, of course, has been similarly treated as the agency of various external determining purposes and bereft of its meaning after the fashion of *allegoresis*; but approaches of this sort have under logical scrutiny gradually lost their warrant. Whether interpretation can cope with the aesthetic object, which is not a priori determined and not even meaningful in the sense of Scriptures, is by no means certain. In this connection, an impressive study of recent date by E. D. Hirsch, Jr., is particularly significant, for he recognizes the problem of determination and attempts to ground interpretation in the concept of the "intrinsic genre," defined as "that sense of the whole by means of which an interpreter can correctly understand any part in its determinacy."[24] This statement, considered in isolation, is not incompatible with the notion that the literary work is determined by formal premises which arise in perception. Hirsch is not disposed, however, to acknowledge the constitutive role of formal premises but rather seeks to demonstrate the objective existence of the "intrinsic genre" as the deliberately contrived instrument of the author's intended meaning. Not self-evident and inferable only from the import of the verbal system which it in fact determines,[25] the "intrinsic genre" is admittedly a self-confirming device requiring the support of external data. Since, in his opinion, "All valid interpretation of every sort is founded on the re-cognition of what an author meant,"[26] Hirsch is prepared to marshal the contestable evidence of biography and milieu. Circularity aside, his "intrinsic genre" appears not to determine the formal construct but only meaning, which, considered as abstract recapitulation, is, at least in reference to literature, ontologically mysterious. Intentionalism is a means by which the interpreter appears able to determine literature without confronting the perplexities of form; it is not an adequate solution but simply one horn of the dilemma created by the concept of the aesthetic object. The other horn, as will appear, is even less agreeable, for it places meaning altogether out of the reach of interpretation.

Interpretation like formal analysis necessarily begins with intuition of the whole; but whereas analysis is largely concerned with the quality of expression as a function of the parts of composition, interpretation commonly describes or intimates a universe of ideas which as context can accommodate the literary object and provide abstract titles for its presumably significant components. So located, a work may be said to mean in the sense of standing for concepts which cohere in a rational order. Yet meaning, philo-

24. E. D. Hirsch, Jr., *Validity in Interpretation* (New Haven and London, 1967), p. 86.
25. *Ibid.*, p. 88.
26. *Ibid.*, pp. 126, 238.

sophically baffling under any circumstances, is doubly perplexing when considered as attribute or constituent of an aesthetic object. While no one can well deny that literature is somehow meaningful or that meaning is theoretically predicable of perhaps most objects of perception or, for that matter, conception, it is far from clear what relation meaning bears to a literary work considered as an inviolable entity. To formalists, such meaning as a work possesses is a function of form and content and accordingly proceeds from the whole; but it is nothing abstractable as a *sententia*. While interpretation sometimes appears to beg the question whether literature is what it means, Hirsch candidly asserts, "neither in fact nor in logic is a verbal meaning the same as any of the countless relational complexes within which it can form a part."[27] It follows that a meaning, as a great or small commonplace, can be embodied in an infinite variety of verbal systems and, conversely, that meaning is theoretically abstractable as an ideological content from any verbal system. This is doubtless the allegorical assumption, but preservation of the integrity of the aesthetic object as such was never a concern of allegory. If, however, the poem or prose work is not determined a priori, and if intuition of the whole entails overarching formal premises, then interpretation somehow answers to form and discovers meaning through its agency. For the reasons previously advanced, no model can exhaust the potential relations of a verbal conglomerate, and, accordingly, rather different models of the same literary event can be defended. Interpretive models, with whatever justification, appear to imitate systems of ideas; and meaning, though theoretically charged with feeling in virtue of context, is yet in the main a function of the abstract and sententious parts of composition. Insofar as this may be the case, interpretation slights the qualities which largely discriminate literary works from overtly determined compositions of practical consequence.

27. *Ibid.*, p. 39.

At first thought, it appears improbable that interpretive models must need exclude the kinds of relations which distinguish verbal systems as aesthetic objects. While interpretation is often accompanied by reports of formal achievement and by value assessments, there is considerable doubt that a necessary relation is often demonstrated between the formal construct as such and its conjectured meaning. The descriptive part of interpretation consists in matching selected components of a literary event with the values of an ideological system which is deemed, from whatever inferences, to have explanatory agency. The ideology determines the work as a conceptual content, provides the terms necessary to description, and sets boundaries to meaning. Interpretation assumes that the particular instance, its claim to uniqueness notwithstanding, is comprehensible in consequence of its adumbration of a more or less familiar set of values. While the factor of resemblance necessarily enters into cognition of whatever kind, the defect of interpretation is that it tends to transform the poem or prose work into epitome and to locate its focus outside the aesthetic perimeter. Meaning, as available to interpretation, can be stated only as a crude approximation; for inasmuch as aesthetic objects are unique their meanings are unique and hence nameless. It is doubtless true that the wholly unique object is invisible—indeed, inconceivable—but this circumstance in the formalist view is insufficient warrant for converting the concrete entity to abstract paraphrase. Formal analysis celebrates literature as a feat not of thought but of language. Linguistic rather than conceptual, the formalist model provides for description in terms of grammatical, rhetorical, and logical relations. External references, always a considerable problem for formalism, can logically exist only as indeterminate glosses which merely complicate the suggestions and overtones generated by the work of art. Formal analysis preserves the aesthetic object at some expense to precise understanding and leaves meaning as an ultimately indefinable function of form and content. Whether the analytical approach is more valid than interpretation is perhaps unarguable, for it too transforms—indeed, paraphrases—literature in conformity with contestable formal premises. What is to be remarked, however, is that formalism as theory and practice was evoked by literature produced with some thought to frustrating reductivism, and not surprisingly it best accommodates the dense and obscure work inspired directly or indirectly by the Symbolist Movement. Limitations notwithstanding, formalism raises serious questions about a great deal of abstract and sententious literature which gathers interest and hence value less from skilled practice of the arts of language than from association with congenial ideologies. Literature of this sort petitions for interpretation and usually suffers from formal analysis. But to argue that interpretation is the proper approach to disclose the value of much literary art is yet to leave in doubt what degree of contingency holds between the quality of ideas and the quality of language.

Whatever value conclusions interpretation entails relate necessarily to cognitive contents rather than to the accomplishment of the whole; and inasmuch as ideas, at least in aesthetic contexts, cannot be plausibly ranked or graded, value is at bottom a mere presumption. Formalists, on the other hand, suppose that in providing grounds for experience of the total literary work they provide therewith grounds for purely aesthetic assessments. Literary value, it stands to reason, ought to be determined not by the supposed excellence of the embodied system of ideas but by the practice of the arts of language. Unfortunately for this theoretically attractive notion, no quality or set of qualities predicable of a literary work can be shown to constitute a universal ground of value. It is doubtless true that literature of established reputation appears usually to possess unity, complexity, and intensity, which M. C. Beardsley proposes as criteria of excellence.[28] Quantification poses a considerable obstacle to the employment of these criteria, but perhaps

28. Op. cit., pp. 462–66. Cf. L. T. Lemon, The Partial Critics (New York, 1965), p. 223.

more seriously their logical warrant may be insecure.[29] H. Morris-Jones asserts, "Certainly no aesthetic evaluation is entailed by their discernible presence in any specific work of art,"[30] and in this view he reflects the distrust, not uncommon among modern philosophers, of aesthetic criteria in general. Though it may be supposed that this philosophical skepticism leaves untouched at least the descriptive part of formal analysis, the truth is otherwise; critical description is through and through evaluative.[31] This must be the case even if critics should maintain a posture of utter detachment, because aesthetic consequences both good and bad are implicit in critical models and the very terms of description are so often value-bound as to create a presumption of value or disvalue.[32] While it is reasonable to maintain that critical exposition ought somehow to make value evident, the awkward circumstance remains that critical exposition cannot substantiate the value claims it ineluctably issues.

To describe the critical enterprise as an inevitably futile search for reasons adequate to support favorable or unfavorable impressions of literature is to slight the very considerable success of modern formalists in coping with what is a perplexing production of the human spirit and to preclude unjustifiably the possibility of logical remedies. Yet this description sorts with and perhaps justifies the deliberate persuasiveness of criticism of all sorts. Without covering laws and without a value-free language, criticism can only be persuasive and, save in small technical matters, not demonstrative at all. As heretofore maintained, the aesthetic object is determined for all purposes, not excluding evaluation, by formal premises which

29. M. C. Beardsley, "On the Generality of Critical Reasons," *Journal of Philosophy*, LIX (1962), pp. 480 f, argues that criteria can have some generality of application and thus support value judgments.

30. H. Morris-Jones, "The Logic of Criticism," *Monist*, L (1966), p. 219. Cf. A. G. Pleydell-Pearce, "On the Limits and Use of 'Aesthetic Criteria,' " *Philosophical Quarterly*, IX (1959), pp. 29–45; and Weitz, *op. cit.*, p. 274.

31. L. A. Reid, "On Talking about the Arts," *Philosophy*, XLI (1966), p. 324.

32. R. M. Hare, *The Language of Morals* (Oxford, 1952), pp. 111–26, doubtless clarifies the descriptive and evaluative functions of terms; but his examples are material objects and not undetermined verbal systems.

rise unaccountably in perception. The critic can safely claim only that the work of art is the cause of his intuition; beyond this point his logical warrant diminishes, and his labor consists mainly in making agreeable an allocation of facts which, with present methodologies, cannot be validated. In a notable essay some years ago, C. L. Stevenson remarked: "No matter how scientific criticism may become, then, and no matter how inexorably its scientific aspects are subject to the canons of inductive and deductive logic, it will bring with it no conclusions that impose a uniformity on the way in which a work of art must be observed."[33] That this should forever be the case is owing to the partialities of form; the form of which the critic speaks—often very confidently—is no less and no more than the means by which he literally recreates the work of art from the potentialities of language. If nothing objectively verifiable and only a paradigm of personal response which may be ultimately incommunicable, the critic's form, inasmuch as it takes account of the quality of language and the complexity of relations, enlarges the possibilities of literary experience. Formalist criticism may fail at last to comprehend all that literature is, but its claims to knowledge of the subtleties of literary language are presently unsurpassed.

33. C. L. Stevenson, "Interpretation and Evaluation in Aesthetics," ed. Max Black, *Philosophical Analysis: A Collection of Essays* (Ithaca, N.Y., 1950), p. 365.

Chapter VIII

The Instruments
of Oracular
Expression
Romanticism fabricated a poet of vast oracular powers largely from superstitious notions and suspicious philosophies which the Renaissance had gathered up somewhat by chance with the rational part of the Graeco-Roman legacy. The model was surely an imposture and, historically considered, a scandal. Seer, sage, prophet, mage—the pretensions varied, but all were titles to transcendent disclosure in times increasingly committed, at least officially, to a unified scientific view. That the poet could be confirmed to any degree in this anachronistic role was probably owing to the circumstance that the general cultural reflex following the Enlightenment reawakened widespread interest in those dark and excluded passages of the human spirit which mystics and seers were thought to frequent. Poets who pretended to voyance benefited from the muffled but persistent rumor of profound mysteries accessible to the high priests of Kabbala and the Corpus Hermeticum, to Illuminists, Rosicrucians, and Neopythagoreans. Western Europe had never ceased to acknowledge, even in such unlikely periods as the later Middle Ages, the aboriginal priestly and prophetic functions of the poet; but romanticism contrived— out of occultism and neoplatonism, antirationalism and anticlassicism—such a warrant for unabashed oracular saying as Antiquity had scarcely imagined. While perhaps none of the romantics was actually prepared to grant the poet his ancient powers in full measure, few seemed inclined to diminish the stature of the heroic abstraction, who symbolically contested the claims of naturalism and positivism.[1]

The pretensions of the romantics to such wisdom as oracles

1. For Poe's exceptional (and dim) view of seers, see R. D. Jacobs, *Poe: Journalist & Critic* (Baton Rouge, La., 1969), pp. 340–42.

possess focused attention on revelation rather than on quality of expression; and modern critics, inclined in the main to support this emphasis, have busied themselves considerably more with interpretation than with stylistic or rhetorical inquiry. It may be that the enduring merit of romantic poets consists in profound insights and not in the mastery of language; and yet their discernible ideas are not in the last half of the twentieth century impressive either as philosophy or as psychology. But to suggest that the form of romantic expression may be, on the whole, more significant than the cognitive part is to appear, on the one hand, to ignore a great deal of slack and imprecise verse and, on the other, to discount such high truths as inspiration supposedly draws down. Whatever the merit of romantic claims to knowledge (and these continue to be stoutly asserted), the language of inspiration has its own peculiar interest and all the more so in the nineteenth century because poets conspicuously neglected to answer whether the gift of the muses included forms of expression as well as of thought.[2] In scattered theoretical conjectures, however, the romantics set thought and expression in a highly problematic relationship and created enduring uncertainties about the perception of verbal properties. But as will appear, their theorizing neglected the means by which on occasion they actually created oracular effects and proved man as responsive as ever to the artful manipulation of language.

1   The romantics, in truth, seldom invoked the muses but rather looked for inspiration to the inner light and the great book of nature. In reclaiming the ancient status of the poet, they signally ignored the disabilities which superstition had laid upon voyants[3]

2. In the *Moralia* (397B–D, 404B), Plutarch recorded a not altogether serious discussion of the relation of inspiration to expression, in which it was concluded that deity provided the inspiration for, but not the language of, oracular utterance.

3. See Mircea Eliade, *Patterns in Comparative Religion*, trans. Rosemary Sheed (London and New York, 1958), pp. 13 f; Ernst Kris, *Psychoanalytic Explorations in Art* (New York, 1952), p. 78.

and proposed out of superior personal powers to make manifest, in Carlyle's resonant phrase, the "sacred mystery of the Universe." It may have been that even so early as Hesiod the muses were only a rich metaphor for the inexplicable creative impulses in man, but they constituted a self-effacing warrant for utterances which surpassed normal human powers. So considered, his *Theogony* was not so much a personal enterprise as a divine mission: "and they [the muses] plucked and gave me a rod, a shoot of sturdy olive; a marvellous thing, and breathed into me a divine voice to celebrate things that shall be and things that were aforetime. . . ." (11.30–33).[4] Two and a half millennia later, the poet was no longer the mouthpiece of the muses but often an approximation of the demigod.[5] William Blake, perhaps the first of the modern oracular poets, was surely less presumptuous than some of his nineteenth-century successors, and yet his seer appears to have had access to the deepest wisdom:

Hear the voice of the Bard!
Who Present, Past, & Future, sees;
Whose ears have heard
The Holy Word
That walk'd among the ancient trees . . .

This is not a passive communicator of divine intelligence but an autonomous voice of doom and destiny, guardian of the Logos and hence of the mysteries emanating from the ambiguous and ubiquitous Stoic concept. Blake's preposterous claim insulates oracular poetry against either critical or philosophical inspection: inasmuch as inspiration is incontestable and the Word impeccable, the Bard's expression is a proper subject only for rapt attention.

The Socratics usurped for philosophers the authority to utter cosmic generalizations and understandably contested the credentials

4. Trans. H. G. Evelyn-White, Loeb Classical Library (Cambridge, Mass., 1950).
5. Cf. William Empson, *Some Versions of Pastoral* (London, 1935), pp. 208 f.

of those competitive classes of sayers, the poets and Sophists. While the Sophists received, perhaps undeservedly, the enduring name of public deceivers, the poets were substantially denied integrity when sane and sanity when authentically oracular. What virtue the poet possessed, the *Phraedrus* (245A) made plain, he possessed at the expense of personal autonomy: "And a third kind of possession and madness comes from the Muses. This takes hold upon a gentle and pure soul, arouses it and inspires it to songs and other poetry. . . . But he who without the divine madness comes to the doors of the Muses, confident that he will be a good poet by art, meets with no success, and the poetry of the sane man vanishes into nothingness before that of the inspired madmen."[6] In the *Republic* (X), the sane poet, represented as a mere imitator, is denied the ability to discriminate between truth and falsity and hence the ability to grasp reality. While prophecy seems to have been very anciently associated with madness, the notion of the *furor poeticus* arose perhaps as late as the fifth century.[7] Invoked together, these superstitions served Greek rationalism by limiting the personal powers of the type of the poet-priest-prophet, exemplified by the mythical Orpheus. Socrates' seeming flippancy suggests considerable skepticism of inspiration, if not of the gods. Not less importantly for romantic theory, his argument thrusts a shrewd barrier between inspiration and conscious art.

Socrates' insistence that the mantic entails the manic, though doubtless a self-serving limitation on pretentious poets, raised indirectly the general question of the warrant for speech of whatever kind. For the Greeks of the fifth and fourth centuries, language, yet invested with magical potency, was an instrument useful

---

6. Trans. H. N. Fowler, Loeb Classical Library (Cambridge, Mass., 1914). Cf. *Ion* (553D–534E) and *Laws* (719); Longinus, *On the Sublime*, VIII. 4.

7. E. R. Dodds, *The Greeks and the Irrational* (Berkeley and Los Angeles, 1951), pp. 70, 82; E. N. Tigerstedt, "Furor Poeticus: Poetic Inspiration in Greek Literature before Democritus and Plato," *Journal of the History of Ideas*, XXXI (1970), pp. 163–78.

not merely for communication but for effecting remote and even
perilous results. Madness tended as a necessary condition to vouch
for inspiration and at the same time to relieve the poet of personal
responsibility for his speech. On the other hand, manifest artfulness
minimized inspiration and raised the question of imposture. The
early romantic preference for simple expression, as opposed to
rhetorical virtuosity, probably owed something to a felt need to
give evidence of ingenuousness and thereby to authenticate the
products of vision. Simple, though not necessarily clear, expression appears to have had a long-standing association with inspired
speech, as the Heraclitean fragment No. 79 suggests: "The Sibyl
with raving mouth utters solemn, unadorned, unlovely words, but
she reaches out over a thousand years with her voice because of the
god in her."[8] Much romantic theorizing about imagination and
inspiration seems in historical perspective to have been an effort
to produce a plausible substitute for the divine source of oracular
utterance and thus a warrant for expression which, otherwise
considered, arose inexplicably and tended uncertainly. Emerson
left in "Instinct and Inspiration" an oblique acknowledgment of
the problem along with a solution which could have been en-
lightening to few: "The poet works to an end above his will, and
by means, too, which are out of his will. . . . The muse may be
defined, *Supervoluntary ends effected by supervoluntary means.*"
While there is no suggestion of madness, Emerson's poet is not
altogether his own man. The statement is significant of the confusions and contradictions encountered by nineteenth-century
theorists in attempting to recover a distant mythic speaker and
therewith such oracular presumptions as rationalism contested.

   Western literary tradition seems not, at first glance, to have
been much affected by the Socratic reservations, for every succeed-
ing period reconfirmed the poet in his exalted functions.[9] Actual

8. Trans. Philip Wheelwright, *Heraclitus* (Princeton, 1959), p. 69.
9. Gwendolyn Bays, *The Orphic Vision: Seer Poets from Novalis to Rimbaud*
(Lincoln, Nebr., 1964), p. 3.

practice, however, was largely governed by imitation theory and by
the Horatian proprieties, which, though variously construed,
probably had the effect of damping down oracular fervor and limiting excesses of expression. If the European poet continued to
invoke the muses, he commonly maintained the posture of free
agent and conscious artist. Boccaccio's *vates*, as sketched in the
Genealogia deorum Gentilium from late classical sources,[10] lost
nothing of either reason or personal freedom from enjoying divine
inspiration. Poetic expression, at least until the end of the eighteenth century, answered directly to the trivium and conspicuously
registered the influence of textbooks of rhetoric. As a practitioner
of verbal art and thus a conscious manipulator of language, the poet
lacked the presumption of infallibility afforded by inspiration and
the muses and consequently stood liable to the suspicions which
Antiquity entertained about rhetoricians. Yet imitation theory,
stressing representation rather than creative initiation, provided a
defense of sorts against charges of hubris or of imposture, though
of course leaving poetry open to correction. The Middle Ages and
Renaissance cannot be said to have removed the old Platonic
doubts, and yet most poets of these eras were manifestly concerned
to uphold virtue in language decorous and rational. Romanticism,
to be sure, rejected none of the good purposes of literature; but
the romantic conception of poetry as product of transcendent
vision tended to free the poet from classical canons of thought and
expression and from such obligations to convention (if not to
objective reality) as imitation theory imposed. Claiming their freedom from the constraints which had allegedly stultified neoclassical poets, the romantics were under strong compulsion to
evolve a contrasting poetics and to adopt an appropriate psychology and metaphysics. Their theoretical labors, although sometimes studied as systematic expositions, are perhaps valuable in the
main for occasional insights. Yet, in attempting to be seers, they
may have rediscovered ancient instruments of oracular expression

10. C. G. Osgood, *Boccaccio on Poetry* (Princeton, 1930), pp. xl f.

and at the same time uncovered serious problems relating to the order of language.

2   The language of romantic poetry, although varying greatly and perhaps agreeing in little, represents out of theoretical necessity some degree of rejection of the norms implicit in classical expositions of grammar, rhetoric, and logic. Inspiration could not in principle be amenable to language rules of unproven universality. Nineteenth-century poets, to be sure, failed to exercise their expressive privileges to the fullest, and it remained for surrealism to demonstrate what extraordinary departures painting the inner reality might entail. Romantics were better justified than they perhaps realized in doubting the lessons of the trivium, for classical expositions of the arts of language were not only normative but, to a considerable extent, deductive. The textbooks neither reflected common usage in any historical interval nor exhausted the possible forms of expression. It is some credit to the intellectual powers of the ancients, however, that their allocations of the facts of language were not overcome in grammar and logic until the twentieth century and in rhetoric not even until the present. Yet they wrought much less impressively with rhetoric, perhaps for the reason that it was less amenable to deductive elaboration than the other arts and was, besides, vexed with ethical perplexities. Expression theory revived all the ancient doubts about the instruments of persuasion, and the romantics, without much apparent reflection, associated them with artificiality and insincerity. If rejected in principle, rhetoric survived conspicuously in practice; and the contemned artifices can be readily illustrated in nineteenth-century verse, even if not so abundantly as in that of the Renaissance, when the old art was unashamedly acknowledged as the basis of effective writing. For the continuing confusion about the character and potentiality of rhetoric, classical philosophers were somewhat to blame; but for reasons not entirely clear poets and critics tended to accept uncritically the dubious notions by means of which the art was

originally prejudiced. Although it is not to be supposed that the nineteenth-century could have given decisive answers to the ultimate questions posed by rhetoric, even superficial inquiry might have raised serious doubts about the literary consequences of inspiration.

While rhetoric as a complete art of composition survived flamboyantly in nineteenth-century oratory, it seems to have signified for the purposes of poetry chiefly elocution or style and the decorative employment of the figures. This was the part of rhetoric which literature incontestably shared with oratory and the part which philosophy has usually viewed with suspicion. In the *Essay Concerning Human Understanding* (III.x.34), Locke had expressed the persisting opinion that figurative language, though not a fault in matter designed to give pleasure, was inappropriate to factual discourse.[11] Examined in the context of doubts about the figures, Wordsworth's wavering discussion of language in the "Preface" (1800) is understandable; but to forgo personified abstractions and otherwise efficacious expressions which inferior poets of the eighteenth century had abused was not *ipso facto* to forgo rhetoric. Nor was the language of men, in which Wordsworth proposed to enshrine philosophical truth, noticeably free of the suspected artifices. If romanticism transcended neoclassicism, it was by means other than the avoidance of rhetorical furniture. Indeed, characteristic romantic poetry, unsupported by divine or pragmatic warrants for expression, could succeed by nothing if not by artfulness, however poorly that circumstance sorted with claims for the inner voice. The romantics actually were far less concerned to deny art than to reconcile it with inspiration. This feat can perhaps be accomplished in a number of varyingly plausible ways, but Baudelaire's is particularly interesting inasmuch as it identifies at least one rather important advantage provided by the mystical philosophies for romantic theory: "Chez les excellents

11. Cf. Thomas Hobbes, *Leviathan*, I.4, 8; T. L. Peacock, "The Four Ages of Poetry"; R. W. Emerson, "Divinity School Address" (1838).

poëtes, il n'y a pas de métaphore, de comparaison ou d'épithète qui ne soit d'une adaptation mathématiquement exacte dans la circonstance actuelle, parce que ces comparaisons, ces métaphores et ces épithètes sont puisées dans l'inépuisable fonds de *l'universelle analogie*, et qu'elles ne peuvent être puisées ailleurs." [12] The doctrine of correspondences and the poet's ability to read the signs accepted, poetic expression is as innocent as the sibyl's utterances—even if it exemplifies all the places, schemes, and tropes of the whole art of rhetoric.

Much the same question about the source of the tropes which Baudelaire answered so very confidently—and sophistically— George Campbell had considered in the previous century without mystical bias and, perhaps accordingly, with more genuine insight into the character of figuration. While not pursued to a significant theoretical conclusion, his proposition marked an advance simply for associating the instruments of poetic production with normal mental activity: "Having now discussed what was proposed here concerning tropes, I shall conclude with observing that in this discussion there hath been occasion, as it were, incidentally to discover,—that they are so far from being the inventions of art, that, on the contrary, they result from the original and essential principles of the human mind. . . ." [13] The eighteenth century doubtless lacked psychological theory adequate to support elaboration of this notion, and Campbell contented himself with a general remark about the problem: "But as to the tracing of those figures to the springs in human nature from which they flow, extremely little hath as yet been attempted." The matter was so little pursued that H. W. Wells could observe early in this century as introduction to a study of poetic metaphor: "Scholarship has here advanced little beyond the work of the classical rhetoricians." [14] A few years later, Paul Valéry rediscovered the same defect in

12. Charles Baudelaire, *Oeuvres complètes*, ed. Yves Florenne ([Paris], 1966), III, p. 573.
13. *The Philosophy of Rhetoric*, III.1.
14. H. W. Wells, *Poetic Imagery* (New York, 1924), p. 2.

scholarship and issued a sharper complaint: "Que si je m'avise à présent de m'informer de ces emplois, ou plutôt de ces abus du langage, que l'on groupe sous le nom vague et général de 'figures,' je ne trouve rien de plus que les vestiges très délaissés de l'analyse fort imparfaite qu'avaient tentée les anciens de ces phénomènes 'rhétoriques'." [15] It was not, of course, correct to say that the poetic uses of figuration had been entirely neglected, for the figures engaged the attention of that considerable number of European scholars who practiced stylistics. Stylistics, however, was then, as earlier, occupied with the differentiae of individual and period styles and not ordinarily with linguistic features in the abstract. Valéry was entirely correct in supposing that analysis of the figures, considered as mental phenomena, had not been accomplished.

Traditional rhetoricians regarded figurative language as an embellishment and thus a departure from the norm,[16] calculated to saturate any alleged truth statement with feeling conducive to audience acceptance. To be sure, Aristotle praised metaphor as an aid to effective discourse,[17] and the medieval Church considered extended metaphor, or allegory, a proper garment for divine wisdom. Nonetheless, the belief persisted that figures were somehow verbal aberrations or, as George Puttenham thought, "in a sorte abuses or rather trespasses in speach, because they passe the ordinary limits of common vtterance, and be occupied of purpose to deceiue the eare and also the minde. . . ." [18] Far from excepting metaphor and allegory from this generalization, he placed them at the head of a list of examples which included aenigma, paremia, ironia, sarcasmus, and hyperbole. Basic to the identification of the figures was the assumption that difference of form entailed difference of effect, and Puttenham acknowledged this circum-

15. Paul Valéry, "Questions de Poésie," *Nouvelle Revue Française*, XLIV (Jan.–March, 1935), p. 64.
16. Quintilian, *Institutio oratoria*, IX.i.4–5; *De rhetorica ad Herennium*, IV.xxxi.
17. *Rhetoric*, III.ii.9.
18. *The Arte of English Poesie*, III.vii.

stance by rendering the Greek terms as epithets descriptive of their discrete functions. His analyses, however, scarcely touched the fundamental questions about the production and perception of figures or, indeed, advanced understanding of their relation to thought much beyond the point at which the ancients left off. In the first century A.D., Demetrius had accounted for the power of allegory by reference to the fear and trembling which obscure and suggestive expression evoked.[19] Quintilian had supposed that hyperbole proved attractive for the reason that no one is content with the exact truth.[20] Eighteen hundred years later Campbell was unable to improve on such superficial explanations, citing synecdoche, for example, as a trope which produced vivacity by reason of fixing on the most interesting part of a subject.[21] The same defect of general theory is conspicuous in Wells, who assessed the effect of the "sunken image," defined as a mere suggestion of metaphor, in vague and affective terms: "It invigorates, elevates and ennobles the language of Shakespere, and makes poignant the lines of Spenser."[22] Conjectures such as these betray the original and largely uncorrected bias of the *ars rhetorica*: forms of expression were classified and illustrated from exemplary authors for pedagogical purposes and without much concern for their effect on the shape of perception.

To judge from a rather indecisive discussion of tropes and figures at the beginning of the ninth book of the *Institutio oratoria*, Quintilian was disinclined to allow to figuration any function other than unselectively exciting the feelings. He dismissed in passing the contemporary opinions that the figures relate to unitary emotions and, more importantly, that cognitive contents are substantially altered by figuration. In the orator's view, thought

19. *On Style*, II.100–101.
20. *Inst. orat.*, VIII.vi.75.
21. *The Philosophy of Rhetoric*, III.i.2. Baudelaire, op. cit., III, p. 600, placed high value on hyperbole and apostrophe "puisque ces formes dérivent naturellement d'un état exagéré de la vitalité."
22. *Op. cit.*, p. 227. Cf. Sister Miriam Joseph, *Shakespeare's Use of the Arts of Language* (New York, 1947), pp. 288 f.

is largely impervious to the various embellishments required by persuasion—"For the same things are often put in different ways and the sense remains unaltered though the words are changed" (IX.i.16).[23] Whether Quintilian divined the implications of the contrary—that is, the unity of thought and expression—is of course unknowable; but he can scarcely have failed to realize that to allow the figures an integral (and hence modifying) function in discourse exposed the art of oratory (and poetry no less) to attack by the philosophers. Considered as mere ornaments, the figures might have been supposed to obstruct rational process in some degree; but considered as actual forms of thought, they celebrated and exploited all those irrational proclivities of mind which philosophy was dedicated to overcoming. Rhetoric could be a sanitary art only so long as it answered to philosophy,[24] but logic could not in Antiquity or afterward be drawn so as to do justice to figurative language.

Whereas the integrity of rhetoric in the rationalist tradition required the theoretical separation of thought and figuration, romantic pretensions required their organic relation. Embellishing the products of inspiration, even though for good and worthy purposes, could be scarcely less than tampering with the order of divine saying. But accepted as integral to the poetic process, the figures, which were sometimes viewed as abuses of language, became by the same token abuses of mind. Rationalism had stood in no danger from the precept that expression should fit thought much like a glove, though the glove might be so ornate and complex as to obscure the hand. The necessary organicism of romantic theory, however, dissolved the distinction between hand and glove and thus implicated poetic vision as never before with the instrument of its expression. The language of poetry, insofar as it depended on figuration and thereby departed from supposed norms of discourse, appeared to be a mode of saying which in

23. Trans. H. E. Butler, Loeb Classical Library (Cambridge, Mass., 1959).
24. Cf. Cicero, *De inventione*, I.i.

principle challenged syllogistic reasoning and thus the criteria for good sense incorporated in traditional expositions of logic.[25] Oracular poets from Blake to Yeats contested the claims of positivists and naturalists to account adequately for the experiential world; but they were not at the same time prepared to maintain on acceptable theoretical grounds that their own intuitive mode of knowing entailed a mode of saying which departed radically from scientific discourse and most conspicuously through figuration. While surrealism ultimately allowed language free rein to celebrate the irrational aspects of experience, early English romantics could not without serious embarrassment fully acknowledge their dependence on artifices long associated with deception or overtly challenge the logical model of thought upheld by rationalism. Constrained by the doctrine of inspiration from separating thought from expression,[26] they meant nonetheless to imitate Sidney's "right popular Philosopher" and accordingly could not allow, without confessing irrationality, that figuration provided the models to which their higher truths conformed. It was thus one thing to reject decoration as false art and quite another to accept such figurative language as poetry necessarily uses as truly commensurate with experience.

If rhetoric entailed manipulation of language in the interest of persuasion, logic entailed the ordering of language according to an axiomatic system which could not in principle accommodate the vagaries of the poetic imagination. While Aristotle's *Organon* provided nothing resembling a description of actual mental process but only a collocation of rules for determining the validity of propositions, it in effect defined right reason for purposes of discourse and imposed norms of rational expression upon poets no less than upon other speakers. Between Virgil and Gray, poets

25. See Elizabeth Sewell, *The Orphic Voice: Poetry and Natural History* (London, 1960), pp. 30–33.
26. In the *Biographia Literaria*, chap. 1, Coleridge may be supposed to have affirmed the inseparability of thought and expression, though in truth his remarks are indecisive.

admitted to no difficulty in registering excesses of spirit, but their ordering of language answered much less to the actual jumble of perceiving and conceiving than to rules of reason. *Elocutio* excepted, the rhetorics were through and through logical, and the figurative forms of even this problematic division were fenced off from thought content by the theory of decoration. The nineteenth century, as Thomas De Quincey remarked in his essay "Rhetoric," tended to identify the old art of persuasion with gaudy figuration, although the figures were the great source of embarrassment to that controversial art. They were an even greater embarrassment to the poets inasmuch as their theory committed them to identification of thought with expression and thus to a mode of saying which to the extent that it utilized figures implicitly contested rules of reason. In the "Preface" (1800), Wordsworth seems to have recognized the problem and to have elected to stay with the rational tradition. While inclined to believe that the language of the poet cannot "differ in any material degree from that of all other men who feel vividly and see clearly," he yet supposed that a poet might "use a peculiar language when expressing his feelings for his own gratification, or that of men like himself." The question of contradiction aside, Wordsworth apparently concluded that the form of expression, whether oracular or otherwise, ought not to depart from the rational order: "Unless, therefore, we are advocates for that admiration which subsists upon ignorance, and that pleasure which arises from hearing what we do not understand, the poet must descend from this supposed height; and, in order to excite rational sympathy, he must express himself as other men express themselves." The antirational character of the romantic stance considered, this is a surprising statement; it supposes that impulses from vernal woods can be rendered according to rules of reason and in relatively transparent language. While Wordsworth doubtless justified his affection for sonorous general statements and his ambition to be taken as a poet-philosopher, he disavowed the very means by which seers have commonly sought to make the ultimate mysteries visible. Neither Coleridge nor Shelley was so far disposed to dilute the voice of inspiration, nor, of course, the *symbolistes*; but these last considered that men are most illuminated by what surpasses their understanding.

Poetic theory and poetic style assuredly vary and perhaps vary reciprocally, but neither the actual mental processes which may be said to cause poetry nor the perception of expressive features can be shown to vary in consequence of theory or other accidental circumstance. As far as anyone could ever know, the habits of mind which poetry uses have not changed since Homer, even though, as supposed, the scientific view of the world has largely replaced the mythopoeic. Far from dissipating the mysteries of poetic production, theory has functioned somewhat to support practical norms but chiefly to define and rationalize the relation of poetry to various conceptions of the real. Thus, nothing significant for composition but rather some degree of commitment to metaphysical realism is reflected in Pope's classical conception of expression as the "dress of thought," in Wordsworth's decision to render vision in the language of common understanding, and indeed, in Eliot's exposition of the "objective correlative." Practically considered, this dichotomizing insulates the ideational essence from the superficies of language, notably the figures, and thus confirms poetry as a conservatory of the eternal truths. While poetry is in some sense an institution of this sort, it is yet not an Academy or Lyceum and could not tolerate dialectical methods for discovering truth. Symbolist and seer, Eliot well understood the liabilities of transparent general statement and understood no less the central position of figuration in oracular utterance. The usefulness of the objective correlative for him, as for Valéry,[27] may have been to demystify the romantic sources of expression rather than to affirm the logical bias of traditional poetry. If doubtful of the "universelle

27. See A. P. Bertocci, *From Symbolism to Baudelaire* (Carbondale, Ill., 1964), p. 68.

analogie," Eliot characteristically demonstrated what Baudelaire regarded as an effective use of language—"Manier savamment une langue, c'est pratiquer une espèce de sorcellerie évocatoire."[28] This is nothing less than a rhetoric of mystification, which, insofar as it frustrates the abstractive process, contests the classical separation of thought and expression. Expression theory, of course, could not easily tolerate so much premeditated artfulness; even so late as Eliot, poetic gift implied, as well as craft, some trafficking with the muses.

Insofar as they were mystics, the romantics could comfortably entertain the notion that the mysteries of the supernatural order which flickered briefly in periods of trance quite surpassed the powers of human utterance. As poets, however, they could not conveniently share the mystic's doubts about the capabilities of language. But if obliged to affirm the capacity of poetry to provide at least intimations of the mystic's deep insights, the poet as mystic yet could not allow that language participated in vision. With his usual caution, Wordsworth confessed himself in "Tintern Abbey,"

> well pleased to recognize
> In nature and the language of the sense
> The anchor of my purest thoughts,

but the thoughts, though testified to by his language, are not in any indicated way responsible to it. Romanticism was capable, however, of generating from its diverse sources an entirely magical view of the function of language, as a wonderfully confused passage in *Prometheus Unbound* evidences:

> Language is a perpetual Orphic song,
> Which rules with daedal harmony a throng
> Of thoughts and forms, which else senseless and shapeless were.

To Shelley at this moment, language was not the futile instrument of the poet mystified by divine splendors but the creative Word of the mage, who, through the manipulation of sign and symbol,

28. *Op. cit.*, III, p. 556.

ordered and thus mastered the mystic's shadowy realm. Mystic
and mage are not entirely opposed roles, as Karl Vossler remarked;[29] and the latter gained the ascendancy, first in Victor Hugo
and subsequently in the *symbolistes*, without extinguishing the
former. By exploiting the magical properties of language—and most
conspicuously the symbol—the seers pretended to make visible
what the mystics could report only in vague terms.[30] Their claim to
perception of patterns of eternity required an impressive warrant,
and this much at least occultism furnished even so late as Yeats.[31]
What actual treasures the distant voices brought can hardly be
ascertained; but voyants were increasingly disposed to refine the
language of inspiration with considerable regard for its expressive
qualities. If Baudelaire, following Poe, insisted on mathematical exactitude, Mallarmé counselled such stratagems as rhetoricians use,
though, to be sure, in the name of Orpheus. In truth, the old,
defeated philosophies, which had enabled the romantics to execute
a more or less convincing revolt from the rationalist interpretation
of experience, entailed a vatic posture and thus considerable
equivocation about the sources of verbal art. A theory of perception which does justice to their oracular voices sorts very awkwardly
with their pretensions to inspiration and revelation and exposes
manipulative skills of an embarrassingly high order.

3   The romantics, insofar as they claimed access to the supernatural, were under some obligation to bring forth new knowledge;
but what they revealed, as the nineteenth century doubtless realized, was not new and not always knowledge. Poets are not, of
course, barred by professional disabilities from significant discovery,
and it is entirely possible that in times past novel insights into
human and cosmic relations were owing to them. Nonetheless, in

29. Karl Vossler, *The Spirit of Language in Civilization*, trans. Oscar Oeser
(New York, 1932), pp. 4 f.
30. See George Mehlis, "Formen der Mystik," *Logos*, II (1911–12), pp.
250 f.
31. See Frank Kermode, *Romantic Image* (London, 1957), p. 131.

recorded times the demonstrable novelty of poetry has consisted in the ordering of expressive elements rather than in truth statements. Although much romantic verse has invited extensive analysis in philosophical terms, the results have been of doubtful significance for literary art and perhaps none at all for systematic philosophy. Such philosophical concepts as poets effectively used in the nineteenth century, as earlier, were great or small commonplaces,[32] and these can scarcely be reckoned the principal ground of poetic success. To discount the debt of the commonplaces to revelation is yet not to deny their poetic uses; if thought, considered as an abstractable entity, furnishes poor indications of literary achievement, the forms which thought takes may be of very great significance for what is loosely called poetic effect. The form of thought is, however, a vacuous concept unless it can be plausibly related to (and at some level identified with) the form of expression. The characteristic forms of poetic expression, as thus far identified, are largely the rhetorical forms; and these, as previously indicated, can be associated with thought only at some expense to rationality. The forms of thought pose a further difficulty inasmuch as they appear to presuppose the form-content dichotomy and thus leave the cognitive part theoretically separable from language. Yet thought is unknowable—indeed, inconceivable—without the terms of its expression;[33] it is more fruitfully regarded as process, in which ideas operate as terms of successive relations. The novelty of poetry, if not ideational, is necessarily formal; and the commonplaces, it follows, have power to move only in consequence of their figured form. Contrary to the opinion of the ancients, however, the figured forms of expression may well be the models of the actual experience of the commonplaces rather than mere verbal ornaments.

32. See E. M. W. Tillyard, *Poetry Direct and Oblique* (rev. ed.; London, 1948), pp. 39–49.
33. M. Merleau-Ponty, *Phénoménologie de la perception* (4th ed.; Paris, 1945), pp. 213 f.

While all acoustical, ideational, and formal properties which analysis can identify in poetic discourse are *ipso facto* accessible to perception, no property or set of properties can be said to enter, by demonstrable necessity, into perception and to occasion specific consequences. Uncovered by warrantable generalizations, statements about poetic effects are of the character of subjective perceptual judgments, advanced as reasons[34] and varying in degrees of persuasiveness. If the expressive values of peculiarly poetic features cannot be objectively determined, the quality of perception is nothing predictable and, indeed, nothing knowable save as personal testimony. Impressions produced by poetic discourse vary so greatly as to permit few fruitful inferences and accordingly suggest, contrary to the assumption of at least one cultural anthropologist,[35] that the forms of perception, whether conscious or unconscious, are not equally available to all individuals. Analysis proceeds without direct reference to differences in perceptual capacity, although implicitly appealing to a well-educated reader; the allocation of facts depends on posited formal relations, which, if not entirely arbitrary, cannot be validated. The defect is to a degree reparable, however, if figuration can be shown with some probability to consist in forms which are crucial for perception. Excluded on principle from scientific discourse and identified as the conspicuous differentiae of poetic language, the figures are inferentially the cause of those effects peculiar to poetry. This proposition entails neither the correlation of figures with unitary emotions nor the acceptance of a common human nature. It is compatible with the view that the forms of expression are the forms of thought, or, to do justice to the total mental and physical response, the forms of experience. So regarded, the figures are shareable perspectives which conjecturally exhaust all the forms of experience which can be articulated; and

34. See William Righter, *Logic and Criticism* (London, 1963), p. 22.
35. Claude Lévi-Strauss, *Structural Anthropology*, trans. Claire Jacobson and B. G. Schoepf (New York and London, 1963), p. 21.

they are, accordingly, components of discourse which in perception have selective consequences. If actual experience runs in the grooves described by figuration, poetry reveals nothing so much as the perspectives from which perception orders the phenomenal world. That that should seem on reflection a world of skewed relations and absurd identifications is probably not owing to the eccentricities of poets but to the circumstance that reflection re-orders perception according to the rational model. If this is indeed the case, the romantics may be said to have affirmed the quality of immediate experience and to have narrowed the gap which Kant held open between thought and perception.

To say that figuration in principle exhausts the forms of expressible experience is not to say that the approximately two hundred figures identified and illustrated between Antiquity and the Renaissance are either inclusive or in all cases perceptually valid. It is altogether probable that some significant forms, though noted in analysis of particular poems as novelties, have not been recognized as legitimate additions to the traditional lists; but it is even more probable that rhetoricians have multiplied distinctions beyond necessity. While experience doubtless registers repetition, for example, in considerable variety, numbering the kinds[36] very nearly to the limit of ingenuity seems as misleading as recording minute allophonic nuances in speech. On the other hand, the possibilities of irony are assuredly not exhausted by antiphrasis, paralipsis, and epitrope. Inasmuch as the rhetorics are practical rather than theoretical in character, sets of related and affectively indistinguishable figures are perhaps valid as means to elegant variation, though to grant as much is to slight the question whether nuances of language bespeak nuances of thought. It is significant that modern critics, while indifferent to the nice discriminations (and bewildering terminology) of the figurists, have singled out some figures as peculiarly agreeable to poetry, most notably metaphor, irony, para-

36. Joseph, op. cit., pp. 305–307, lists fourteen figures of repetition.

dox, and ambiguity,[37] which, it is important to recognize, may appertain to the whole as well as to the part. Although there is no obvious reason for preferring these over (say) auxesis, hyperbole, paronomasia, and simile, they may be in fact salient members of a thus far unverified class of verbal forms which describe the more important perspectives available for human experience. To state the matter in general terms, some forms—whether classified as tropes, *figurae verborum*, or *figurae sententiarum*—appear to be crucial for the shape of perception and others a matter of relative indifference. It cannot be assumed, contrary to the view of some linguists, that a verbal distinction by the fact of its discoverability is realized in experience. The significant figures, if identifiable, might be expected to connect language and experience in meaningful relations and to expose thereby the properties of the aesthetic object which effectively determine the quality of perception.

If figuration is commensurate with perception, then the world of sense impressions—the only world directly knowable—is plagued irremediably by indeterminacy, contradiction, and mutability. In representing these properties, poets, by the Platonic view, imitated not reality but mere appearance and accordingly stood condemned as falsifiers. Nonetheless, postclassical poets, although possibly more acutely aware than the ancients of the multifarious character of existence, for a good many centuries accepted and sustained an orderly and rational world picture in the best Platonic sense. Artful and resourceful manipulators of language perhaps without peers, Renaissance poets may have very nearly exhausted the formal perspectives from which the human condition can be plausibly contemplated; but for all their contriving to make manifest the complexity of the world as perceived, the rational real remained intact and supreme. In principle at least, reason ruled rhetoric, not

37. Herbert Read, *Collected Essays in Literary Criticism* (London, 1938), p. 98; I. A. Richards, *The Philosophy of Rhetoric* (New York, 1936), p. 40; Cleanth Brooks, Jr., *The Well Wrought Urn* (New York, 1947), p. 3; William Empson, *Seven Types of Ambiguity* (2d ed.; London, 1947), p. xv.

excepting *elocutio*;[38] and figuration was allowed no other virtue
than dressing up the plain terms of propositional truth. The actual
relation of forms of expression to experience was, of course, unaffected by the theory of decoration; but in the Renaissance—and,
to be sure, in the Enlightenment—verbal display conformed to the
firm logic of rational argument. While the romantics cannot be
said to have generally advocated expressive license, their language
in principle answered to inspiration and the problematic vagaries
thereof; the figures, accordingly, acquired unprecedented and un-
foreseen integrity and implicitly called in question the primacy of
rules of reason. It is unlikely that the romantics were ever prepared
to accept the full consequences of George Campbell's conjecture
that the figures "result from the original and essential principles of
the human mind," for the world thereby adumbrated neither flat-
ters the human condition nor offers much hope of improvement.
Regarded simply as forms of expression and played against rational
norms, such figures as paradox, irony, ambiguity, oxymoron, and
antithesis may be supposed to describe the perverse and accidental
quality of existence; regarded as forms of experience and models of
the real, these figures shatter confidence in cosmic order and raise
up the prospect of incoherence, malfunction, and irrationality in
the very nature of things. Somewhat less portentous, the tropes
metonymy and synecdoche have an essentializing function and
often appear to apprehend the essential real; yet knowledge of
essence thus won entails deformation and even caricature of
simple appearance. Analogy, by contrast, seems perfectly innocent,
knitting up the animal, vegetable, and mineral kingdoms in fruitful
and logically agreeable one-to-one relations. But if analogy is the
road even to scientific insight, the rampant metaphors of the poets
call common sense in doubt and collapse the nice partitions of
objective viewing. Martin Foss some years ago remarked the potentiality of metaphor for simultaneous illumination and obfusca-

38. Joseph, *op. cit.*, p. 398.

tion.[39] While the poets freely confound the kingdoms of kind, animizing and de-animizing, dwarfing and magnifying, their ordering of language usually seems incommensurate with their unlikely perspectives. The grammar of absurdity differs so little from the grammar of reason that the preposterous identifications and predications of the poets in some fashion parody the standard forms of the logicians. If, however, figures are models of the perceptual real, it may be the logicians who unconsciously parody the forms of ordinary experience.

The ancients sought by exploiting the affective properties of language to make truth agreeable; the romantics sought by uttering the inspired word to make a higher truth visible. Rhetoric, as classically conceived, presupposed basic mental infirmities which could be played on by means of verbal artifice. Romanticism celebrated feeling—in effect denying the infirmities—but barred poets from practicing on perception with features of language which smacked of persuasion. If it is granted that early and late their revealed truths consisted in recast commonplaces which ordinarily required neither defense nor extensive exposition, then it can be accepted that the practical concern of the romantic seers was not persuasion but creating problematic occasions without recourse to dialectical methods. While revelation seemingly disavows such aids as rhetoric uses, commonplaces, considered simply as abstract statements, have small affective virtue. Wordsworth proposed to generate interest by the "coloring of imagination," and other romantics cultivated suggestiveness and étrangeté apparently for the same purpose. All things considered, their frequent success can have been owing only to their magnifying, by whatever means, the projective tendencies of perception. If so, such liberties of expression as poets claimed by virtue of inspiration the romantic audience matched with commensurate liberties of perception; and

39. Martin Foss, *Symbol and Metaphor in Human Experience* (Princeton, 1949), p. 56.

in the absence of rational norms there were no obvious restraints on the energies of re-creation. While the romantics staked a good deal on the power of suggestive imagery, it is yet likely that projection is most active when perception encounters firm, but nonetheless problematic, Gestalten, that is, such relations as figures describe. Poe is supposed to have commenced with form, allowing sense to emerge, if at all, in consequence of suggestion;[40] but it is observable that his formal perspectives are often so ill defined that sense is in doubt. In that romantic poetry which best sustains oracular pretensions and creates accordingly the impression of deep wisdom, it is fair to say that form is sense; and figuration, both of the part and of the whole, provides the only practical formulating alternative to the logical order which romanticism generally eschewed. These circumstances perhaps explain Valéry's unelaborated approval of Mistral's statement, "What is 'form' for anyone else is 'content' for me."[41] While the brain, as Anton Ehrenzweig maintains with the Gestalttheoretiker, "projects that definite configuration into the chaos which we perceive as the forms and shapes around us,"[42] verbal conglomerates achieve Prägnanz (and hence affective success) only as the forms of expression confirm the forms of experience. If perception can discover in a verbal system only what it has placed there, "il faut," as Maurice Merleau-Ponty remarked, "que l'objet perçu renferme déjà la structure intelligible qu'elle dégage."[43] Whatever the claims of the romantics to vision, it is apparent that their oracular performances best succeeded when figuring the familiar perplexities of human experience. In an important sense they made truth visible, although the paralogical order defined by their figures

---

40. See Hugo Friedrich, *Die Struktur der modernen Lyrik von Baudelaire bis zur Gegenwart* (Hamburg, 1956), p. 38.

41. Paul Valéry, *The Art of Poetry*, trans. Denise Folliot, Bollingen Series, 45.7 (New York, 1958), p. 183.

42. Anton Ehrenzweig, *The Psycho-Analysis of Artistic Vision and Hearing* (2d ed.; New York, 1965), p. 22.

43. *Op. cit.*, p. 35.

offered no means of resolving the perplexities which the truth
consisted in.

4   The successful oracular poems of the romantics cannot in
reason be discriminated from or, indeed, preferred over, their
poetic expositions of metaphysical and psychological theory if
what purports to be revelation is presumed to rule art. Considered
as testimonials to transcendent vision, Wordsworth's "Tintern
Abbey" and "Immortality Ode" are not qualitatively different;
and their value derives less from the artful manipulation of language than from supposed philosophical insights. By maintaining
a philosophical focus, critics have directed attention to a considerable body of discursive verse which may be said to rationalize
rather than to demonstrate oracular speaking. Poems which illustrate the affective potentialities of the oracular attitude, while
scarcely neglected, have been studied more often than not as
ideological contents documenting systems of thought. The circumstance that the "Tyger," for example, is most apparently a
formal achievement is considerably obscured if the dark antinomy
lurking therein is explicated by reference to Blake's hermetic or
political lucubrations. If, however, the autonomy of the poem is
granted, the mystery turns out to be a commonplace perplexity
which has been wonderfully energized through the ordering of
affective elements. The terms of the relation are good, evil, and
a benevolent Creator; and the relation is both paradoxical and
ironical. The symbol of the tiger rules the poem, though in consequence of investment as well as of intrinsic affective value. The
succession of incantatory questions invests the symbol with sinister
connotations which set Creator and creature in an equivocal relationship. The function of these questions is not precisely described by any of the interrogative figures of the rhetorics; for the
oracular voice is not persuasive or demonstrative but ostensibly
revelatory. Northrop Frye has defined the attitude and granted
the romantic presumption: "He [the poet] is a priest of a mystery;

he turns his back on his hearers, and invokes, chanting in a hieratic tongue, the real presence of the Word which reveals the mystery."[44] To reveal the mystery is not, however, to resolve it. The oracular poet succeeds by exhibiting perplexity and precluding resolution, not by devising happy equations to reconcile the jarring oppositions and incongruities of experience. The "Tyger" no more calls for answers than Villon's poem of similar construction, the "Ballade des dames du temps jadis"; both are verbalizations of forms of experience which can only be intellectualized (and hence falsified) by philosophical inquiry.

Rhetorically considered, the symbol is a verbal sign which, much like the analogical figures, posits more or less arbitrary relations between disparate entities of the material and immaterial orders; by contrast, the symbol in some romantic theory is the fruit and proof of transcendent vision, at once the means of discovering remote truth and its inviolable embodiment. While it was evident after the example of Keats that an irrational conception of the symbol was not crucial for the uses of poetry, romantic symbolism continued to manifest a pronounced affinity for occultism.[45] Yeats has left an eloquent testimonial to the inherent potency of the symbol which, it should be remarked, accords much better with his occultist speculations than with his verse: "I cannot now think symbols less than the greatest of all powers whether they are used consciously by the masters of magic, or half unconsciously by their successors, the poet, the musician and the artist."[46] However agreeable to the archaic societies which venerated the Word and its manipulators, this supposition is wholly unnecessary. Indeed, the ancient superstition reflected by Yeats, that the sign can somehow

44. Northrop Frye, "Three Meanings of Symbolism," *Yale French Studies*, No. 9 (1952), p. 14.
45. Bertocci, *op. cit.*, p. 18; John Senior, *The Way Down and Out: The Occult in Symbolist Literature* (Ithaca, N.Y., 1959), p. xxiii.
46. W. B. Yeats, *Essays and Introductions* (New York, 1961), p. 49. Cf. Hermann Pongs, *Das Bild in der Dichtung* (Marburg, 1927–39), II, pp. 3 f; Jean Danielou, "The Problem of Symbolism," *Thought*, XXV (1950), pp. 427–30.

contain the essence and therewith the potency of its reference, diminishes the role of art, for it entails acceptance of more or less
fixed symbolic values which require nothing from artifice. To be
sure, romantic symbolism is not usually fixed but rather fluid, and
it succeeds, if at all, by artful investment. This is not to suggest
that symbols are merely neutral receptacles which owe nothing
to tradition and association. Blake's "forests of the night" recall
the "selva oscura" of the *Divina Commedia* and ultimately the
archetypal garden defiled through human error, and the tiger
inhabits the same menagerie of large and fearsome carnivores as
Dante's lion, leopard, and wolf, which are the one-dimensional
instruments of allegory; but it is by the relations which figuration
describes, not by magical properties or established usage, that the
symbols of the "Tyger" are energized. Yeats provides no obvious
exceptions to the generalization that successful romantic symbols
are familiar objects of perception or conception which have been
charged by rhetorical means with relations significant for human
experience. To take a conspicuously artful instance, the focal
"rough beast" of the "Second Coming" is not antecedently determined but becomes a relational content as a direct consequence
of the paradox, irony, antithesis, and auxesis which shape and fit
the road down which it "slouches." The parade of ill-defined and
improbable symbols through Blake's prophetic poems underscores
the plain fact that *Prägnanz* is a function of aptness in the perceptual object and relational complexity. And aptness is not necessarily
strangeness: Edwin Muir's "The Road" and Wallace Stevens'
"Anecdote of the Jar" demonstrate that the largely unregarded
objects of common existence are as efficacious as unicorns or even
fauns. It is perhaps superfluous to dwell on the self-evident function
of symbols, but the Baudelairean "forêts de symboles" have been
so shrouded in mystery as to obscure the technical accomplishment of oracular speaking.

  To praise the romantics for having demonstrated the capacity
of the symbol for focusing complex relations is to disturb the

metaphysical grounds of their expressive warrant. What inspiration somehow discovers and revelation utters is not verbal artifice but the Word, and the Word is most conspicuously the symbol. While the symbolist achievement nowhere entails "Vergöttlichung der Worte," symbolist theory can tolerate no other formulating principle; beyond reason and the paralogical order of figuration there can be no conceivable order except that provided by language infused with spirit, that is, with divine form. From the temple of nature, according to Baudelaire's sonnet "Correspondances," issue "confuses paroles"; these are sacred words, which mysteriously encompass the natural and the supernatural, the profane and the divine.[47] The symbolic titles gleaned by the poet from nature both signify the correspondence between two orders of the real and effect their union. Though, as *Geistersprache*, the language of symbolism is warranted against all suspicion of absurdity, the integrity of the symbol cannot be altogether safeguarded in an age given to dissipating mystery. It is perhaps significant of concern over the pervasive analytical habit that Goethe and Coleridge in approving the symbolist mode should have opposed it to allegory;[48] for *allegoria*, though close kin to the symbol, is an intellectualizing figure which dissolves the perceptual real into abstract values. While distinguishable, symbolism and allegory have a common origin and a marked affinity.[49] Behind the Swedenborgian doctrine of correspondences, as behind medieval allegory, lies the neoplatonic (and occultist) assumption that the visible world figures the invisible.[50] If determinable either from context or established

47. See the valuable discussion of Hermann Güntert, *Von der Sprache der Götter und Geister* (Halle, 1921), pp. 3–50.

48. Coleridge is supposed to have created the preference for symbolism and the prejudice against allegory in the *Statesman's Manual*, though earlier Goethe had expressed much the same opinions, according to René Wellek and Austin Warren, *Theory of Criticism* (3d ed.; New York, 1956), p. 300. Yeats repeatedly denigrated allegory, as opposed to symbolism—*op. cit.*, pp. 116, 146–48, 160–61.

49. Cf. A. G. Lehmann, *The Symbolist Aesthetic in France, 1885–1895* (Oxford, 1950), pp. 282–86.

50. See Edgar de Bruyne, *Etudes d'esthétique médiévale* (Bruges, 1946), II, pp. 368–70.

usage, the symbol is readily convertible to allegory; and the only
cogent objection is that conversion changes the modality and thus
violates the integrity of the aesthetic object. Under the circumstances, it is ironic that Goethe's *Faust* should have developed in
the second part a Platonic thinness characteristic of allegory and
that Coleridge with his marginal notes and occasional platitude,
should have tempted his readers to allegorize the "Rime of the
Ancient Mariner," which is in most respects an exemplary oracular
production. Allegory, it is sometimes forgotten, was first a method
of interpretation and only later a principle of composition. If no
longer habitual, as in the Middle Ages, allegory is always available
to confirm the recurrent assumption that literature bodies forth
divine truth. *Geistersprache* ineluctably evokes allegorizing. The
claim of the romantics to the possession of magically infused
language was entailed not by the actual requirements of expression
but by their oracular pretensions. Although nothing was actually
lost to poetry by this awkward circumstance, in mystifying the
sources and instruments of poetic production, the romantics di-
verted attention from their manipulative powers and from the
central truths which they proved against rationalism.

The strategies employed by the *symbolistes* to create an impression of oracular speaking and at the same time to thwart allegorization resulted in a number of instructive confusions. Whereas
English poets tended, at whatever risk from reductionism, to
invest their symbols very fully and precisely, the French were inclined to float theirs, relatively undefined, in a sea of suggestion
and musical effects. The consequence of this practice is readily
apparent in Valéry's clever admission, "Mes vers ont le sens qu'on
leur prête."[51] Yet the French neither early nor late renounced the
old romantic obligation to make a special truth visible. But if
committed as voyants to revelation, they were committed as mages
to mystification; and this difficulty embarrasses Jean Moréas'

51. Paul Valéry, "Préface à un Commentaire," *Nouvelle Revue Français,*
XXXIV (Jan.–June, 1930), p. 218.

exposition of the relation of idea to image: "la poésie symbolique cherche à vêtir l'Idée d'une forme sensible qui, néanmoins, ne serait pas son but à elle-même, mais qui, tout en servant à exprimer l'Idée, demeurerait sujette. L'Idée, à son tour, ne doit point se laisser voir privée des somptueuses simarres des analogies extérieures; car le caractère essentiel de l'art symbolique consiste à ne jamais aller jusqu'à la concentration [conception?] de l'Idée en soi."[52] The result is necessarily obscurity, which is tolerable—indeed, congenial—so long as its source and thrust can be discerned. The symbolists, however, placed excessive reliance on sound and suggestion, following the dubious example of Poe; and focus, accordingly, is very often problematic—even in such brilliant exhibitions of verbal virtuosity as the "Après-midi d'un faune" and the "Cimetière marin." Unusually sensitive to acoustical values, the French have frequently testified to the pitch and cadence of experience; but Mallarmé surely exaggerated the power of verbal music, "L'air ou chant sous le texte, conduisant la divination d'ici là, y applique son motif en fleuron et cul-de-lampe invisibles."[53] He succeeded in subordinating the intelligible to the poetic sense—to employ a distinction made by Jacques Maritain[54]—but at the price of perceptual confusion. And yet obscurity could afford the hermetic secrets of the French symbolists no lasting security,[55] for allegory as explication or interpretation has always fed on obscure relations. Eliot provides an instructive contrast to the French: while cultivating their subtle harmonies and illustrating the most efficient uses of the symbol, he yet respected the allegorical mode[56] and made no apparent effort to prevent

52. Quoted from Guy Michaud, *La doctrine symboliste* (Documents) (Paris, 1947), p. 25.
53. Stéphane Mallarmé, *Oeuvres complètes*, ed. Henri Mondor and G. Jean-Aubry (Paris, 1945), p. 387.
54. Jacques Maritain, *Creative Intuition in Art and Poetry*, Bollingen Series, 35.1 (New York, 1953), p. 259.
55. Anna Balakian, *The Symbolist Movement: A Critical Appraisal* (New York, 1967), p. 164.
56. T. S. Eliot, *Selected Essays, 1917–1932* (New York, 1932), pp. 204 f.

abstractions from surfacing. Perhaps the explanation is that Eliot's poetry verges on allegory in quite obvious ways but at the same time little rewards search for obscure values. Tiresias, the seer of the "Waste Land," achieves an authentic oracular voice not so much by hinting at hermetic secrets as by reiterating what all the world knows too well. While the language is suggestive and often suggestively musical, the symbol of the wasteland is invested by a procession of paradoxes, ironies, and antitheses, that is, by the forms of widespread, if not universal, experience. Since the obscurities of the "Waste Land" are local rather than general and the figured perplexities commonplace, converting the poem to a set of unremarkable cultural propositions serves neither understanding nor aesthetic purposes.

If by some mysterious chance the romantics occasionally recovered the original oracular voice—the voice of Orpheus before poetry entered on what Mallarmé considered "la grande déviation homérique"[57]—they obviously could not resurrect the audience susceptible to magical language and mantic exhibitionism. Romantic theorizing and posturing doubtless created an audience fairly tolerant of the poet in the role of seer or mage, but there is no reason to suppose that the response to the poetry owed a great deal to faith in the poet's transcendent powers. In a whimsical moment Eliot declared, "I myself should like an audience which could neither read nor write";[58] but his success with skeptical intellectuals suggests that education is no real bar to the effects peculiar to poetry. His usual strategy, though often obscured by learned allusiveness, is as simple as—and not so different from—that of the brief Middle English song, "Earth upon Earth," which by means of incantatory repetition, paronomasia, and paradox figures the reciprocal relation of man and common clay. Without occultist

57. See Georges Cattaui, *Orphisme et prophétie chez les poètes français, 1850–1950* (Paris, 1965), p. 111.
58. T. S. Eliot, *The Use of Poetry and the Use of Criticism* (London, 1933), p. 152.

props, Eliot confirmed the basic romantic discovery—the continuing receptivity of mind, even in an age of science, to language which departs radically from logical order and opposes skewed perspectives to simple appearance. In the "Four Ages of Poetry" Thomas Love Peacock could dismiss poetry as an anachronism on the assumption that mind had advanced very nearly to the final Comtean stage, but the romantics proved mind as prone as ever to project irrational patterns on the phenomenal world. Against all probability, they succeeded in engaging the interest of a considerable audience by refiguring a small store of ancient and banal perplexities, such as the coincidence of opposites, unity in diversity, irrecoverable time and eternal recurrence, mutability and discontinuity, permanence and decay. For science these are not real problems and not therefore solvable, but it is doubtful if the prospect of solution affects the perception of poetry which exploits perplexity. Nor should the oracular poems which actually pretend to prophecy be thought exceptions, for poetic prophets are ordinarily cyclical theorists and accordingly project the perverse (and familiar) forms of past events into the future. Far from dissipating the mystery of the unknown, the oracular poet intones the forms of expression which appear to be the forms of experience and thus confirms the reality which unreflecting perception creates. To insist on the primacy of figuration as form is to appear to discount the independent affective value of the Baudelairean symbol and the Jungian archetype as well. If the archetype, which, of course, materializes as symbol, is a recurrent feature of (and, indeed, colors all) experience, it is necessarily commonplace and not demonstrably evocative except as a term in a significant relation. The archetype may be a necessary, but hardly a sufficient, condition of audience response. If figuration as significant relation is the essential instrument of oracular speaking (and perhaps the true measure of art), the romantics succeeded by the same and not so strange means that the *priscus poeta* used to stir the primeval throng.

The romantics confirmed the worst fears of the ancients—and more: for man, if a victim of beguiling speech, appears to cooperate enthusiastically in his own deception. It cannot be that the seers and mages succeeded in restoring the magical power attributed to language before the advent of literacy;[59] more likely, by freeing figuration of obligation to reason they were enabled to enchant man with the crooked perspectives of his own psychic history. To be sure, their achievement sometimes outrages common sense, for expression which eschews logical references cannot in principle be distinguished from hallucination. The poets have been examined repeatedly for symptoms of dissociation—Rimbaud's "dérèglement de tous les sens"—though the consequences for art of this old shamanistic ploy are probably slight.[60] Of signal importance is the circumstance that the romantic audience—to judge from its agreeable response—could be implicated in seeming mental aberrations. There is no occasion to concur in the conjecture offered by T. B. Macaulay in "Milton," "Perhaps no person can be a poet, or can even enjoy poetry, without a certain unsoundness of mind. . . ."; but there is no reason to doubt that much of the time experience runs in the eccentric patterns of the figures. To take a passage from Rilke's *Die Sonette an Orpheus* (Pt. I, No. xii) out of context: "wir leben wahrhaft in Figuren." Not only have the implications of this insight been largely ignored, but romantic poetry has often been denatured through unreflecting interpretation. To lift ideas out of their figured relations and to refer them to metaphysical systems is to change their modality and to expose poetic truths to such analysis as ordinary-language philosophers perform.[61] Yet romantic poetry is perhaps the less problematic and disturbing in consequence of the usual critical transformations, for a world structured by irony and paradox,

59. See J. C. Carothers, "Culture, Psychiatry, and the Written Word," *Psychiatry*, XXII (1959), p. 311.
60. N. K. Chadwick, *Poetry & Prophecy* (Cambridge, 1952), pp. 20, 61.
61. See R. W. Hepburn, "Literary and Logical Analysis," *Philosophical Quarterly*, VIII (1958), pp. 342–56.

synecdoche and metaphor is frighteningly at odds with the world located by science through empirically verifiable identifications and predications. While logical models of the external real are pragmatically superior to the relations described by the figures, figuration may be a better index to the quality of perception and thus of experience. So much accepted, the romantics may be said to have revealed the secrets not of the universe but of the inner reality, and this considerable achievement entailed as much artful contriving as ever the Sophists used.

Chapter IX

The Theoretical
Liabilities of
Literary Criticism

The critical enterprise in the twentieth century—the well-named Age of Analysis—has far surpassed its conceptual legacy and by means of rare exploratory instruments probed the unsuspected recesses of the most redoubtable literary monuments; but the theories supporting the multitudinous analyses appear to be individually defective and mutually invalidating. Clearly, theoretical formulations have not been adequate to practical gains, and I. A. Richards' depreciatory summation of critical concepts promulgated since Aristotle has now scarcely less validity than it possessed nearly half a century ago.[1] Richards was hopeful of bringing order to the "chaos of critical theories"; but his most immediate followers largely rejected his scientific presuppositions, and lately book-length studies have magnified his misconceptions. While Richards and others in the next generation supposed that adequate theory was possible, there is now far more skepticism than confidence—though, oddly, no appreciable alarm. It is an intriguing coincidence that *PMLA*, a monument to unembarrassed historicism and never an organ for literary theorists, should lately have printed an article which, though of considerable speculative interest, contains an almost triumphant dismissal of comprehensive theory: "For we are all now in a position to judge the sterility of efforts to devise a coherent, positive, universally valid theory of literature, of attempts to work out some universal combination good for all times and places by weighing the various critical 'methods': the illusion of Method has come to seem just as abstract and systematic an enterprise—in the bad sense—as the older theories of Beauty

1. I. A. Richards, *Principles of Literary Criticism* (New York, 1947), p. 6. First published 1924.

which it replaced."[2] The author's striking judgment speaks from the record of telling assaults on all the principal critical positions and may well go unchallenged even by theorists with large vested interests. The serious practical considerations aside, the radical notion that literary theory, from whatever mysterious circumstances, must need be flawed aborning has moderate philosophic interest; for it stands to reason that entities possessing numerous properties in common can be associated through warrantable and operational generalizations. To accept the contrary is to commit criticism forever to the free state of disorder, in which assertion and refutation hang in equipoise.

Any work of literary art is evidently a verbal production and inferentially a member of a set with properly defining (i.e., necessary and sufficient) properties. Covering theories are antecedently feasible, and the incontestable fact that none has altogether passed logical inspection suggests the presence of complications from which collectivities are ordinarily free. It is possible that literary objects are conventionally but not essentially related and bear only a family resemblance. Some years ago Morris Weitz invoked Wittgenstein's insight in order to associate plausibly the widely different objects denoted by the term *art*;[3] but when narrowed to literature, the analogy becomes sterile, if not misleading. Granted the proneness of general terms to metaphorical creep and consequent confusion with alien entities, literature yet answers approximately in all its supposed exemplars to rules governing the arts of language. Nor is this necessary condition threatened by grammatical, rhetorical, or logical aberrations, for these are understood, if at all, as purposeful variations from norms. But if incontestable relations are observable among literary works, they yet may not yield such generalizations as criticism profitably uses; theories are simply

2. Fredric Jameson, "Metacommentary," *PMLA*, LXXXVI (1971), p. 10. Cf. Wallace Martin, "The Hermeneutic Circle and the Art of Interpretation," *Comparative Literature*, XXIV (1972), p. 117.
3. Morris Weitz, "The Role of Theory in Aesthetics," *Journal of Aesthetics and Art Criticism*, XV (1956–57), pp. 30 f.

vacuous unless conferring special significance on observation, which is substantially to say, unless appearing to entail or at least to sanction productive methods of analysis. The likeliest obstacle to the formulation of general theory, however, is the unwillingness of critics to accept in principle limitations on the authority of literature and their insistence that theory incorporate metaphysical assumptions, which, if neither confirmable nor refutable, are endlessly disputable. These preconditions considered, it is scarcely surprising that theory cannot define its object or dictate truly objective observational procedures but only provide pretexts for tendentious construing.

1   Considered simply as verbal production of a distinctive kind, literature poses for theory formidable, though probably not insuperable, difficulties; considered as institutionalized discourse, it loses definable shape and melts into the tormented whirl of conflicting and changing cultural sympathies. It is in the latter condition that literature—more particularly poetry—has been maintained at least since the Homeric epics, and in the latter condition that for all their radical perceptions and principled dissensions modern critics have been content—if not determined—to leave it. The institutional character of literature accepted, it appears to follow that theory can leave this circumstance out of account only at the risk of falsifying the collectivity. But if theory assumes the burden of providing for—that is, of incorporating at face value—such unlikely assumptions as institutions unavoidably embody, it must need define literature with metaphysical predicates and leave the procedures of analysis to the shaping force of premeditated conclusions. Institutions of whatever kind are self-justifying and self-aggrandizing; definitional and valuational propositions issued from within their confines are not disinterested but persuasive and covertly apologetic. Cultural phenomena, in contrast to natural, doubtless cannot be adequately understood outside the ideological climate of their occurrence, but literary theory is not bound by

this self-evident truth to accommodate the values and relations assumed by the institution. This would be the case only if literature were constituted by the institution. The converse is possibly true, though this is not a circumstance which strict literary theory can take into account. It may be possible to devise a defensible theory of literature and of the institution as well, though not a theory comprehending both which leaves the former sufficiently distinct for methodical observation. This is simply to deny that bifocal theories are feasible.

The institution of literature is a supervening cultural fiction propagated in defenses from Aristotle's to Allen Tate's and sustained in principle by wide (and largely uncritical) acceptance; it is not presupposed by individual works or necessary to their understanding. The institution varies considerably from critic to critic with respect to dimensions and emphases and periodically shifts its axes at considerable expense to existing criticism. It is not a limiting concept which provides for the logical and modest subsumption of exemplars but one which allows literature to mingle with and often to be absorbed by domains of reputedly systematic knowledge. When implicated evidentially with institutional values, literature becomes exceedingly ambiguous and unamenable to theory of any aesthetic kind. So much conceded, the institution of literature can be regarded only as an unnecessary and altogether troublesome set of assumptions which frustrates theorizing and leaves applied criticism with uncertain grounds. Although the institution creates more problems than it solves, its preservation can hardly be a historical accident. Literature is not purposeful in the usual sense of the word and therefore not readily justifiable; its ends are either obscure or possibly in didactic instances better served by logical modes of expression. Its integrity and relevance can be called in question and on the basis of selected specimens seriously shaken. Guardians of the institution have always been able to locate adversaries—traditionally the strict moralists but more recently those who would minimize the claims of literature to serious attention and those who would burden it with intolerable obligations. Polemical purposes doubtless require that literature be defined honorifically and invested with transcendent values, although the effect is probably to quieten rather than to convert the doubters. That literature is a significant human production not even philistines can deny, but they are not logically compelled by such reasons as institutional defenders give to grant it superior claims on human interest.[4] To the confusion of criticism, the properties of literature which defenses present as values are not defining but at most only sometimes accompanying and, accordingly, not the immediate objects of critical observation. The institution is constituted by such problematic values as truth, goodness, and beauty, which literature presumably embodies collectively; but none of these, considered as properties, can be unconditionally predicated of the individual work. Moreover, the incontestable properties which analysis in principle observes never entail the excellences on which the institution counts.

While literature may be collectively good, individual works are not equally good; and some, lacking either verbal felicity or redeeming social virtue, are supposedly unworthy of critical attention. The metaphysical predicates with which institutional defenders assail detractors are obviously useless for separating the fit from the unfit exemplars and for sorting the approved residue hierarchically. Although ranking has been accomplished after a fashion by history, the historical process as affecting literary value is constituted by individual judgments, which remain to be explained and validated. Critics characteristically give reasons for their preferences, and these can be generalized so as to yield criteria. Serious questions remain, however, relating both to the actual generality of proposed criteria and to the evidence adduced to satisfy them; and indeed it has been denied that any identifiable properties

4. Critics are inclined to approve the spirit of defenses even when rejecting the specific claims. See Benedetto Croce, *The Defence of Poetry: Variations on the Theme of Shelley*, trans. E. F. Carritt (Oxford, 1933).

entail value judgments.[5] Literary criteria are usually unquantifiable; more importantly, they are usually ambiguous and cannot be otherwise so long as literature is unidentified save as a collectivity of metaphysical entities. No determinate conclusions can be expected in any case from criteria (e.g., unity, complexity, intensity) which sometimes apply indifferently to the creative process, to the verbal object, and to audience reception and which can be satisfied only through subtle (and dubious) analytical strategies. Yet the flexibility of criteria, though ultimately a source of contradiction, suits the general thrust of analysis, which usually is to make evident further excellences of literature already admitted, by whatever curious consensus, to the institutional canon. The critical attitude dictated by the institution is encomiastic, and conformably the coordinates defining the locus of analysis tend to be properties which can be represented as satisfying standards of excellence. While no one would deny that the most useful end of analysis is discovery and not the confirmation of foregone conclusions, criticism is nonetheless favorably disposed toward its subject even to the point of prejudice. Interpreted as interest in verbal performance, value poses a possibly manageable problem; implicated with the institution of literature, the problem of value is nothing theoretically solvable and probably not a genuine problem at all.[6]

Institutions exist to support values (and vested interests) against real or imagined detraction and are defined in some measure by what they oppose. The most theoretically sophisticated opposition to the claims of literary apologists has been provided since the Socratic strictures by exact science and analytical philosophy, although literature has seldom been the immediate concern of either. The assumptions of eighteenth-century rationalism appeared to exclude literature from the domains of reliable knowledge

5. See H. Morris-Jones, "The Logic of Criticism," *Monist,* L (1966), p. 219; and Morris Weitz, *Hamlet and the Philosophy of Literary Criticism* (Chicago and London, 1964), p. 274.

6. See A. J. Ayer, *Language, Truth and Logic* (2d ed.; New York, [1957]), p. 50.

and the severe verification rules of modern science to minimize
the consequences of inspiration and revelation. While the arrogant
certainty of science has considerably abated, apologists are yet
capable of assertions of the immoderate kind which provoked poets
and theologians in the last century. Ernest Nagel allows "no antecedent limits" on the "power of scientific reason to acquire theoretical mastery over natural and social processes" and stigmatizes
demurrals without exception: "Every doctrine which pretends to
set such limits contains within itself the seeds of intolerance and
repression."[7] The uses of sophistic duly noted, it is abundantly
evident that institutional claims, though doubtless fortifying true
believers, may have the unfortunate effect of creating hostile and
largely artificial barriers between areas of human interest and,
accordingly, of precluding cooperation. Obsessed with the fiction
of the mechanical model and convinced of its universal truth,
classical scientists overreached themselves, and representatives of
religion and the arts reacted predictably.[8] It is nonetheless a historical error and one symptomatic of the poverty of theory that
defenses of literature should have staked a great deal on knowledge;
for knowledge, at least incontestably, is knowledge of objective
reality, which science defines to the satisfaction of the rational
world and not surprisingly masters. Literary theorists are now
perfectly aware of the unfortunate consequences of thrusting
poets and novelists into the domains of systematic knowledge, and
in fact very little applied criticism has exposed them of late to
competition with scientists and philosophers. While the cognitive
problem as usually stated no longer seems of much theoretical
interest, the relation of criticism to science has been a chronic
perplexity since Richards set out to reorder theory along psychological lines. The presumption of science to "explain" human

7. Ernest Nagel, *Sovereign Reason and Other Studies in the Philosophy of Science* (Glencoe, Ill., 1954), p. 308.
8. Werner Heisenberg, *Philosophic Problems of Nuclear Science*, trans. F. C. Hayes (New York, 1952), pp. 22 f.

enterprises makes no exception of literature, and the critic is forced either to deny its relevance for his work or to accept the cooperation of an institution which appears to threaten his own.

Whatever the logical and ethical objections, the penetration of science into literary study has been extensive; and a large fraction of the history of modern criticism is occupied with approaches based more or less competently on psychology, sociology, and cultural anthropology. If none of these withstands theoretical scrutiny, all survive in critical practice without noticeable embarrassment. The assumptions and methods of the social studies have on the whole produced such crude and partial results that contextualists have been strengthened in their general disposition to decline the services of science, but in truth the crucial issues raised for literature and criticism by science as such lose nothing of significance from absurdities committed in the name of disciplines which lack secure theoretical foundations. Scientific methodology simply underscores the circumstance that the determination of the verbal object, the logic of analysis, and the limits of inference pose for criticism questions which have not been decisively answered. Doubtless criticism cannot be a science in the strict sense of the word, although it seems no more liable to failure than some noisy pretenders. Whether it is logically affected by the example of the physical sciences, together with the caveats of analytical philosophy, has been answered by implication in the negative; but when occasionally confronted, the question has proved an embarrassment and a temptation to equivocation. Undertaking to oppose the stultifying limitations imposed on aesthetics by linguistic (philosophical) analysts, M. H. Abrams manages at one and the same time to locate criticism in the neighborhood of the more liberal conceptions of science and to acknowledge how slackly theory regulates practice: "A valid poetic theory is empirical in that it begins and ends in an appeal to the facts of existing poems, but it is not a science, like a physical science; it is an enterprise of discovery, or what Coleridge called 'a speculative instrument.' Its statements are not to be judged by their empirical verifiability out of context, but by their function as stages in the total process of illuminating the qualities and structure of diverse poems. The definitions from which most theorists set out . . . in practice have served as an indispensable heuristic device for blocking out an area of investigation and establishing a point of vantage; they have functioned also as a critical premise, or elected starting point for reasoning about poetry and for developing a coherent set of terms and categories to be used in classifying, describing, and appraising particular poems."[9]

If literary theory is necessarily tentative in character, it is not exceptionally so; science long ago abandoned the illusory goal of complete certainty and recognized theories simply as logical constructs which, though organizing experience conveniently, could never be entirely verified by experience. Dogmatists doubtless survive in science and no less in criticism, but the philosophic liberality displayed by Richard von Mises characterizes the modern attitude: "I am prepared to concede without further argument that all the theoretical constructions, including geometry, which are used in the various branches of physics are only imperfect instruments to enable the world of empirical fact to be reconstructed in our minds."[10] Scientists, moreover, are perfectly aware of the pervasive influence of belief and expectation on observation.[11] But in principle at least, science has detached the pursuit of knowledge from ideology, that is, from political, social, and religious philosophies which can thoroughly confuse what is with what ought to be and may appeal to sentiment as much as to reason.[12] While the complexities of literature may preclude rigorous analytical methods,

9. "Poetry, Theories of," *Encyclopedia of Poetry and Poetics*, ed. Alex Preminger *et al.* (Princeton, 1965), p. 648.

10. Richard von Mises, *Probability, Statistics and Truth*, trans. J. Neyman, D. Scholl, and E. Rabinowitsch (2d ed.; London, 1957), p. 8.

11. See C. R. Kordig, "The Theory-Ladenness of Observation," *Review of Metaphysics*, XXIV (1970–71), pp. 448–81.

12. See H. G. Nutini, "The Ideological Bases of Lévi-Strauss's Structuralism," *American Anthropologist*, LXXIII (1971), p. 539.

criticism is not thereby exempted from the canons of logic or spared
the necessity of using theoretical language with some degree of
precision. To recommend definitions of literature as heuristic
fictions valuable for exposing productive angles of vision is to slight
the circumstance that they are usually not defining but implicating;
the predicates are vague concepts which ultimately bespeak views
of man and the world and leave unacknowledged the primary and
altogether perplexing datum of language. Old and new definitions
of literature—as imitation, moral suasion, expression, communication, social behavior, displaced mythology—can never have been
valuable as limiting concepts but only as propositions congenial to
supervening cultural theories. As such, they have not been true
warrants for methodical observation but, rather, dubious excuses for
accommodating literature to various notions of the contemporary
real. If analytical criticism has surpassed rank impressionism, the
gains have been owing more to improved reading than to improved
theory; for theory has most evidently provided a pretext rather than
a regulative principle. In truth, the function of theory has usually
been to determine literature as evidence or expression in relation to
ideology and in some instances to provide such barriers to alien
modes of inquiry as enable the critic to assume a priestly role and
to mediate the mysteries of the literary imagination without serious
competition.

2   Separating the observation of literature from its assumed
values and assumed implications for other intellectual domains,
although logically justifiable, entails considerable limitation on its
authority and on the liberties of criticism. Examined from without
the institution, literature loses its pretentious surrogate role, which
sometimes infringes even systematic knowledge; and criticism is
left with an unsorted bag of undetermined verbal objects, about
which very little of significance can be asserted with sufficient
reason. When deprived of determining references, literature is to
all appearances autonomous and autotelic. This condition, postu-

lated by contextualists, assuredly frees literature from the clutch of
irrelevant considerations and assuredly raises the question whether
aesthetic entities can be logically determined for the purposes of
analysis. Thus far, attempts to determine form and content in
meaningful relations at the empirical level, that is, in the case of
the individual work, have scarcely escaped subjectivity and covert
appeals to institutional values. Whatever the problem of applied
criticism, the supposed work of literary art is, if coherent, a verbal
system and further a relational sketch, hypothetical in that it conjectures something of an imaginable state of being but not in that
it is either verifiable or falsifiable by acceptable procedures. Since
the writer's formulation of experience is untestable (and inarguable), the literary work can be described only as quasi-hypothetical;
but in principle at least it could be a significant hypothesis just as
well as a mere descriptive generalization of limited experience.
While literature, as compared with scientific writing, usually falls
on a relatively low level of abstractness, it may nonetheless reflect
the average, the typical, the general; and this possibility has long
been acknowledged in the concept of the concrete universal. Yet
universality, once invoked as a value criterion, can be no more than
an assumption and cannot therefore be supposed to verify a literary
construct. The relation of literature to the real may be very narrow
—as an *ad hoc* hypothesis—or very broad, but it is always problematic. If nothing ascertainable or demonstrably crucial for the quality
of perception, truth status yet remains an unspoken concern for
criticism; and some degree of general truth is at least an implicit
claim of most thematic expositions. As a verification strategy,
however, the claim for generality shifts literature onto contestable
grounds and envelops it in the confusion of mere opinion about
abstractions. While appearing to overcome indeterminacy, verification tends to convert literature to ideology and to limit its characteristic semantic potentiality.

Verification presupposes understanding, but the language of
literature is so far equivocal as often to leave in doubt what is to be

verified. Although criticism proceeds, perhaps necessarily, on the assumption that semantic waver can be overcome, there are in fact no better tests for determining the sense of a literary construct than for determining its relation to the real. While freely admitting that literary language is not logical, critics have paused, quite properly, before the conclusion that it is illogical. Indeed, it is characteristically paralogical, that is, figurative, with respect to the part and even to the whole, and therefore in contrast to scientific discourse, which, it is supposed not always correctly, uses univocal identification and predication. If the mode of expression leaves meaning in doubt, there can be no doubt that literature somehow means; and critics have claimed as their special competence the resolution of even the most stubborn ambiguities. Their conclusions, however, are often at variance and sufficiently so as to raise the question whether intuition does not in fact rule methodology. If a decisive role is denied to intuition, discovering meaning must be simply a rational procedure which at least roughly obeys the canons of logic; and indeed modern critics generally create the impression that their inferences follow legitimately from linguistic data. At the same time, they are inclined to deny that literature is liable to such methods as logicians use either to determine meaning or to assess it for logicality and factuality. Nonetheless, meaning, taken as truth statement, can be neither stated nor tested by the logician or the critic until translated into standard form. While the same thought may be for some purposes variously expressible, reductive conversion violates the paralogical order and unavoidably the writer's model of experience. Logically questionable and, to judge from the dissimilar results, quite unreliable, conversion in various subtle forms of paraphrase and interpretation is widely practiced, though over the protests of contextualists. If "a logician cannot do justice to the infinite subtlety of language,"[13] as R. M. Hare readily concedes, the critic, using ordinary analytical procedures in the pursuit of meaning, cannot pretend to cope much more successfully with

13. R. M. Hare, *The Language of Morals* (Oxford, 1952), p. 126.

the indirections of literary language. In any case, the formulation of meaning for the purposes of criticism entails the substitution of hypothetical statements of a logical order for a paralogical construct, although criticism has no theory of equivalences to warrant substitutions of any sort.

This theoretical sketch permits the conclusion that the poet or novelist as a maker of constructs occupies the same position in the somewhat mysterious realm denoted by literature as the theorist in science and the critic's pursuit of meaning, beset with difficulties enough, may also be mistaken in principle. It may be supposed that the critic, although often disavowing rigorous methods, is in fact the counterpart of the scientist who applies and verifies existing theory, and to an extent perhaps largely unsuspected and wholly unjustified this may indeed be the case. While the scientist invokes theory to explain the regularities of phenomenal behavior, the critic invokes theory to rationalize his observation of what is actually theory, though of uncertain force. The critical exposition describes, explains, and interprets what is, if only sketchily, already description, explanation, and interpretation. Embarked unavoidably on infinite regress, the critic envelops the literary work with theoretical overlays of an increasingly abstract character; but his hypotheses succeed merely in reformulating at an abstract level the complex of experience to which only the writer's construct testifies. Literature is not a complete account but rather a model of experience, which, like the scientific model, sieves sense-impressions in conformity with formal perspectives. Though originating in experience, it cannot be confirmed empirically. The literary construct, like the scientific theory,[14] surpasses the author's experience and even understanding and indeed may teach him what he means without in the least exhausting its potentiality for other meanings. Critics have traditionally proceeded on the assumption that the author's meaning is recoverable, but what is actually re-

14. See Michael Polanyi, *Personal Knowledge: Towards a Post-Critical Philosophy* (Chicago, 1958), pp. 43–48.

coverable is only one or another location in the semantic spectrum
which a literary model in theory describes. The paralogical order
of literary language incorporates in the writer's construct irremediable semantic free-play and therewith irremediable indeterminacy.
As ascribed to literature, objective meaning can be only an illusion;
and analysis is perhaps to a considerable extent a procedure to
rationalize the discovery of what the critic has himself supplied.
By its very diverse conclusions criticism testifies to the circumstance
that meaning is not a content but a potentiality and by the same
token to the capacity of literary language for organizing perception
in eternally interesting *Gestalten*; but it has no reliable methods
to ascertain the extensional meaning and thus the theoretical scope
of even the simplest poem.

3   The concept of the unverifiable verbal construct obviously
deprives so-called extrinsic criticisms of reliable referential data
and thus of competence for genetic explications; whether formalist
methods, which on principle occasion a minimum of disturbance
to the formal order of literature, are less vulnerable to logical
objections remains in question. Although rather dissimilar with
respect to their analytical techniques, contextualists and structuralists agree in undertaking to make evident a necessary relation of
part to whole, of formal properties to significance, presumably
without recourse to doubtful a priori assumptions. The literary
work, it is supposed, consists of internal relations which somehow
define and in some curious fashion are upheld by a central organizing principle, essence, or meaning, which becomes evident only
after methodical observation—and, necessarily, interpretation. The
concept of the inviolable organic whole appears to confer self-
sufficiency on the literary work and to guarantee the coherence and
interdependency of parts; but the whole and the part are alike
abstractions, which can seldom be incontestably confirmed in
experience. Part-whole analysis partitions the verbal conglomerate
and orders the parts after a variety of reputedly valid principles,

though, in truth, without overcoming arbitrariness. Whether acoustical, grammatical, or semantic, the part is not, with rare exceptions, definable as an irreducible and at the same time significant property; nor is the putative part invariably indispensable, as assumed, to the whole. In all probability, perception accomplishes the unification of the literary work at considerable expense to the parts, in which event the empirical whole is not greater but indeed less than the sum of the available parts. To argue the contrary is to assume that nothing escapes perception, though selection is the actual price of perception. Holism is enormously persuasive simply because it agrees with experience, for perception has no power to disorganize and perhaps seldom fails to impose unity upon verbal objects. Methodical observation of the supposed parts, however, never entails certain conclusions about the theoretical whole. The critic's structuration has only the status of an unverifiable hypothesis about a model of experience.

The ostensible concern of formalists is to scan the parts of a literary work in order to establish its relational system and thus confirm the integrity of the whole; their paramount concern, however, is to locate a central significance, which may be supposed to exist in consequence of formal relations and at the same time to constitute an organizing principle. The inevitable claim for unity is much less a claim for formal excellence than for the discovery of a center which rationalizes the partitions and allocations of analysis. Granted that a verbal structure without meaning is implausible and in any case as abstract as a mathematical formulation, it is yet not evident that the parts, singly or collectively, attest determinately to meaning in either its syntactic or semantic dimension.[15] This could be the case only if literary language manifested relation and reference unambiguously. The thin intuitional warrant for proceeding from part to center on the basis of linguistic evidence was embarrassingly disclosed some years ago by Leo

15. On this discrimination, see F. E. Sparshott, *The Concept of Criticism* (Oxford, 1967), p. 130.

Spitzer: "Any one outward feature, when sufficiently followed up to the center, must yield us insight into the artistic whole, whose unity will thus have been respected. The choice of the particular phenomenon, then, would appear to be of secondary importance: any single one must, according to my ideology, give final results."[16] Spitzer was perfectly aware of the risks of the hermeneutic circle but not apparently of a disastrous implication of his reasoning—that the parts, each a microcosm, are not interdependent but mutually dispensable. More recent practitioners of *stylistique* have diminished confidence in the explanatory power of linguistic data;[17] and indeed it may properly be doubted that "final results" in the sense of central significance are logically available to linguistic analysis—and for the simple reason that no general laws have been forthcoming which correlate sense with such data as linguistics can rigorously describe.[18] The problem of meaning for formalism, whether grounded in phonology and grammar or in rhetoric, is further complicated by the circumstance that part-whole analysis is obligated to complete description, which, even if possible, could only be obfuscating. In practice, of course, analysis is always selected and selective of features judged significant for the center; but selection implies alternatives, and the very

16. Leo Spitzer, *Linguistics and Literary History* (Princeton, 1948), p. 42.
17. See Charles Bruneau, "La stylistique," *Romance Philology*, V (1951–52), pp. 11–13; and A. G. Juilland's review of Bruneau's *L'époque réaliste; première partie: Fin du romantisme et Parnasse* (Paris, 1953), in *Language*, XXX (1954), pp. 321–23.
18. The pretensions of linguists to provide adequate accounts of literary productions have not been made good, and their disposition has become increasingly to accept a corroborating (and thus subordinate) role for linguistics in criticism. See René Wellek's "Closing Statement," ed. T. A. Sebeok, *Style in Language* (New York and London, 1960), pp. 410 f; F. W. Bateson, "Linguistics and Literary Criticism," ed. Peter Demetz et al., *The Disciplines of Criticism* (New Haven and London, 1968), pp. 3–16; Nicolas Ruwet, "Linguistics and Poetics," ed. Richard Macksey and Eugenio Donato, *The Languages of Criticism and the Sciences of Man: The Structuralist Controversy* (Baltimore and London, 1970), pp. 296–304; Seymour Chatman and S. R. Levin, "Linguistics and Poetics," Preminger's *Encyclopedia of Poetry and Poetics*, p. 451; and Roger Fowler, *The Languages of Literature: Some Linguistic Contributions to Criticism* (New York, 1971), pp. 35–40.

different appraisals which aesthetic objects permit underscore
the hard fact that there are no tests for discriminating features
which are decisive for meaning from those which are merely
incidental.

Structuralisme, the most pretentious (and variable) formalism
of all, proposes to overcome the problematic observing subject by
positing the objective existence of systematic totalities which in-
form man and nature and describe the very shape of reality.[19]
While effectively limiting the resourcefulness of perception, this
hypothesis requires the widely respected and altogether unverified
assumption promulgated by Claude Lévi-Strauss, that the "unconscious activity of the mind consists in imposing forms upon
contents" and that these forms are "fundamentally the same for
all minds."[20] In theory self-regulating and thus endlessly trans-
formable, structure in whatever phenomenal complex remains
intact and fully accessible to systematic observation.[21] To judge
from Roman Jakobson's presuppositions, as elaborated by Michael
Riffaterre, literature consists in levels of articulated parts, which,
if not equally expressive, are mutually elucidating and confirming
and, as far as can be determined, equally registered in perception:
"Which is to say that the recurrence of equivalent forms, *parallelism*, is the basic relationship underlying poetry. Of course, since
language is a system made up of several levels superimposed one
on top of the other (phonetic, phonological, syntactical, semantic,
etc.), parallelism manifests itself on any level: so then, a poem is
a verbal sequence wherein the same relations between constituents
are repeated at various levels and the same story is told in several
ways at the same time and at several times in the same way."[22]

19. Maurice Corvez, *Les Structuralistes* (Paris, 1969), p. 11.
20. Claude Lévi-Strauss, *Structural Anthropology*, trans. Claire Jacobson
and B. G. Shoepf (New York and London, 1963), p. 21.
21. Jean Piaget, *Le Structuralisme* (3d ed.; Paris, 1968), p. 7.
22. Michael Riffaterre, "Describing Poetic Structures: Two Approaches to
Baudelaire's *Les Chats*," *Yale French Studies* (Structuralism Issue), Nos. 36, 37
(Oct., 1966), p. 201.

Riffaterre has inadvertently accomplished the *reductio ad absurdum* of the familiar formalist claim that meaning proceeds from all parts of a literary work and inadvertently granted that the various levels, since reiterative, are mutually dispensable. Quite as vulnerable is the assumption, pervasive in so-called linguistic criticism, that, at least in principle, description of linguistic properties can locate meaning, though, in truth, no sketch of such relations as linguists observe entails semantic conclusions. *Structuralisme*, it is apparent, arrests the free-play of the center with a rigid determinism, theoretically excluding the vagaries of perception from consideration with the assumption of universally shared and altogether unavoidable conceptual schemes.[23] In depriving observation of choice, structuralists appear to neutralize Maurice Merleau-Ponty's troublesome insistence on the liberties of the viewing subject: "On répète que les sons et les phonèmes ne veulent rien dire par eux-mêmes et que notre conscience ne peut trouver dans le langage que ce qu'elle y a mis";[24] but the widely dissimilar results of analysis regularly contradict the notion of the helpless observer. Unconfirmed in experience and unsupported by general laws, structuralism as represented, particularly in some sectors of the French "nouvelle critique," is properly describable not as a warrantable methodology but as "une sorte de dogmatisme sans fondement véritable."[25] It is nonetheless instructive as an ambitious attempt, buttressed by existentialism and phenomenology, Saussure and Lévi-Strauss, to overcome the indeterminacy of liter-

23. Literary structures, when identified, turn out to be neither fine-grained nor particularly novel discriminations—e.g., logical or causal order, temporal order, spatial order. Moreover, structural analysis, though often illuminating with respect to linguistic and interpersonal relations, seems not to entail, or to be entailed by, the primordial structures, which in theory determine the literary object and expose the characterizing properties of literary discourse. See Tzvetan Todorov, "Poétique," in Oswald Ducrot et al., *Qu'est-ce que le structuralisme?* (Paris, 1968), pp. 101-102, 123–32.

24. Maurice Merleau-Ponty, *Phénoménologie de la perception* (4th ed.; Paris, 1945), p. 445.

25. Corvez, *op. cit.*, p. 110.

ature on formal grounds and to expose what is certainly signified as a necessary consequence of structuration.

Even if structures were empirically verifiable and precisely describable, the center, considered as semantic focus and organizing principle, would remain problematic; for it is not, in truth, entailed by or strictly answerable to formal relations. While structure without center is inconceivable, it does not follow that either precisely defines the other. Inherent in formalism, the problem of the center can hardly arise so long as literature is determined as expression or effect of external forces; the central significance of a work so located is simply a function of its references. The exclusion of external determining references, logically justifiable and necessary to preserve the aesthetic integrity of literature, forces formalist critics to argue that theoretically meaning is a consequence of and an entity inseparable from structure or to accept the severe alternative that the literary work is an indeterminate verbal construct which leaves meaning to vary unpredictably with observation. The antinomy created by suppression of the referential dimension of meaning may be supposed resolved by a corollary of holism, that meaning proceeds from all parts of a verbal whole; but this somewhat mysterious accounting for meaning merely compounds the difficulties of the part-whole concept. To spread meaning through all the parts is in some sense to deny the center, at least as a regulative constant. If the center is held to be an entity testified to by structure but not implicated in it, then the location of the center within the verbal system is in doubt. With the dilemmas of *structuralisme* in mind, Jacques Derrida has wonderfully complicated the notion of the center, which in his usage is somewhat broader and less precise than meaning: "Thus it has always been thought that the center, which is by definition unique, constituted that very thing within a structure which governs the structure, while escaping structurality. This is why classical thought concerning structure could say that the center is, paradoxically, *within* the structure and *outside* it. The center is at the center of the totality, and yet, since the center does not belong to the totality . . . the totality *has its center elsewhere*. The center is not the center. The concept of centered structure—although it represents coherence itself, the condition of the epistèmè as philosophy or science—is contradictorily coherent. And, as always, coherence in contradiction expresses the force of a desire."[26] Without the presumption of the center, analysis could only be indecisive, if not blind; with the presumption of the center, analysis is committed to limiting semantic free-play and thus to deforming its object. Analysis of literature seems feasible only on the presumption of determinate meaning; but in arresting the flux of literary experience, analysis tends to lose meaning in gaining it. Again, Derrida has commented perceptively: "*Comprendre* la structure d'un devenir, la forme d'une force, c'est perdre le sens en le gagnant. Le sens du devenir et de la force, dans leur pure et propre qualité, c'est le repos du commencement et de la fin, le paix d'un spectacle, horizon ou visage. En ce repos et en cette paix, la qualité du devenir et de la force est offusquée par le sens même."[27]

Parts and wholes and centers, to exist in theory, exist in consequence of formal principles, which is to say no more than that form is a necessary condition of existence—and, it should be added, of perception. While never involving themselves deeply with the perplexities of form or with the problem of the observer, formalists have pretended to comprehend literary relational systems with lawlike propositions about unity in variety, reconciliation of opposites, and binary oppositions. Perhaps for the reason that literature so often responds persuasively to these models, which, of course, belong to organic contextualism and structuralism, practicing critics have tended to assume their objective reality and literal truth,

26. Jacques Derrida, "Structure, Sign, and Play in the Discourse of the Human Sciences," ed. Richard Macksey and Eugenio Donato, *The Languages of Criticism and the Sciences of Man: The Structuralist Controversy* (Baltimore and London, 1970), p. 248.

27. Jacques Derrida, *L'Écriture et la différence* (Paris, 1967), pp. 44 f.

although they are in fact analogies of doubtful generality and authority.[28] Theorists have long recognized the metaphorical character of Coleridge's exposition of organic form and are unlikely to overlook the geometrical metaphor upon which Roman Jakobson has hinged his structuralist model of linguistic distribution: "*The poetic function projects the principle of equivalence from the axis of selection into the axis of combination.* Equivalence is promoted to the constitutive device of the sequence."[29] Whether scientific or literary, models are irremediably metaphoric;[30] and critics need suffer no embarrassment on this score. It is a circumstance of considerable interest, however, that the language of criticism as metalanguage implicated with metaphor should be deemed appropriate to mediate language already situated in the paralogical mode, for it is not evident that metaphor has the power either to describe or to explain metaphor. The impression is often created that the organic model possesses very great generality and thus constitutes a fair approximation of the relational system of any literary work, though this could be the case only if literature were in fact limited to the formal perspectives, notably irony and paradox, for which organicism provides an adequate account. While in science the function of analogy is presumably to illuminate and not to create concepts,[31] the critic's metaphor as a formal construct laid over a formal construct necessarily reformulates and to some extent cre-

28. For the history—and liabilities—of organicism in literature and science, see James Benziger, "Organic Unity: Leibniz to Coleridge," *PMLA*, LXVI (1951), pp. 24–48; and D. C. Phillips, "Organicism in the Late Nineteenth and Early Twentieth Centuries," *Journal of the History of Ideas*, XXXI (1970), pp. 413–32. See also R. J. Shoeck, "Mathematics and Languages of Literary Criticism," *Journal of Aesthetics and Art Criticism*, XXVI (1967–68), pp. 367–69, on the abuses of the organic metaphor.

29. Roman Jakobson, "Closing Statement: Linguistics and Poetics," ed. T. A. Sebeok, *Style in Language* (New York and London, 1960), p. 358.

30. See Owen Barfield, *Poetic Diction: A Study in Meaning* (new ed.; New York, 1952), p. 135; and Douglas Berggren, "The Use and Abuse of Metaphor," *Review of Metaphysics*, XVI (1962–63), pp. 237–58; XVI (1962–63), pp. 450–72.

31. J. E. Schlanger, "Metaphor and Invention," *Diogenes*, No. 69 (Spring, 1970), p. 24.

ates—and with a degree of indeterminacy commensurate with the theoretical waver of the literary object. A desperate expedient, the spatial metaphor affords a means for arresting the flux of the literary continuum and for determining form and meaning in plausible relationships; but it has no warrant in perception and in theory falsifies what it purports to master. Unfortunately for the logic of the case, analysis cannot easily accommodate the propositions that formal principles are plural beyond provable limit, varying with the literary work and the observer, and that they do not entail conclusions of any narrow sort.

Yet to discount formalism in its several versions as a congeries of false assumptions and justified pretensions is to slight its very considerable usefulness as a loose discipline for observation and as the matrix of nice discriminations and sometimes brilliant insights. Theory is never immaculate and perhaps never wholly adequate to understanding. Redrawn and refined, formalism in all probability can cope with the indeterminate verbal construct, though not so far as to overcome semantic waver. To seek to determine meaning precisely is to surpass the literary object and to expose it to the deforming force of ideological considerations. The much-reprehended extrinsic approaches can accomplish as much and without the pretense of rigor and objectivity. To be sure, formalists are privileged—indeed, obligated—to conjecture the semantic spectrum and thus the range of implication of a literary work, but to decide in favor of one or another location of meaning is to extend formalist theory beyond its capability. Yet uncertainty is apparently intolerable to the critical temper, for the seeming aim of perhaps most analysis is to shatter the mystery of the artist's contriving and to fix its final significance in a system of belief which presumably has explanatory power. That literature is implicated with social, political, and religious thought seems inarguable, but to say precisely how exceeds all theoretical warrants and risks ideological bias. Nonetheless, theory which infringes the liberties of construing cannot be entirely agreeable. Criticism, like the *sciences humaines*, has always been value-bound, with the consequence that theory has been admired for its compatibility with specific cultural attitudes as well as for its claims to validity. Whatever it may prohibit in principle, *structuralisme* in practice falls into subjectivity and, moreover, in seizing the "entire coherence" of a work admits into consideration social and political factors of doubtful relevance.[32] More circumspect in practice, the leading American formalism, contextualism, has been supposed by its most distinguished advocates, W. K. Wimsatt and Cleanth Brooks, to possess a significant correspondence with dogmatic religion: "It appears to us, however, relevant . . . at least to confess an opinion that the kind of literary theory which seems to us to emerge the most plausibly from the long history of the debates is far more difficult to orient within any of the Platonic or Gnostic ideal world views, or within the Manichaean full dualism and strife of principles, than precisely within the vision of suffering, the optimism, the mystery which are embraced in the religious dogma of the Incarnation."[33] While offered as opinion, this rather surprising (and irrelevant) statement suggests apology and assuredly invites comparison with a later defense of Wimsatt's following on an adverse appraisal of *structuralisme*: "I report in conclusion my persisting, perhaps paradoxical, but I think not perverse, conviction that the critic who wishes to retain his humanism and his identity as a literary critic will have to persevere in his allegiance to the party of Coleridge and Croce."[34] These recommendations for theory are presumably not supposed to outweigh validity. But whatever the case, their introduction betrays a widespread and apparently incorrigible tendency among critics to draw into con-

32. See Serge Doubrovsky, *Pourquoi la nouvelle critique* ([Paris], 1966), pp. 71 f.
33. W. K. Wimsatt and Cleanth Brooks, *Literary Criticism: A Short History* (New York, 1957), p. 746.
34. W. K. Wimsatt, "Battering the Object: The Ontological Approach," *Stratford-upon-Avon Studies*, No. 12 (1970), p. 81.

sideration the consequences of literary theory for larger cultural matters. If burdened with ideological responsibility, theory can only be vulnerable to logical scrutiny and observation open to the charge of bias.

Since the allegorization of Homer in the sixth century B.C. there has been evident in perhaps every large interval of Western culture a disposition to reformulate in abstract (and agreeable) terms the monuments of the literary legacy. Reinterpretation in modern times has usually occurred on the pretext of improved historical understanding, and assuredly historicism has exposed many an absurd assumption; but the new view of the old work is likely to be in considerable part a preference reflecting the tensions of the new times. Thus Shakespeare, whose Christianity seems not to have been of contemporary concern, appears doomed to be unbaptized and rebaptized in many a strange eddy by scholarship warmed in the heat of ideological dispute. Doubtless every period will conserve the achievements of the past, though in and on its own terms, which will vary with contending parties; and theory, though not of a strict literary kind, will never be lacking to support personal interest. What is irremediable in humanity is not to be censured but rather taken into account. The practical understanding of literature is finally an accomplishment of intuition, and intuition varies necessarily with its conceptual freight and with the formal perspectives permitted by the literary object. Observation seeks a good *Gestalt*, which is to say an agreeable arrangement of sense-impressions; and analysis undertakes to defend against all alternatives what is in fact individual experience. Perfectly consistent with the concept of the indeterminate verbal construct, this conclusion can be contested only on the assumption that critical performances, since widely divergent, are widely erroneous and that improved analytical techniques can in time resolve the differences and master the verbal entity. The notion of certainty belongs to a somewhat primitive era of science; in reference to unique literary objects it is in any case logically absurd. Considerable advancement may be possible at the theoretical level, though not before the problem identified by Jean-Paul Sartre's pregnant contention has been overcome: "Tout fait psychique est synthèse, tout fait psychique est forme et possède une structure."[35] It may be assumed a priori that the forms or conceptual schemes available for artistic creation are the same as those available for observation, but this likely truth brings with it no certain conclusions about the individual creative process or means for predicting the quality of individual perception. Formalism may one day be vindicated in some part, though not before the forms, whether the figures of the classical rhetoricians or some more precise cataloguing, have been confirmed as instruments of perception. Fortunately, the study of literary figuration logically implicates the observer, to whose neglect critical strife is considerably owing; to understand the grounds of variation in observation is to understand how the same work of literary art can induce very firm and very different impressions. It is scarcely possible, however, that criticism can achieve an adequate theoretical grasp of literature and its consequences without assistance from supposedly alien disciplines, for the history of modern thought teaches nothing if not that the divisions of knowledge break down at theoretical levels.

35. Jean-Paul Sartre, *L'Imagination* (4th ed.; Paris, 1956), p. 160.

Index

Abrams, M. H., 22, 56, 216–17
Addison, Joseph, 105
Alanus de Insulis, 88
Alexander, Franz, 53 n
Anceschi, Luciano, 161
Aquinas, Thomas, 88
Aristotle, 21–22, 25, 30, 61–62, 133–37, 161, 184, 187, 212
Arnold, Matthew, 49, 87, 95
Auden, W. H., 14, 24, 48–49, 58–59, 69–70, 85, 91–92, 96
Audience, 45–48, 52–53, 70–87 passim, 129–30, 140, 206
Augustine, Bishop of Hippo, 61, 98
Ayer, A. J., 214 n

Bacon, Roger, 88
Balakian, Anna, 204 n
Baldi, Sergio, 103, 123
Baldwin, C. S., 62–63, 65
Ball, P. M., 24 n
Ballad, popular: criticism of, 99–100, 109; defined, 100–102, 110, 112–13, 122–24; origin of, 101–104, 107–108; and tradition, 103–104, 111–12; art of, 104–107, 121; analyzed, 113–21
Barfield, Owen, 229 n
Barry, Phillips, 102–103
Bateson, F. W., 36 n, 224
Battenhouse, R. W., 53
Baudelaire, Charles, 78, 182–83, 185, 190–91, 201–202
Bays, Gwendolyn, 179
Beardsley, M. C., 22–23, 34, 43–44, 156 n, 172–73

Beer, Ernst, 25
Behrens, Irene, 160
Benn, Gottfried, 34–35
Benziger, James, 229
Beowulf, 84, 137–43
Berggren, Douglas, 229
Bergson, Henri, 158
Bertocci, A. P., 189, 200
Bishop, J. P., 92
Blake, William, 93, 95, 177, 187, 199–201
Blomfield, Joan, 137 n
Bloom, E. A., 53 n
Boccaccio, Giovanni, 88, 92, 180
Bonjour, Adrien, 142 n
Brémond, Henri, 63
Brewer, D. S., 148
Brodeur, A. G., 142 n
Bronson, B. H., 147
Brooks, Cleanth, 27, 136–37, 231
Browning, Robert, 47, 68, 81, 86
Bruneau, Charles, 224 n
Bruyne, Edgar de, 88, 202
Burgum, E. B., 75 n
Burke, Kenneth, 60, 68–69, 96, 156

Caffrey, John, 96
Caillois, Roger, 30
Campbell, George, 61, 183–85, 196
Camus, Albert, 67
Carlyle, Thomas, 96, 177
Carothers, J. C., 207 n
Cary, N. R., 53
Cassirer, Ernst, 128
Cattaui, Georges, 205
Chadwick, N. K., 207 n

Chapman, George, 87, 90, 93
Chatman, Seymour, 224 n
Chaucer, Geoffrey, 46, 100, 108, 126, 146–47, 151–53
Child, Arthur, 139, 167
Child, F. J., 100–102, 105–106, 123–24
Chrétien de Troyes, 45
Cicero, 186
Clements, R. J., 22
Coleridge, Samuel Taylor, 133, 136–37, 187, 189, 202–203, 231
Communal theory, 102–103
Conquest, Robert, 71–72, 75
Contextualism. See Formalism
Cooper, Neil, 163
Correspondences, doctrine of, 183, 202
Corvez, Maurice, 225–26
Criticism: state of, 3–5, 9–10; and other disciplines, 5, 10, 39–40, 215–17, 220–21; and speaker, 31, 33–35; biographical, 33–44 passim, 48, 51–55; as glossing, 41–42; limits of, 42–43, 173–74; biased, 49–50, 146–53 passim, 214, 232; obligations of, 51–55, 153–54, 217–18; of popular ballad, 99–100, 109; of medieval literature, 126–27; and literary history, 130–31; and unity, 133, 139–40; and form, 157–60, 165–66; and theory, 209–10; and value, 213–14; perplexities of, 220–21; and language, 220–21; and analogy, 228–30; and intuition, 232
Croce, Benedetto, 23, 61, 157, 161, 213, 231
Crosby, Ruth, 108, 130
Curtius, E. R., 88

Danielou, Jean, 200
Dante Alighieri, 46, 51, 93, 97, 126, 143, 145, 201
Davis, Jr., A. K., 103
de la Mare, Walter, 39
Demetrius, 185
DeQuincey, Thomas, 188
Derrida, Jacques, 227–28

Description, 139, 155, 158, 164–67
Dewel, John, 156 n
Dionysius the Areopagite, 128, 135
Dodds, E. R., 178
Donaldson, E. T., 144
Donne, John, 17, 19, 34, 47, 61, 81, 88, 104
Doubrovsky, Serge, 231
Du Bois, A. E., 140–41
Duhamel, P. A., 64–65, 79

Eastman, Max, 74
Ehrenzweig, Anton, 198
Eliade, Mircea, 176
Eliot, T. S., 18–19, 27–28, 47, 50, 57–59, 66, 69, 71, 74–76, 79, 81, 86, 96, 189–90, 204–206
Emerson, Ralph Waldo, 179, 182
Empson, William, 177, 195
Entwistle, W. J., 112
Erlich, Victor, 34
Explanation: and criticism, 167
Expression: theory of, 26, 181, 190; and thought, 176, 185–99 passim; and grammar, 181; and logic, 181; and rhetoric, 181

Faral, Edmond, 129–30
Figuration: opposed, 182; unanalyzed, 183–86; theory of, 184–86; and thought, 185–87, 192–99 passim; and logic, 186–89; and perception, 207–208; and form, 233
Figures of expression: allegory, 88–89, 144, 170, 202–205; ambiguity, 29, 70, 137, 195; antithesis, 196, 205; auxesis, 195; hyperbole, 184, 195; irony, 29, 70, 137, 184, 194, 196, 205, 207; metaphor, 183–85, 194, 196–97, 208, 229; metonymy, 196; oxymoron, 196; paradox, 137, 194, 196, 205, 207; paronomasia, 195, 205; repetition, 194, 205; simile, 195; synecdoche, 196, 208
Fisher, P. F., 142
Flint, F. S., 23
Fónagy, Ivan, 37
Form: organic, 136–37, 148–50, 153, 186, 229; and description, 155,

158–59, 165–67; perplexities of, 155, 161–66; defined, 156; aspects of, 157–59; and intuition, 157–59, 162; and analogy, 163; and interpretation, 167–70; and meaning, 198, 223; and figuration, 233
Formalism: as methodology, 155, 222–23; and meaning, 170, 227–28; and interpretation, 172; defended, 230; and value, 172–74
Foss, Martin, 97, 196–97
Fowler, Roger, 224
Frank, Jr., R. W., 144, 147
Fraser, G. S., 59–60, 79
Friedlaender, Marc, 74
Friedrich, Hugo, 77, 198
Frost, Robert, 17–18, 83
Frye, Northrop, 39–40, 144, 199–200
Fussell, Jr., Paul, 156 n

Gang, T. M., 142
Gascoyne, David, 80
Genre theory, 160–61
Georgian poetry, 59, 83
Gerould, G. H., 100–24 passim
Goethe, Johann Wolfgang von, 202–203
Goldsmith, M. E., 137, 143
Gosse, Edmund, 59
Gourmont, Rémy de, 23
Grammar, 181, 197
Graves, Robert, 57, 61, 79, 83
Gray, Thomas, 187
Gummere, F. B., 102–103

Hamburger, Käte, 34, 47
Hardy, Thomas, 58
Hare, R. M., 173, 220
Harrison, J. R., 48
Hart, W. M., 101
Hausman, C. R., 69
Hawes, Stephen, 88
Heisenberg, Werner, 215
Hempel, C. G., 167
Henryson, Robert, 121
Hepburn, R. W., 95, 207 n
Heraclitus, 179
Hermeneutic circle, 169, 224
Herrick, Robert, 47

Hesiod, 177
Hirsch, Jr., E. D., 168–70
Hobbes, Thomas, 182
Hodgart, M. J. C., 106, 112
Holtz, William, 158
Homer, 189, 205, 211, 232
Hopkins, Gerard Manley, 36
Horace, 129
Howell, W. S., 65 n
Hudson, W. H., 62–63
Hulbert, J. R., 138
Hulme, T. E., 59, 96
Hungerland, I. C., 136
Huppé, B. F., 143–44

Ideology, 28, 44–45 passim, 59, 63–67
Imagist poetry, 29, 59
Imitation theory, 180
Imitative form: fallacy of, 79, 145
Inspiration, 88, 176–96 passim
Intentional fallacy, 22, 43–44, 149, 169
Interpretation: and biography, 37; and unity, 139–49 passim; patristic, 143–45; and description, 167; and form, 167–70; and formalism, 172
Intuition, 232

Jacobi, Jolande, 96
Jacobs, R. D., 175
Jaeger, Hans, 28, 34, 36, 82
Jakobson, Roman, 225, 229
James, T. G., 100–101
Jameson, Fredric, 209–10
Jarrell, Randall, 58–59, 91–92, 98
Jeanroy, Alfred, 88 n
Jebb, R. C., 21
Jonson, Ben, 87, 89, 98
Jordan, Elijah, 29
Jordan, R. M., 151
Joseph, Sister Miriam, 185, 194, 196
Juilland, A. G., 224
Jung, C. G., 206

Kant, Immanuel, 194
Keats, John, 42, 112, 200
Kell, Richard, 161

Ker, W. P., 124, 133
Kermode, Frank, 191
Kittredge, G. L., 102, 105–107, 121, 151–52
Klaeber, Friedrich, 137–38
Kordig, C. R., 217
Kridl, Manfred, 34, 82
Krieger, Murray, 93
Kris, Ernst, 176
Kuhn, T. S., 11

Langland, William, 133, 143–45
Language. See Literature
Lawlor, John, 145
Leach, MacEdward, 106–108, 112, 122
Lear, Edward, 52
Lehmann, A. G., 202
Lemon, L. T., 72
Lerner, Laurence, 26
Lévi-Strauss, Claude, 193, 225–26
Levin, S. R., 224
Lewis, C. S., 23, 42
Linguistics, 195, 224–26
Literature: uses of, 4; justified, 4; references of, 4; as institution, 4, 189, 211–15; indeterminacy of, 7, 145–46, 227; as ideology, 44–55 passim, 46–48; restrictions on, 45–46; and knowledge, 49, 93–95, 215; and rhetoric, 61–62; and society, 129–31; and form, 159; and philosophy, 177–78; defined, 210, 218–21; and science, 214–15; determination of, 219; language of, 219–21; and interpretation, 232
Literary history, 11, 38–39, 41–42, 130–31
Locke, John, 182
Loerke, Oskar, 156 n
Logic, 65, 181, 186–89, 197, 220–21
Longinus, 178
Lord, Catherine, 135
Lorenz, K. Z., 163
Lowes, J. L., 151
Lumiansky, R. M., 146–52 passim
Lydgate, John, 51
Lyric: privileges of, 12; justified, 12, 18–22; and rhetoric, 13, 63; and

logic, 16–18; sincerity of, 22; modern, 30, 33; subjectivity of, 32–33, 43; speaker of, 32–43 passim; form of, 160–61

Macaulay, T. B., 207
MacDonald, Dwight, 93
McKeon, Richard, 64, 70
McLaughlin, C. A., 128
Macrobius, 88
Mallarmé, Stéphane, 191, 204, 205
Malone, Kemp, 142
Malory, Thomas, 147–51
Mann, Thomas, 25
Marcabru, 88
Maritain, Jacques, 204
Martin, Wallace, 210 n
Mary Frances, Sister, 138
Maugham, W. S., 87
Mazzeo, J. A., 144
Meaning, 169–72, 198, 220–30 passim
Mehlis, Georg, 191
Meindl, R. J., 153 n
Merleau-Ponty, Maurice, 192, 198, 226
Metaphysical poetry, 76, 84, 87
Methodology, 5–6, 11, 42, 174, 222
Meun, Jean de, 108
Meurs, J. C. van, 142
Miller, J. H., 158
Milton, John, 24, 46, 52, 69
Mises, Richard von, 217
Mistral, Frédéric, 157, 198
Model: critical, 134–35, 162, 164–65, 170; literary, 159, 228–30; scientific, 164, 221
Modernist poetry: character of, 12–14, 28–31; and speaker, 17–20, 33–34; criticism of, 43–55 passim, 97–98; and rhetoric, 59, 65–67; commitment of, 69–70; obscurity of, 73–84 passim, 95; and society, 86–87, 89–94, 97–98; discounted, 93–97; and science, 93–95; analysis of, 95–96; and symbolism, 96; aims of, 97
Moore, Geoffrey, 72
Moore, George, 63
Moore, J. R., 111

Moorman, Charles, 148–50
Moréas, Jean, 203–204
Morgan, D. N., 132
Morris-Jones, H., 173, 214 n
Mourgues, Odette de, 28
Muir, Edwin, 201
Müllenhoff, K. V., 141

Nagel, Ernest, 215
"New Lines" poets, 71–72, 75
Nutini, H. G., 217

Obscurity: defended, 73–75, 88–89;
opposed, 73–75; and culture, 73–
74, 79, 84–93 passim; causes of, 74;
undemocratic, 74, 87–93 passim;
and education, 75–76; and rhetoric,
75–84 passim; and logic, 75–84
passim; technicalities of, 75–84
passim; precedents for, 87–92
O'Connor, W. V., 78
O'Loughlin, J. L. N., 142
Olson, Elder, 74
Oppenheim, Paul, 167
Oratory, 21–22, 63, 66. See also
Rhetoric
Osborne, Harold, 132

Part-whole analysis, 222–30 passim.
See also Form, Formalism
Peacock, T. L., 182, 206
Pepper, S. C., 158 n
Perception, 191–99 passim, 207–208,
223
Percy, Thomas, 104–106, 109
Perry, R. B., 14 n, 139, 154
Persona. See Speaker
Peyre, Henri, 29–30 passim
Phillips, D. C., 229
Philosophy, 93–95, 177–78, 181–82,
186, 191–92
Piaget, Jean, 225 n
Pizzo, Enrico, 137
Plato, 60–61, 94, 135–36, 161, 178
Pleydell, Pearce, A. G., 151, 173
Plutarch, 176
Poe, Edgar Allan, 63, 78, 175, 191,
198, 204
Poésie pure, 13, 48, 63–64, 68

Poet: responsibility of, 73, 86, 89–93;
and muses, 176–77, 190; and
speaker, 17–22 passim, 33–34; and
sincerity, 24–31; and audience, 53,
70–71; and society, 79, 89–93; as
rhetorician, 57–60, 62–64; as oracle,
175–80, 198–200, 205–206; and
madness, 178–79; and scientist, 221
Polanyi, Michael, 221
Pongs, Hermann, 200
Pope, Alexander, 61, 67, 189
Pound, Ezra, 23, 48, 50
Pound, Louise, 100, 102–103, 111
Press, John, 74
Propaganda, 24
Prudentius, 88–89
Psychology, 35, 39–42, 198, 207–208
Purcell, J. M., 39
Puttenham, George, 76, 184–85

Quintilian, 21, 30, 64, 184–86

Ransom, John Crowe, 19
Raymond, Marcel, 34
Read, Herbert, 27–28, 58, 67, 70, 79,
84, 136, 195
Reid, L. A., 173
Revelation, 65, 191, 199
Rhetoric: opposed, 20, 56–59, 67–68,
181–82; and sincerity, 27, 30, 57;
as deception, 57–61; as ideology,
59, 63–67; defined, 60–63; and
literature, 61–62; and culture, 62,
65–72 passim; as decoration, 64;
and logic, 65; alternatives to, 68–70;
and philosophy, 181–82, 186
Richards, I. A., 27–28, 30, 79, 95,
195, 209, 215
Riding, Laura, 83
Riffaterre, Michael, 225–26
Righter, William, 193
Rilke, R. M., 207
Rimbaud, Arthur, 207
Robertson, Jr., D. W., 143–44
Roellinger, F. X., 95 n
Rogers, H. L., 142
Romanticism: and sincerity, 22, 24,
26; and speaker, 31, 33; and rhe-
toric, 57, 65; revolt against, 67;

claims of, 175–77; and occultism, 175, 191; and expression, 180–82; and language, 181–83, 190–91; and figuration, 182–83; and knowledge, 191–92, 197; and inspiration, 196
Rossetti, D. G., 121
Rousseau, J. J., 25
Ruggiers, P. G., 153 n
Rumble, T. C., 149
Ruwet, Nicolas, 224

Sartre, Jean Paul, 233
Saussure, Ferdinand de, 226
Schlanger, J. E., 229 n
Schlauch, Margaret, 91
Schlegel, A. W., 136
Schoeck, R. J., 229 n
Schröder, Edward, 124
Schwartz, Delmore, 74
Science, 93–95, 196, 206, 214–17, 221, 229
Scriven, Michael, 151
Senior, John, 96, 187
Sewell, Elizabeth, 187
Shakespeare, William, 34, 53, 61, 104, 185, 232
Shapiro, Karl, 75, 86, 91, 98
Sharp, R. L., 87
Shelley, Percy Bysshe, 34, 92, 95, 189, 190
Shenstone, William, 100
Sidney, Philip, 187
Sincerity, 22–31 passim, 56
Sisam, Kenneth, 128, 142
Sontag, Susan, 158
Sophocles, 128
Sparshott, F. E., 167, 223
Speaker: and poet, 14, 18–22, 28; in medieval lyric, 15–16, 44–45; in Renaissance lyric, 16–17; identified with author, 32–34, 47–48, 54, 82–83; analyzed, 34–43; in modern lyric, 45–46
Spenser, Edmund, 89, 185
Spitzer, Leo, 223
Sprigg, C. S., 61
Staiger, Emil, 12–13
Stankiewicz, Edward, 41–42
Stein, Arnold, 87

Stevens, Wallace, 46, 50, 201
Stevenson, C. L., 174
Stillwell, Gardiner, 147
Stoll, E. E., 89
Structuralism, 222–27 passim. See also Formalism
Sturluson, Snorri, 51
Stylistics, 184, 224
Surrealism, 26, 181, 187
Symbol, 68–69, 191, 199–203
Symbolism, 143, 147, 200
Symbolists, 29, 65, 96, 189, 203–206
Symons, Arthur, 27

Taine, H. A., 41
Tate, Allen, 50, 66 n, 90, 95, 212
Tatlock, J. S. P., 128
Taupin, René, 23, 59
Tennyson, Alfred, 67–68, 76, 83, 85
Theory, literary: confused, 5; defects of, 5, 209–10; need for, 5–7; neglect of, 9–11; obstacles to, 210–11; and institution of literature, 211–12; character of, 217; function of, 218; and criticism, 230–32. See also Criticism
Theory, scientific, 221
Thomas, Dylan, 18, 50, 72, 75, 80, 96
Tigerstedt, E. N., 178
Tillyard, E. M. W., 23, 192
Tindall, W. Y., 46, 76
Todorov, Tzvetan, 226 n
Tolkien, J. R. R., 141–42
Tolstoy, Leo, 23
Towers, T. H., 153 n
Trilling, Lionel, 53, 98
Tupper, Frederick, 151
Tuve, Rosemond, 78

Ullman, Stephen, 35 n
Unity: defined, 127–28; and interpretation, 139–49 passim; and symbolism, 143, 147; and models, 165; and perception, 223
Universal, concrete, 219
Urban, W. M., 95

Valéry, Paul, 77, 157, 183–84, 189, 198, 203–204

Value: moral, 4; aesthetic, 4, 214; established in lyric, 12–22; non-aesthetic, 42–43, 213; criteria of, 154, 172–73, 214; and formalism, 172–73
Villon, François, 200
Vinaver, Eugène, 132, 147–50
Vinsauf, Geoffroi de, 129
Virgil, 51, 187
Vogelweide. See Walther von der Vogelweide
Vossler, Karl, 191
Vries, Jan de, 138

Waggoner, H. H., 93
Walther von der Vogelweide, 45
Warren, Austin, 155–56, 202
Warren, R. P., 63
Weitz, Morris, 136, 167, 173, 210, 214 n
Wellek, René, 106, 156–57, 202, 224

Wells, E. K., 103–104, 107, 124
Wells, H. W., 133–34, 183, 185
Whitman, Walt, 50
Whyte, L. L., 156 n
Wilde, Oscar, 31
Williams, Oscar, 57
Wimsatt, W. K., 22, 27, 43–44, 96, 112, 136, 231
Winters, Yvor, 59, 70, 79
Wittgenstein, Ludwig, 210
Wordsworth, William, 14, 17, 20–21, 25–27, 30, 34, 39, 61, 67, 74, 82, 182, 188–90, 197, 199
Wrenn, C. L., 131
Wright, G. T., 33, 52
Wright, H. G., 142
Wutz, Herbert, 14 n

Yeats, W. B., 19, 36, 48, 50, 59, 69–71, 86, 96, 187, 200–201